KILLING WEALTH, FREEING WEALTH

KILLING

HOW TO SAVE AMERICA'S ECONOMY

WEALTH,

...AND YOUR OWN

FREEING

WEALTH

Floyd Brown and **Lee Troxler**

WND BOOKS

KILLING WEALTH, FREEING WEALTH
WND Books

Published by WorldNetDaily
Washington, D.C.

WRITTEN BY FLOYD BROWN AND LEE TROXLER
JACKET DESIGN BY MARK KARIS
INTERIOR DESIGN BY NEUWIRTH & ASSOCIATES, INC.

WND Books are distributed to the trade by:
Midpoint Trade Books
27 West 20th Street, Suite 1102
New York, NY 10011

WND Books are available at special discounts for bulk purchases. WND Books, Inc. also publishes books in electronic formats. For more information, call (541) 474-1776 or visit www.wndbooks.com.

First Edition

ISBN: 978-1-935071-81-5

Library of Congress information available

Printed in the United States of America

10 9 8 7 6 5 4 3 2 1

Dedicated to our parents,
Floyd and Nadine,
Dale and Marilyn,
who have lived by the first principles
that we must now fight to preserve.

■

We wish to thank our friends and family
who contributed so much time and talent, especially Mary Beth
Brown, Jim Moore, Christine Lakatos, and Karen Harling.

CONTENTS

Introduction

ix

1

Rise of the "Killionaires"

1

2

Engineering the Great Financial Panic of 2008

20

3

Crooked Culture Feeds These Killionaires

35

4

The Sugar/Sugar/Shaft Strategy

65

5

President Obama's Economic Brinkmanship—Stimulus or Depressant?

77

6

Fast-Patching or Euro-Trashing America?

94

7

Get Ready for the Forty-Cent Dollar

126

8

Power to Tax, Power to Destroy

139

9

The Monstrous Guilt of Labor Unions Past

158

10

The Biggest Financial Bubble in History

173

11

Giving Lawyers License to Strip Small Business

185

12

The Perils of One-Party Government

195

13

How Will America Be Changed?

206

14

Your Personal Clawback Strategy

225

15

Freeing Wealth

235

Notes

247

Index

257

INTRODUCTION

WE'VE SPENT A lifetime pushing boulders up mountains, often failing—that is how entrepreneurs succeed. But this mountain of success we call the American dream is trembling beneath our feet, and everything we've worked a lifetime to achieve is now crashing down, or threatening to. So it is time to pay closer attention and get clear on next steps. For starters, we have to ask some basic questions, such as, "How the hell did America slide so far?"

We have some ideas, and that's what this book is about.

It's about a *nation* that has divided into two camps with two very different scripts for our American future—and neither script works.

It's about a *system* that rewards cleverness and lies and mocks our traditional work ethic—setting up a terrible fall.

It's about a *society* eroding under the sanctioned acid drip of fashionable morality hardly different from the acid trips of the 1960s—with dire consequences.

Beyond these generalities, it's about environmentally Down-syndromed automakers and union bosses who gave us gas-guzzling SUVs and junky sedans. It's about the privileged preppies in their penny loafers at Citi|BofA|Chase|Morgan|Whatever who dreamed up inventive ways to fleece the public. It's about professional politicians who've never held a real job or done an honest day's work. Okay, if these folks want their billion-dollar bailouts and their unlimited spending accounts all provided by hardworking taxpayers, here's how we do it:

We tie a rope to their necks, and each rope leads into one of our living rooms. Every time a noncompetitive American car rolls by our window, we give that rope a yank. Every time a creditworthy borrower is turned away at a taxpayer-financed bank, we yank again even harder. Every time some political windbag sneaks another earmark onto a bloated piece of legislation, we all yank in unison.

But this book is about much more than simply getting even.

It's about the terrible realization that all of the financial hell we've endured is literally Bush league in comparison to what's ahead. For as we'll see, a new and even larger Ponzi scheme is *only now* unfolding, and this one is being funded by taxpayer dollars.

This scheme is now bubbling up from the diseased swamps of the nation's capital, just south of the last heist pulled off in plain sight in the cold-blooded canyons of Wall Street. For months we have smelled the foul stench of this financial wickedness, but not seen it. Now it is visible to the eye.

Seeing the direction it takes will stop you short.

It is at once frightening and maddening, and it is beginning to drive many good people beyond the bounds of civility and restraint. We're getting angrier by the hour. We will act. Soon.

HOW DID WE SLIDE SO FAR?

Yes, how did America get here? Forget putting that question to the Democratic leadership, or the Republican leadership, either. The former have a vested interest in the problem; the latter can't be trusted to keep their word. Today's political parties have become meaningless, if occasionally entertaining, abstractions. They may yet get their collective acts together, but if the history of vaudeville is instructive, don't count on it anytime soon.

From our perspective, the folks in Washington and in statehouses and municipal buildings across the land have taken whatever drug Michael Jackson was taking—able to dance on stage, asleep the rest of the time.

That's not to say that there are easy answers to the financial crisis that our elected leaders confront. In fact, there are only hard answers. Our nation is sick. The national ticker has stopped.

Ask yourself, what would you do if you were president?

Perhaps if you found yourself in the role of a citizen doctor presented with a patient in cardiac arrest, your first instinct would be to apply the paddles to the heart. Not the left arm or the right leg—the way the politicians are doing with big showy flourishes. No, the heart. At full crank.

Entrepreneurs and investors have long been the beating heart of America, responsible for creating 80 percent of all *new* jobs. To restart the national ticker, then, wouldn't it make the most sense to stimulate entrepreneurship and investment?

What's the gain in handing welfare checks to the nonworking poor? At some point, the check-writers will have to stop signing, and those poor will still be poor.

Likewise, what's the value in shoveling cash into dinosaur companies that cannot stand straight, much less compete in the global marketplace?

Wouldn't it be wiser—far wiser—to take those billions and invest in the 13 million small businesses of America to create new jobs and opportunities for future growth?

Of course it would. But it won't come from the current bunch in Washington. We'll see in these pages how the politicians give their fine and nifty speeches in favor of all things wonderful and then turn around and pass laws robbing from the producers and giving to the speculators, the borrowers, and the irresponsible. It's the era of the fleece blanket. Barack Obama is simply Bernie Madoff with political power and a printing press—he has automated the fleecing. And it's making those of us who produce things angrier by the hour.

It's truly amazing to watch politicians in Washington stand up and insist, straight-faced, that they can solve the financial crisis by throwing trillions of dollars at it. We got into this mess by borrowing and spending too much; how can we logically get out of this mess by borrowing and spending so much?

We need to *think* our way out of this mess.

Here's a modest proposal to add to the national conversation about our nation's future. With Barack Obama bent on nationalizing one industry after another, we think he might just appreciate this. Perhaps there is an industry or two he has overlooked?

Why not nationalize all the lawyers and Wall Street bankers and pay them a minimum living wage, and then privatize all the doctors and teachers and pay them a couple million a year? In that way we'll be healthy and wise, and the wealthy will take care of themselves!

Gosh, that was fun. What else could we do for our country?

Issues of Importance to Entrepreneur Investors

Stop the corporate bailouts and sweetheart deals. "Too big to fail" has become code for "bend over, taxpayers." Big business can sink or swim, just like the rest of us. The folks who collapsed the economy in 2008 now tell us that the economy will collapse if we let big companies fail. Huh? We'll dig into their lame arguments in these pages, and we'll expose the conniving charlatans and their sorry charades.

Whatever "cap and trade" is, cap it and trade it. We could spend our every waking minute wading through the highfalutin language in the "global warming" legislation. But it still wouldn't make sense. That's because "global warming" is being marketed to us by some of the same people who, thirty years ago, marketed "global cooling." They were hucksters then, they're hucksters now. Energy is a core issue—too important to be left to political fiddlers.

We should be pressing ahead on all fronts—drilling for oil and natural gas, *and* developing alternative energy sources, including nuclear. Several inventors are hot on the alt-en trail, zeroing in on genuine alternatives to fossil fuel, and we'll be there investing and cheering loudest. But until then, we must make the fullest use of our domestic natural resources.

Health care needs to be fixed, but it won't be. The current system is unworkable and will only become more so. No amount of good intentions will result in lower costs or improved care. Baby boomers will see to that. They will insist on increasingly expensive medical treatments well into their nineties and beyond. Democrats will argue for rationing—believing that worse care for more people is best. Republicans will argue for the free market— but when they had the power to reform a broken system, they fiddled. The solution, still long in coming, is to institute a three-tier system of care: Poor, Passable, and Privileged. In the meantime, at least two American companies have figured out health care and we'll see why they're earning big applause from management *and* employees.

Secure our borders and stop coddling illegal immigrants. Board up the underground tunnels and build big walls if necessary. Slow the border violence and drug trafficking. Amnesty made sense in 1980, but not in 2010. We are a nation of immigrants and have long welcomed people from all nations—but too many millions now abuse our welcome. We know of this firsthand. When one of us still lived in California, we found the American flag on our porch cut down one night . . . and clumsily taped back in its place was a Mexican flag.

These are *not* the immigrants President Reagan once championed. These folks aim to change the fabric of the nation, and so their activities are a matter of national security.

Right now nothing is done about the border problem because big business benefits from the cheap labor and Democrats benefit from the easy votes. But enough! Managing the borders is a tough task—so let's throw some entrepreneurial ingenuity at it. We have ideas.

Help the states compete nationally. Bitterly extreme partisanship will not wane for decades, for reasons we'll investigate. Fact is, folks like a good political fight. Oh, they say otherwise. But they lie.

Fighting has become more important than the outcome. So it hardly matters which side you root for. The guys you vote for don't do any more than the ones you vote against. Remember how poor Lara responded as she stumbled through snowdrifts in *Dr. Zhivago*? Was she running from the White Army or the Red Army? She said, "White, Red, what does it matter?"

So while Washington bickers and fiddles, why not give the states a chance to offer their own solutions to the problems? Permit them to craft their own individualized "welcome to" packages, attracting the kind of people they like. Several states will be hungry and savvy enough to create small-business-friendly environments. We'll tell you about some innovative strategies some states are devising to attract talent and enterprise.

We're headed for those states ourselves, inviting you to join us.

THE NEW BLACK MAGIC COMING OUT OF WASHINGTON

Barack Obama has been in office long enough to make his intentions known. It's now clear that in Mr. Obama's view:

- Those of us who made the right decisions in the past and saved our money now have to bail out all the people who didn't.
- People who overspent their paychecks shouldn't have to cut back or pare down but should go on living the good life.
- The same people in government who allowed the financial crisis to unfold are the best suited to solve it.

After all that has happened, the folks who've been working in Washington for decades are still claiming that they know what's best for us. One administration went, and another came in. But there was hardly any difference in their financial agendas. In their view, the only solution to the financial crisis was to take on trillions of dollars in new debt, more than we could ever pay back, more than our children can ever pay back, more than our grandchildren will ever pay back. Trust us, they say.

But how can we?

John Maynard Keynes called himself an economist, but he proved to be something of a magician. In the early twentieth century, he convinced the world that in bad economic times—like the ones the United States faced then, and now—the government could spend $1 and create $8! All kinds of folks latched on to this magical thinking. Political idealists liked it the most. They gave it a fancy name—the "Keynesian Multiplier." It gave them cover and an excuse to "tax and tax, spend and spend, elect and elect," as Ronald Reagan called it before driving the final nail in the failed coffin of Keynesianism.[1]

But nothing succeeds like a bad idea.

With a new spending crew in Washington, that old Keynesian

black magic has again been elevated to the status of official policy. So it was that the Obama administration threw several trillion dollars at the economic crisis in hopes of creating many trillions in economic activity. Will it happen?

A better question might be: "How could it?"

WHO REALLY STIMULATES THE ECONOMY?

When it comes to revving up free enterprise, who is really at the controls? The entrepreneur who creates products that people buy, or the financier who creates money out of thin air? The entrepreneur who has provided 300 people good-paying jobs over the years with flourishing businesses, or the politician who takes from the productive and gives to the unproductive? The entrepreneur who stays late at the office to write that extra proposal that opens a new market opportunity, or the freeloader sitting at home pregnant with her fourth child waiting for her next welfare check?

According to the Obama administration, the latter group is the economic stimulus this country needs. If we just have faith, they say, everything will return to 2007 soon. Maybe it will. But we don't see it happening for entrepreneurs and investors, especially with all the new taxes coming our way.

We don't have a problem with taxes, per se. We like paved roads, and the national power grid, and a standing army. And we have to pay for these. But the Obama administration thinks we don't pay enough. And we can't seem to shake that big red circle on our back— it's as though Big Brother has a laser pointer trained right on us. The poor have been told they won't have to pay taxes. They've got to be happy about that. The super-rich have dozens of loopholes arranged for them, so they won't be paying much in the way of taxes. The "pay 'til it hurts" honor seems to fall to those of us stuck in the middle— not poor enough, not rich enough, but just right for the taxing. So we'll be hit with higher federal taxes to add to state taxes, property taxes, sales taxes, payroll taxes, unemployment taxes, workers' compensation taxes. How much will it add up to before Mr. Obama is finished?

We'll look at the tax plans coming your way. But here's the thumbnail: We'll soon be back at above 50 percent confiscatory taxation.

If you were to demand of government workers or university professors to give up 50 percent of their pay voluntarily, what do you think the response would be? Outrage and anger? Strikes, protests, charges of discrimination, lawsuits? Sure, all of these.

Yet entrepreneurs and investors are being told we can only keep half of what we earn while working longer hours and forfeiting any hope of ever having any free time or real life. Is this right?

Here's an idea. Let's say *Company A* pays $200,000 a quarter in taxes; but instead of sending it off to Washington, *Company A* is allowed to spend it on new business ventures, hiring more employees, generating economic growth. Their employees and the local community will gain a lot more than they ever could through some government redistribution program. Think it will happen?

Neither do we.

REGULATIONS KILL
THE ENTREPRENEURIAL SPIRIT OF AMERICA

Everybody hates red tape, right?

Actually, big business loves it when regulators overdo the regulating and then lapse into a bureaucratic coma when smaller businesses try to navigate the mess of red tape.

Those who are eager today for new regulations to control greedy bankers may not realize that big business likes heavy regulation. They have the resources to comply with all the pettifogging minutia. And they have the clout in Washington to get the regulations written in a way that prejudices their entrepreneurial competitors.

Case in point: a small business owner in Old Town Alexandria, Virginia, wanted simply to change the lettering on his street sign. He had to apply for a "ladder permit," at a cost of $50, and a "building permit," at an additional cost of $55. The process took several weeks and dozens of hours, even for a task as simple as replacing the "e" on your "Ye Olde Sandwich Shoppe" sign.

Such onerous rules, however well-intended, hit entrepreneurs hardest because we lack the time and resources required to jump through bureaucratic hurdles, hire lawyers to fight City Hall, or make the right campaign contributions.

Old Town is but an example.

All across America, the old unfamiliar names—that is, the shops with distinctive merchandise and local owners and unique tastes and a red, white, and blue patriotism, have been smashed into a vanilla eyesore of familiar chains and franchises. They've been Big-Boxed and Gap-i-fied, replaced by a Chipotle, Starbucks, Wal-Mart, and Olive Garden—the same stores you can find in every other city in America.

All these big chains can afford heavy-handed regulations—and even welcome the burden. The entrepreneur, who is already overwhelmed by all the obstacles thrown in the path, is the real loser. And so is America. On this count, many of the critics of American culture are right. Our customs have been corrupted, our ways and means bankrupted. Dip a toe into the American homogenization, and you'll find the real culprit. It is the big-money people behind the scenes, pulling the strings, playing the politicians, having their way with us all. In this book we will identify these people and slap a label on them—*Killionaires*—for not only have they killed billions in wealth, they've also discredited free enterprise.

But there is a way to K.O. these Killionaires, a way to beat them on different terms, and in so doing, free up billions in wealth. That is also what this book is about.

We've had enough wealth killing; it's time for wealth freeing.

It's time to take up arms and, like the Minutemen in the woods along the road to Lexington, pick off these new enemies of freedom and genuinely *free* enterprise. Our goal together can be as simple as it is urgent—to set a vision for a just America that delivers equality of opportunity to all.

KILLING WEALTH, FREEING WEALTH

1

RISE OF THE "KILLIONAIRES"

Next to my fantasies about being God,
I also have very strong fantasies of being mad. . . .

—GEORGE SOROS

GEORGE SOROS HAS not produced a single thing in his entire life. Instead, like some grotesque vulture, he has feasted on the financial vulnerabilities of others. But he knows how to make money, or more appropriately, he knows how to kill wealth. Nobody has been more active in undermining the U.S. economy than Mr. Soros. We will see how the activities of Soros the vulture led directly to the Great Financial Panic of 2008 in which $8 trillion in wealth—a once inconceivable sum—was destroyed in a matter of hours. For this handiwork of his, Mr. Soros pocketed $1.1 billion in trading profits in 2008. Soros himself bragged without shame to the *Australian*: "I'm having a very good crisis. . . . It is, in a way, the culminating point of my life's work."[2]

It is never a wonder to see men wicked, as Jonathan Swift noted, but it is a wonder to see them not ashamed. Mr. Soros, and by extension his many willing accomplices, know no shame. Washington insider John Feehery further explains: "Soros is no Warren Buffett, a white knight who rides to the rescue. He is more like the financial version of Darth Vader, driving markets down for his own profit."[3]

Mr. Soros was the first of the Killionaires, but far from the last. Indeed, he set an example for others to follow, as we will see.

Subverting the principles of free enterprise through a process known as "asset-stripping" is a favored tactic of these Killionaires. (Those readers who are also gamers know that in *Halo 3* the "Killionaire" medal is awarded for multi-kills. It's not so different in our use here.) As exemplified by Mr. Soros, Killionaires are focused on killing off the wealth of millions to increase their own personal wealth. Mr. Soros himself sums it up best: "I am basically there to make money. I cannot and do not look at the social consequences of what I do."[4]

Since Mr. Soros is widely acknowledged to be the single largest benefactor of the Democratic Party, with President Obama on his speed dial, his cavalier disregard for the "social consequences" of his actions is most relevant to our investigation here.

IT CAN NEVER HAPPEN IN AMERICA

For the dubious honor of the "four most dangerous words" in the English language, we nominate *"It's different this time."*

When someone with a financial product to sell gets up in front of a room with breakthrough news, insisting that the ideal conditions have all fallen into place, and the old obstacles have all been overcome—making it *different* this time, the room should empty. A con is being worked.

Of course, the room does not empty. Instead the audience inches forward in their seats, curious, even intrigued and eager for the pitch. Few among us can resist a good con. Deep down, we revel in the daring cheek of the flimflam man, even if we know better than to take the bait. We may protest loudly to the contrary, but we want to believe.

On the streets of Kiev in the early 1990s, the people wanted to believe the oligarchs who promised brighter tomorrows from vast revenues generated by rapidly escalating oil and gas prices worldwide. And they kept believing, even as the oligarchs stripped the nation and left in their wake a hyperinflation raging north of 10,000 percent in 1993. Instead of fulfilling Ukrainian hopes of rejoining the community of nations, the country fell backward into Stalinist-era destitution.

In 1997, along the jungle paths leading into Bangkok and the wide lanes into Seoul, the people wanted to believe that economic miracles promised by distant elites would soon come to pass, elevating their Pacific nations to new levels of prosperity. Deeper and deeper the nations plunged into debt until, one day, foreign creditors cranked off the spigot. And the economies of Thailand and South Korea tanked.

Who were those distant elites?

The *Financial Times* reported that Mr. Soros was "blamed for the destruction of the Thai economy in 1997," and according to a Thai political activist: "We regard George Soros as a kind of Dracula. He sucks the blood from the people. The Chinese call him 'the crocodile,' because his economic and ideological efforts in China were so insatiate, and because his financial speculation created millions of dollars in profits as it ravished the Thai and Malaysian economies."

To which Mr. Soros replied: "When you speculate in the financial markets, you are free of most of the moral concerns that confront an ordinary businessman."[5]

Disregard of "social consequences." Free of "moral concerns." Democratic Party "benefactor." Is there a conclusion taking shape here? Yes, but not yet. For our purpose here and now is to make clear the enormous change that has happened to America.

For years, we Americans heard these horror stories of economic devastation and life-crushing hyperinflation. We took solace in believing that the hell could never be delivered here. Well, those could also be the four most dangerous words:

"Could never happen here."

Because it clearly did. We wanted to believe the financial promoters who insisted that the post-9/11 multimarket extravaganza was credible, different. We had faith that a systemic failure of the financial system would never happen in our fair nation, or at least not in our lifetimes. But it did, and "it" is far from over.

What does our gullibility say about us?

That we are human and fallible? Sure. But it says something entirely different about the guys making the killings—the Killionaires and their supporting cast of politicians and promoters. They knew full well what they were doing. They were following a long-established script, updating it only slightly with especially disturbing plot twists, hitting all their marks, and delivering their lines like consummate pros.

SCRIPTING A FINANCIAL CRISIS

This script is a timeless one, and has for ever and a day read something like this:

Some fancy-talking fellow borrows a vast sum of money from bankers and investors on the belief that prices for (salt, tulips, lumber, gold, derivatives, carbon credits, or whatever the latest craze) will soon froth and bubble in a glorious new springtime of furious profit-taking. Fancytalker takes the cash he's given and quickly spends almost all of it, gobbling up other companies in his targeted industry and launching his ambitious plans. In doing so he creates all kinds of jobs, and invites the local politicians to attend festive ribbon-cutting ceremonies and glam for the cameras. Fancytalker's importance to the local economy, and to the politicians, gains critical momentum.

Not one to waste time, Fancytalker leverages this growing political support to obtain new and even more lucrative business deals, tax breaks, and subsidies. Nobody is more pleased with Fancytalker than his original investors. Investing is, after all, a risky enterprise, and so investors would much prefer that their capital go into companies gliding along on the good graces of government—even if there are faint whisperings of favoritism and corruption to be heard.

Well, as surely as the blue haze of summer gives way to red autumn leaves, Fancytalker gets carried away with his own self-importance, and he loads on new mountains of debt to expand his vast kingdom to some newly imagined horizon. The whispers of favoritism become inquiries by troubled auditors. How can he manage all this debt, they wonder?

Not missing a step, Fancytalker enlists his new political pals to lean on local banks to keep the credit lines open—just long enough to make a grab for the brass ring. Local bankers go along, having little choice. And that newly imagined horizon? It does what horizons always do—it continues receding into the distance.

Fancytalker is now painfully aware that his grand scheme is about to be exposed. All the wealth he killed will be trotted out on public display in an endless news loop. His prospects now look bleak and empty, although his offshore bank accounts are full and secure. So he throws himself dramatically to his knees, and in a compelling act of contrition, begs forgiveness and mercy. He gets it, as he knows he will (*it's written in the damn script, after all!*). But he finds that seemingly overnight the conditions for borrowing have become tighter. Nobody will lend any money on affordable terms. His gig is up as the first act closes out.

Cue the mobs. Taking to the streets in righteous indignation, the angry crowds thrust skyward their clever poster boards proclaiming "Death to Capitalism" and "Kill Corporations." It's all quite entertaining but irrelevant to the central problem now facing the nation: Fancytalker was just one of many, and, as it turns out, his story has unfolded in thousands of communities across the land. Now, everywhere, there's only a trickle of credit available to businesses—no matter how solid their balance sheets. So businesses pull back on purchases, letting the shelves go bare. And consumers aren't spending what little money is left in their pockets, anyway. Economic paralysis ensues. A gloomy wintery chill falls over the public and each day feels like February, dreary and unending.

Politicians push their way to the microphones and hurtle blame at Fancytalkers everywhere for causing such a mess. Show trials are quickly organized to demonstrate how seriously the leaders take this betrayal of the public trust. Politicians take pause and then lift their eyes in adoring supplication to the mighty money machine, the Federal Reserve, where magical things are said to happen. The Fed wastes no time in asking the Bureau of Engraving and Printing to put some nice graphics on nice paper and proclaiming: *"Money!"* Or more in the modern mode, the Fed purchases securities or other assets from securities dealers in exchange for electronic credits that amount to cash and are deposited in banks. All this new "money" is then used to prime the import pump, get goods into the stores, make debt payments, bail out companies, and deliver sweet relief across the land. All that's required of us is that *we believe.*

Recall how they believed in Kiev, Bangkok, and Seoul. And the result in each case was a staggering financial collapse that slammed years and years of unending economic misery down upon the working people. Is that what's in store for the United States, now that we've been taken to the brink? We find out in the next act—after a brief intermission and an introduction of our leading characters.

NOT YOUR FATHER'S ROBBER BARONS

In the 1980s the American economy was transformed from a manufacturing powerhouse into a financial services powerhouse. With little in the way of public discussion, we decided as a country that "financial services" were the new "plastics" and we wanted to own that future. A few lone sentries, such as Patrick Buchanan, warned that a country that makes nothing will inevitably amount to nothing. But America wasn't listening, and instead launched a massive sector and skills migration.

Mark Thoma, an economist at the University of Oregon, reported that in 1970 about one in four American workers were reporting to have jobs in the manufacturing sector, but by 2005 that number had dropped to one in ten. And even that number understates: "Since perhaps half of the workers in a typical manufacturing firm are involved in service-type jobs, such as design, distribution and financial planning, the true share of workers making things you can drop on your toe may be only 5%..." [6]

An email made the rounds on the Internet in 2009 capturing the harsh truth of the emerging, post-industrial America:

John Smith started the day early having set his alarm clock (Made In Japan) for 6 am. While his coffeepot (Made in China) was perking, he shaved with his electric razor (Made in Hong Kong). He put on a dress shirt (Made in Sri Lanka), designer jeans (Made in Singapore) and tennis shoes (Made in Korea). After cooking his breakfast in his new electric skillet (Made in India) he sat down with his calculator (Made in Mexico) to see how much he could spend today. He got in his car (Made in Germany) filled it with gas (from Saudi Arabia) and went looking for a good paying American job. At the end of yet another fruitless day, Joe decided to relax. He put on his sandals (Made

in Brazil) poured himself some wine (Made in France), turned on the
TV (Made in Indonesia) and wondered why he couldn't find a good
paying job in America . . .

Yes, manufacturing jobs were pouring out of the country in the
1980s onward, and it didn't seem to matter to anybody. "Why worry,"
the sirens sang, "when we can all be as happy as lottery winners with
a financial services economy that spreads the wealth like dandelion
seeds in a warm wind?"

To help spread some of that so-called wealth with cyclone effect,
President Clinton agreed to rip away a century of market-guiding, free-
enterprise-promoting regulations. These regulations had long guided
the markets and checked the abuses of the greedy and corrupt few.

But Mr. Clinton shoved them aside.

And the first baby boomer president found willing accomplices from
the Republicans in Congress at the time. Few there had any love of
government regulation. They were fond of recalling President Reagan's
great line about government excess: "Government's view of the economy
can be summed up in a few short phrases: If it moves, tax it. If it keeps
moving, regulate it. And if it stops moving, subsidize it."[7]

But what Mr. Clinton and the Republicans chose to ignore was Mr.
Reagan's intent in characterizing government so. He was offering an
overarching view on the proper role of government in our lives; he was
not making specific policy with those words. Mr. Reagan understood
that many regulations are obviously good and essential to a functioning
society. It's illegal to shout "Fire!" in a crowded theater unless there
is a fire—and that's a good thing. It's also illegal for stockbrokers to
make trades on a company if they have inside information on that
company—another good thing. With these simple examples we see
that the issue is not regulation itself, but the manner and kind of
regulation.

For decades America's financial markets had been governed by
effective regulations, making the U.S. stock exchanges the most stable
in the world. But Mr. Clinton had political debts to pay to certain
people on Wall Street who had a very selfish agenda to promote. And
the Republican Congress was all too happy to oblige in unleashing

a river of deregulatory policies that marked the beginning of the Killionaires' assault on the hard-working people of America. Here were the five biggest attacks:

1. The Glass-Steagall Act was repealed in 1999. Since the Great Depression this law had forbidden banks, brokerages, and insurance companies from intertwining their businesses. The big money financiers were set free to take risks that could only end in financial disaster and cost taxpayers countless trillions of dollars to clean up the mess.

2. Capital was allowed to move more freely across borders— making it easy for the very wealthy to hide assets from the IRS, contributing to the class envy that rotted the core of the American psyche.

3. A little-understood product called a "credit default swap" became major business on Wall Street, potentially impacting the entire economy; efforts to regulate it were squashed— allowing a bunch of speculators to crash the eighteenth-largest public company in the world.

4. Investment banks were allowed to turn every dollar in their portfolios into forty dollars. This stroke of unprecedented financial alchemy created the potential for banks to net stratospheric profits on the ride up, and unbearable losses on the fall back.

5. Folks at the Securities and Exchange Commission hung out a GONE FISHIN' sign—sending a signal to Wall Street that, except for an occasional show trial from a New York Attorney General eyeing higher office, anything goes.

Each new attack on the protective strictures of free enterprise strengthened the financial industry and boosted its clout on Capitol Hill. It was a grand time to be young and ambitious on Wall Street. Up until 1985, the financial sector had never represented more than 16 percent of all U.S. corporate profits. A decade later, the profits generated by financial companies had doubled to 30 percent, and by the August 2008 financial collapse, those profits topped 40 percent.

This merits a pause.

At the pace financial service profits were accelerating, they could have, by the time of this writing, represented half of all the profits generated by all U.S. companies in all industrial sectors—had they not been cut short. Half! And for what? Packaging little pieces of paper, or in many cases, packaging pixels. Not making anything, just packaging and repackaging. A fabulous new economy—the service economy. And of course, the pay was grand. Folks on Wall Street had been paid about the same as other industries in the postwar period through the 1980s, but by 2007 those working in finance were making 181 percent of what their friends in private industry were making—almost double the pay.[8]

Wall Street had a good thing going.

With each ratchet in power, the public cheered louder and lined up more expectantly at the Killionaires' flowing fountains, in hopes the nectar of these new gods of money might deliver a little effervescence to their portfolio numbers. Cunningly made tipsy on the heady brew, the public was then easily conned.

In days of old, those seeking to relieve the public of their earnings had to threaten violence, and occasionally deliver on it. Then, as democratic institutions caught on in the western world, the con men and fancytalkers turned to more sophisticated methods of persuasion—campaign contributions, backroom dealings, and wire transfers to offshore bank accounts. But the modern Killionaires shot right past such awkward inducements. They were the beneficiaries of a "new belief system" that they themselves helped usher in, a belief that whatever was good for Wall Street was now good for the country.

This belief system was adopted all the way to the highest levels of government. And should some lone government regulator try to apply a dose of common sense to the good cheer of fancytalking persuasion, there would be hell to pay.

Take the case of Brooksley Born, former chairwoman of the Commodity Futures Trading Commission. Ms. Born's biggest error appears to have been warning that unchecked trading in the credit markets could lead to a huge disaster.[9] She saw the fantastic growth in the use of "derivatives" and she believed they should be regulated.

But her superiors, Robert Rubin, Larry Summers, and Alan Greenspan would hear nothing of that. We can imagine them barking after her as she was dismissed, "Don't let the door hit you on the way out."

Even when respected authors raised the yellow flag, in titles such as *Barbarians at the Gate* and *Bonfire of the Vanities*, they had the opposite effect.

Engines revved.

Liar's Poker author, Michael Lewis, commented in December 2008 that his exposé of Wall Street shenanigans had resulted in a flood of "letters from students at Ohio State who wanted to know if I had any other secrets to share about Wall Street. They'd read my book as a how-to manual."[10] Young students, laborers nearing retirement, and executives with cash to burn all read about, and swallowed whole, this fabulous new belief system. Money-making became honored and celebrated by all, because now everyone could participate. Everyone. Because *it's different this time*.

In fact, it *was* different.

But not in a good way. Even though a new belief system was sweeping the country and everyone bought in, not all belief systems are created equal. There were social and political undercurrents at work, taking the players in diverging directions.

TWO SCRIPTS FOR ONE AMERICAN DRAMA

Since our nation's earliest days, we Americans have believed very deeply in the concept of "freedom," even though from time to time we have defined it very differently. "We all declare for liberty," Abraham Lincoln noted, "but in using the same word we do not all mean the same thing."[11] And so today two camps declare for freedom, but in very different ways.

One camp, let's call them *Traditionalists*, can be most easily identified by a steadfast belief that America is a good nation; that with all its faults, America is a nation to be honored and exalted. In the sensible and accepting eyes of *Traditionalists*, America has no equal in showing the world how best to create a free, open, and generous society with opportunities for all.

These opportunities are maximized, the *Traditionalists* hold, by expanding the power of our financial institutions and allowing money to flow freely across global markets. This unleashing of enterprise is good for America and good for advancing the American promise around the world, as well.

The *Traditionalist* view is steeped in, well, tradition. So it has been chronicled many times, perhaps most famously in 1956 by C. Wright Mills in *The Power Elite*. Mills was an avowed Marxist but nonetheless famously correct in suggesting that the highest echelons of business, government, and the military in America were run by an "interlocking directorate," with the leadership jumping from one highly responsible position to another, with an unerring commitment to the national interest. These were the "deciders," and their decisions carried major consequences that rippled throughout society. Conservative in outlook, they allied naturally with the Republican Party. *Traditionalists'* ideals and approach to power have remained rather consistent since Mr. Mills' chronicling, and they continue to retain a core belief in the goodness of America.

When being perfectly frank, *Traditionalists* can accept and even endorse the idea of an American empire and the universality of American values. Because a good and strong America, in their view, is an America also rightly responsible for bringing order to the world and confronting evil if necessity demands it. Not every *Traditionalist* is overjoyed with the idea of America playing global cop. But generally they consider it the price that must be paid for the freedoms we enjoy in this world.

The second camp in this American drama could not disagree more.

Call them *Revisionists*, they were playing marbles and jacks when Mr. Mills published his work. These *Revisionists* first made their mark in the rebellious 1960s. Their views on America were shaped by the difficulties of the war in Vietnam, and any mistakes made by our political and military leaders in that war became the prism through which all future judgments would be made. Suddenly they viewed the unquestioning acceptance of American goodness as sappy and naïve. Suddenly these *Revisionists* were devoting themselves to exposing a long litany of wrongs and abuses that Americans had committed, going right back to 1607 Jamestown.

Our supposedly shameful heritage became such an embarrassment to *Revisionists* that they insisted on interjecting it into every public debate and letting it color every policy consideration. If they were capable of any balance or perspective in their views on America, they showed none of it. As the superb radio personality and author Michael Medved wrote in *The 10 Biggest Lies About America*, the turbulent 1960s created among the *Revisionists* a self-loathing that was as corrosive as it has been long-lasting:

> The unprecedented U.S. failure in Indochina gave credibility, if not confirmation, to those protestors who had decried our "imperialist" foreign policy, and chose to identify their nation as "Amerika"—the Germanic spelling meant to evoke the Nazis, while the inserted k recalled our homegrown KKK. Once you've associated your native soil with genocidal fascists and white supremacist thugs, it's tough to return to singing the praises of the land of the free and the home of the brave—even after ultimate victory in the Cold War and the evanescent surge of unity following the terror attacks of 9/11 . . .
>
> By that time the tribalism and identity politics of the 1960s had become a well-established feature of our national life, with jostling interest groups largely taking the place of homogenizing notions of Americanism. African Americans, feminists, Latinos, gays, Asians, the disabled, hippies, Native Americans—each aggrieved segment of society demanded justice and redress, competing for recognition as the most victimized and gypped.[12]

And so the *Revisionist* agenda was born—to seek redress for two centuries of perceived wrongs. In the early days of the 1960s, these *Revisionists* were still few in number, and their influence limited. To accomplish anything, they had to act like the old Chinese storyteller's fox that was unable to befriend a tiger. The wily fox created the illusion of good friendship by always trailing just behind the tiger, speaking often of his great concern for the tiger's well-being. In so doing, the fox could often get his way.

But then *Revisionists* caught a huge break: the emergence of a natural ally in the pursuit of their goals—the modern Democratic Party. Democrats shared many of the *Revisionist* views, and the Democrats were keen on regaining relevance on the national stage after being convincingly discredited by the Reagan Revolution.

So they began laying their plans and waiting for their break. How fortunate for them that two giant opportunities converged around the 2008 timeframe.

First, George Bush the Second did a scrupulous job of destroying the credibility of the Republican Party in most people's eyes.

And second, the United States underwent a massive demographic shift that literally changed the face and character of a nation.

If the Democratic Party and *Revisionists* became as one, the planners figured, they could pounce on these twin opportunities and assure themselves of electoral dominance. They could control the national agenda—no longer the wily fox, now the ferocious tiger—for decades to come.

On the demographic front, America is now for all intents and purposes a majority-minority country in which fewer than half the people claim European ancestry. For the first time in our nation's history, the new immigrants don't want to "fit in." First to prominently identify this phenomenon was the late historian Samuel Huntington. In *Who Are We? The Challenges to America's National Identity*, Mr. Huntington argued that America's great success had been the result of successive generations choosing to honor the ideals of the founding fathers, but that honor was fading into the past: "By 2000, America was, in many respects, less a nation than it had been for a century. The Stars and Stripes were at half-mast and other flags flew higher on the flagpole of American identities."[13]

Revisionists don't care if Huntington is reporting the facts or sounding an alarm, they know opportunity is knocking—because demography is destiny. Millions upon millions are streaming across borders, feeling no attachment to American traditions, no concern for American culture, no understanding or belief in American exceptionalism.

Revisionists can work with this.

Immigrants like these can be turned against those stale old "Anglo" values, and turned onto a revised view of America.

For the *Revisionists,* these have been yeasty times. They have used a grassroots organizing tool known as ACORN (more to come in Chapter 3) to tilt the electoral map their way and ensure the election of *Revisionists* to key government posts. Controlling government ensures the delivery of a desired legislative agenda. With the right legislative holes to run though, *Revisionists* have become free to act on twin fronts: They can undermine the traditional values they so despise, and they can sidestep the guiding principles of free enterprise. Taken together, they are building the kind of nation they desire while growing exceedingly wealthy.

When asked about this agenda, *Revisionists* can be quite candid.

Bill Clinton's Labor Secretary, Robert Reich, admits, "America's highest income earners . . . have been seceding from the rest of the nation."

University of Chicago's Martha Nussbaum insists "patriotic pride" is "morally dangerous."

Dr. Amy Gutmann of Princeton is repulsed that students are still forced to study civics, when their allegiance "should not be to the United States or to some other politically sovereign community," but to "democratic humanism," whatever that is.

Robert Jensen, professor of journalism at the University of Texas, writes, "It is crucial to scrap patriotism in today's empire, the United States, where patriotism is not only a bad idea but literally a threat to the very survival of our planet."

Chalmers Johnson, professor emeritus of political science at the University of California, San Diego, recalls Ronald Reagan's depiction of the Soviet Union as an evil empire to make his point that "today it is the U.S. that is widely perceived as an evil empire, and world forces are gathering to stop us."

MIT professor Noam Chomsky concludes, "If the Nuremberg laws were applied, then every post-war American president would have been hanged."

These are a few of the thought leaders of the *Revisionist* view.[14]

Clearly we now have two scripts for one American drama. One group believes in the essential goodness of American institutions; the other considers them corrupt and valueless. One group sees America learning from her mistakes and constantly improving as a result, the other is rewriting history books to focus with a primal vengeance on America's most glaring mistakes. One group believes in making money the old-fashioned way—earning it; the other is intent on asset-stripping a nation they have little regard for. Do we generalize?

Sure, and quibble with the details if you really need to. But in the pages ahead you will see how two radically different plans for our national future are unfolding, and what these plans each mean for your own personal financial prospects.

FROM THE SCRIPT TO REALITY

For the past two decades, players from both the *Traditional* and the *Revisionist* camps, each with their own scripts in tow, have moved with extraordinary ease between their offices on Wall Street and Washington. When in the "Northern Office" they've created new tools of wealth. When in the "Southern Office" they've protected those creations.

When Bill Clinton swept into the presidency, he tapped Robert Rubin for his Treasury Secretary, a man who had made millions as a trader and executive at Goldman Sachs. While at Goldman, Mr. Rubin had lobbied hard to persuade Washington to loosen its regulatory hold on Wall Street. While in Washington, Mr. Rubin was positioned to keep the wealth flowing *from* Main Street—where generally responsible people labored to create it, *to* Wall Street—where the new class of Killionaires stole it. When Mr. Rubin returned to Wall Street, he joined Citigroup's executive committee. From there he participated in what would become the grandest asset-stripping exercise in modern history—the Great Financial Panic of 2008, which killed an estimated $8 trillion in wealth.[15] When later asked whether he made any mistakes during his tenure at Citigroup, Mr. Rubin gave it some thought, hemmed and hawed a bit, then concluded "I'm inclined to think probably not."[16]

When George W. Bush became president, he appointed Paul O'Neill as Treasury Secretary. But dear Mr. O'Neill had the audacity to point out the obvious—that the United States was flirting with disastrous budget deficits exceeding $500 billion (then an almost unbelievable figure). Mr. O'Neill called for sharp tax increases and massive spending cuts to restore fiscal sanity to government. Well, that was surely the last thing anyone in Washington or Wall Street wanted to hear. Mr. O'Neill was given a one-way ticket back to Main Street or wherever it was he had come from with such hilarious notions.

Mr. Bush turned next to John Snow, a talented man who could be relied upon to preserve the new status quo ante. Indeed he did, until departing to become chairman of Cerberus Capital Management, at the time a large private-equity firm. Companies such as Cerberus specialize in seizing control of valuable corporations, running them hopelessly deep into debt, and stripping out their most valuable assets. After sucking away billions for themselves, they leave the host companies as near-lifeless corpses, completely defenseless should the economy weaken. Private-equity firms like Cerberus publicly tout their "creative destruction" as capitalism at its best, and good for everyone. But they know better. They know that in the lead-up to the 2008 panic, they were short on "creating" and long on "destroying."

Mr. Snow took the greased-turnstile tour of Washington and was quickly back in the private sector. His replacement was Henry Paulson, CEO of none other than Goldman Sachs. It was then the summer of 2006, and all the players knew the financial gravy train would soon derail. So with the feverishness of engineers facing another train bearing down on the same track, they intensified their efforts to strip clean the assets of Main Street.

All of which led to the Great Financial Panic of 2008.

Entering office with the economy in the toilet, Barack Obama promised a clean break from all this crony capitalism. So how did that work out? For his Secretary of the Treasury, Mr. Obama chose Timothy Geitner. *Such* a breath of fresh air. Mr. Geitner had (1) worked under Mr. Rubin in Clinton's Treasury Department, (2) been a policymaker at the International Monetary Fund, (3) been President of the New York Federal Reserve, and (4) been cheating on his taxes—seriously cheating, though we're told that doesn't matter. A line from an old song comes to mind, "Meet the new boss, same as the old boss."[17]

So is there any difference between Mr. Bush and Mr. Obama in the critical economic decision-making that affects us all? Not much.

When we examine Mr. Obama's appointments to senior policy posts, we are struck by how many aides are in the position to refill the punch bowl for their pals in the Northern Offices while they enjoy the cherry blossoms and black-tie fetes of the Southern Offices:

- **Larry Summers** was brought in to chair the Council of Economic Advisors, which is very important to the nation's prosperity—and to his former hedge fund, which added $5.2 million to his wealth in 2008.
- Deputy National Security Advisor **Tom Donilon** earned $3.9 million at law firm O'Melveny & Myers in 2008 for ably representing Citigroup and Goldman Sachs, among others. Now inside government, Donilon is positioned to continue guarding the interests of his banking clients.[18]
- **Stoven Rattner** stepped away from his fortune, estimated at between $188 million and $608 million, to run Mr. Obama's auto task force. Among Mr. Rattner's holdings was a Cerberus Capital Partners fund that owned Chrysler, until Chapter 11 bankruptcy. Mr. Rattner's tenure was cut short by scandal, but not before he helped orchestrate the nationalization of a company Cerberus had earlier stripped.[19]

THE PURPOSE OF THE FINANCIAL CRISIS

The Great Financial Panic of 2008 is commonly believed to have resulted from one of the following: the lowering of U.S. interest rates after the Dotcom Crash of 2001; all the cheap goods flowing out of China; loose purse strings at Fannie Mae and Freddie Mac; regulators being fast asleep at the switch; foolish accounting rules that turned a mere mountain of a problem into an overnight Mt. St. Helens; and dastardly mortgage brokers cramming home loans down the throats of people who couldn't afford them. And indeed, all are to blame—to an extent. But only as a headache is a symptom of a tumor. That's the beauty of this economic collapse in the eyes of the people who engineered it. While folks bicker and ballyhoo over who is most responsible, the scoundrels behind the curtain, pulling the strings, are getting off scot-free.

For a peek behind the curtain, follow the money.

We know that most of the major commercial and investment banks, and the hedge funds that play in the unregulated shadows, now appear largely broke. But these players were clearly the biggest financial beneficiaries of the housing bubble. Each time a home loan was sold, packaged, securitized, and resold, banks took their transaction fees, and the hedge funds buying those securities reaped ever-larger fees as their holdings grew. Keeping those fees coming was Job #1 on Wall Street, as well as in Washington. So it was that Fed Chairman Alan Greenspan made regular trips to Capitol Hill to mumble sweet nothings that nobody understood but everyone agreed meant the good times were still rolling. Commissions were still coming in. All was swell. When Mr. Greenspan finally hung it up, his chair was filled by Ben Bernanke, the scholar who had studied the Great Depression (and so everyone agreed that he ought to know a thing or two). As late as June 2006, Mr. Bernanke proclaimed: "The management of market risk and credit risk has become increasingly sophisticated . . . banking organizations of all sizes have made substantial strides over the past two decades in their ability to measure and manage risks." [20]

Mr. Bernanke made these comments just a few weeks before the banks' risk-taking created the largest financial crisis in modern history. Did Mr. Bernanke, like Mr. Greenspan before him, make a colossal error in judgment? Were they naïvely ignorant to what was happening? Or was there another explanation?

We gained some insight into these questions on April 2, 2009, when Mr. Obama traveled to London for a meeting of the G-20 (shorthand for the twenty major industrialized nations). The meeting took on added importance because it was Mr. Obama's first big international show, and the world's central bankers were playing to the folks back home, looking to lay public blame for the global financial crisis squarely on the United States. G-20 was a grand spectacle, with security details and protesters making life miserable for Londoners for weeks over a four-hour meeting. It was a curiously short meeting, given the gravity of the situation, but not without its accomplishments.

For one, the group issued a communiqué that received little attention, by design. This communiqué created a new bureaucracy named the Financial Stability Board (actually a facelift on the old Financial Stability Forum, around since 1999) to better supervise markets and make them more stable. This new bureaucracy would be able to peer into the workings of banks in the twenty member countries, and somehow prevent a repeat of the 2008 financial catastrophe.[21] Sounds rather boring, so what's the impact of this new binding rule?

In the fine print, it says the bureaucrats can implement "tough new principles on pay and compensation and support sustainable compensation schemes and the corporate social responsibility of all firms." [22] So Mr. Obama agreed to give an international body the power to interfere in the management of U.S. corporations. That means a group of central bankers, neither elected by U.S. voters nor accountable to the U.S. government, are now in the position to dictate policy on management issues such as shareholder rights, employee records, and corporate responsibility. Even while critical of the practices of big business in the financial collapse, the last thing we want is international busybodies dictating policy to U.S. companies. Yet now Mr. Obama has signed a communiqué making it possible.

The question is begged: Why?

We suspect, and will lay out in coming chapters, a working thesis: that after years of chatter about a single world government, run by central bankers who know what's good for us all, Mr. Obama is moving ahead to make it a reality. That would, in fact, be the prize Mr. Obama's biggest campaign contributors have been working for years to obtain.

Let's look closer at Mr. Obama's benefactors, and their agenda . . .

2

ENGINEERING THE GREAT FINANCIAL PANIC OF 2008

Money. It's so last year. But cheer up. Consider the following. So we were wrong about, well, everything: real estate, leverage, deregulation, derivatives, risk management. I mean, really, who's perfect?[23]
—*The Deal*, a Wall Street newsletter

THERE HAVE BEEN many and varied accounts of the Great Financial Panic of 2008. The epic destruction of $8 trillion in global wealth has been pinned on a Chinese menu of culprits:

- Overly expansionist monetary policy that put too much easy money into too many people's irresponsible hands following the tech crash of 2001
- Financial shenanigans at the government-backed home promoters Fannie Mae and Freddie Mac
- Government watchdogs paying no attention whatsoever to all the signs of terrible excess
- Foolish accounting rules that turned a mere mountain of a problem into an overnight volcano
- Mortgage brokers coaxing folks into buying homes they couldn't afford
- And on and on.

All in all, there was blame enough to go around. But there was more to it. We believe these *official* stories of the financial crisis were intended to avert your eyes from the *real* story. Sure, there is truth enough to the official stories—who would suggest otherwise? But there is also a feeling of looking at the façade of a building—like in the old spaghetti westerns, with the lean-to storefronts and flimsy boardwalks and all kinds of stage hands scurrying around in the dirt behind the doorways. Yes, there is an artificiality to those official "explanations" that begs for closer review.

Our search for the truth behind the mask takes us back to the 1960s birth of mass counterculture. Baby boomers tend to look back upon those glory days with an idealistic pride, a sense of having accomplished something important. To this day, many of the generational cohorts that came of age in the 1960s continue to believe that America and its institutions had veered badly from the noble path—both at home and in overseas battles. A certain segment of these boomers who fancied the *Revisionist* view of American "dysfunction" turned against those institutions with a vengeance and spite so overwhelming that they sacrificed all perspective in the bargain.

They vowed to never trust anyone over thirty . . . until they turned thirty. Suddenly they found themselves in the role of "the Man" and were quite self-conscious about it. They were up against the wall, and they had a choice to make. Either they could channel all that generational idealism into society-improving institutions, or they could stoke the rebel *Revisionist* fires that burned just below the surface. A great many—an astoundingly great many—chose the latter course and drifted into some kind of reflexive acceptance of the *Revisionist* script we've referred to.

In interviews, some *Revisionists* have even admitted to being inspired by Arthur Penn's 1967 movie *Bonnie and Clyde*. Lead characters Warren Beatty and Faye Dunaway were cool cats taking on the corrupt power structure. They were gorgeous, wildly liberal in real life, and they robbed banks. So if it worked in the movies, these *Revisionists* reasoned, why not dream up new and exciting ways to rob banks?

Why not, in short, take full advantage of emerging technologies to break money out of vaults? An ambitious agenda, sure. But hell, they were young, bright, and motivated. First task? Try to tear down the *real* economy and replace it with an *artificial* economy. Real economies are hard to control. Manufacturing products with thousands of component parts, building homes with physical products from nature, inventing medical devices that could extend our healthy years—all these things are tangible and easily valued. Everyone knows the deal. But an artificial economy could be easier to game. Fancy mathematical models could be designed to create the pretense of value. And salesmen could be paid handsomely to convince everyone that it was all real.

WHAT MADE THE GREAT PANIC OF 2008 DIFFERENT

What made the 2008 crisis so unusual was not the collapse of real estate prices. Heck, real estate has been collapsing since they invented Florida. And it wasn't the toppling of once-proud banks. They've been failing since the outcasts of medieval Europe ingeniously set up card tables on the banks of rivers at the edge of towns and began lending people money at interest—to wit, "bankers." The difference in 2008 was how little was *real*, and how much was *artificial*.

In the housing industry, things like dirt are real, mortgages less real, mortgage-backed securities much less real, collateralized debt obligations not really real at all. Artificial, in fact. These are tools used to break money out of vaults.

The folks who dreamed up these tools are the ones who transformed America from a real to an artificial economy, profiting handsomely at every turn. They are the rogue scoundrels who've dedicated their adult lives to subverting free enterprise, asset-stripping the hardworking people of this country, and laughing all the way past the bank they collapsed to their awaiting yachts. They are the Killionaires we seek to name by name and then drag to the whipping post—giving them their just due.

These Killionaires early-on sought to create a partisan food fight, offering cash incentives to the crazies on the Far Left and their counterparts on the Far Right to fight like mad dogs, keeping everyone distracted while the Killionaires privately set about killing wealth. Two of the bigger distractions these private political alliances created were CRA and BDS.

CRA is short for the Community Reinvestment Act, President Carter's 1977 initiative that twisted the arms of bankers and forced them to make loans to lower-income folks who couldn't afford the payments. Was this the root cause of the housing bubble and the financial collapse? People demanded to know. Congress held hearings. No less a luminary than Alan Greenspan told legislators that if they wanted an explanation for the mess, "It's instructive to go back to the early stages of the subprime market, which has essentially emerged out of CRA."[24] Conservative think tanks, lobbying organizations, and media outlets grabbed soundbites like this and ran their mouths with them. Funding for their "blame CRA" campaigns came from many sources, including Killionaires who had much to gain from all the commotion.

In fairness to Mr. Carter, CRA was born of good intentions, even if it devolved into bad law. CRA gave rise to a permanent network of "affordable housing" advocates who kept pushing banks to lend to people who couldn't afford houses. And CRA did its thing through five administrations over three decades before the housing bubble exploded. So CRA contributed to the housing mess, but it's a stretch to suggest that it was a top cause.

As theater goes, CRA will never make it to Broadway. But that's okay for conservatives who pine more for the moral of the story than for the production values, anyway. Not so, liberals. They need to swoon and foment. They got their chance to rage psychotically with BDS—Bush Derangement Syndrome.

Former President George W. Bush, for all his strengths and weaknesses in an honest appraisal, was capable of driving card-carrying liberals stark raving mad. Whether it was his inability to deliver a public speech with any elegance whatsoever; or public demonstrations of his faith in a God in heaven who's very different from their ecofriendly gods; or his audacity to take our nation into war of any kind, liberals could fly off the handle at the very mention of the word Bush. So whatever the societal ill, it became Mr. Bush's fault.

Or Dick Cheney's fault. A fixation on Mr. Cheney was a backstage pass at liberal carnivals. As liberal blogger David Sirota wrote, only half jesting: "Drought in Oklahoma? Cheney. Terrorist attack in Yemen? Cheney. The Great Chicago Fire of 1871? Cheney."[25]

The Great Financial Panic of 2008 became The Bush-Cheney Robbery of 2008 to these foaming-at-the-mouth Pomeranian liberals. Nobody could tell them any different. And who was organizing all the radical left mouth-foamers? A number of organizations, but principally MoveOn.org. And who was standing in the shadows behind MoveOn.org, underwriting millions in costs? A number of Killionaires, but principally George Soros.

If this kind of analysis tips your BS-meter, we understand. Many people will blithely suggest that the obsessions with CRA or BDS have less to do with the evil machinations of Killionaires and more to do with the respective parties trying to belittle their opponents. And there is plenty of truth in this, as far as it goes.

But political parties are expensive parties, right?

Dependent on the gifts of big money benefactors, right?

So is the real question one of political "access" and high-level "connections"—who had them, who used them, and what came of it?

Did the Killionaires insert themselves into the political machinery at strategic points in hopes of extracting maximum financial gain?

Can we trace back any fingerprints to the asset-stripping machinery that we contend has been under construction for many years?

A TWENTY-FIVE-YEAR CAMPAIGN TO KILL CAPITALISM

It's difficult to put start and end markers on the campaign to subvert the capitalist order in America. But one very suspect event came at such a critical point in the build-up to the $8 trillion wealth grab that it deserves special attention.

The year was 1993, and the Federal Reserve Bank of Boston had just published *Closing the Gap: A Guide to Equal Opportunity Lending*.[26] Officially this report talked about ways to better assist low-income and minority households through better staff training and outreach programs and similarly boring banking housekeeping issues. Also contained in the report was a message to lenders. It was more in the form of an "urging," actually, in the sense that a bulldozer (government) urges dirt piles (banks). The message was clear: Lower the amount of income your customers need to qualify for a mortgage. This key report was followed by others of a similar vein. All were carefully designed to begin lifting the price of housing above historical levels of appreciation and create an eventual housing bubble.

So who was putting gas in that bulldozer, effectively pulling the levers from behind the curtain that year?

Interestingly, just a few months earlier, George Soros had singlehandedly crashed the Bank of England and left working-class Brits in a bad way. His goal, at which he succeeded, was to make a billion dollars in a single day. Mr. Soros proved that he could cripple England by playing fast and loose with the financial regulations of the time. He set his sights next on the United States—*a far bigger prize*. But there was a little problem. There were investment restrictions that were strictly enforced and meant to thwart the likes of Mr. Soros. The United States boasted a first-rate regulatory framework—it was, in fact, the model that every legitimate national economy aspired to. If Mr. Soros was going to make an even bigger killing in the United States, the crotchety old billionaire knew, he would have to circumvent those financial controls.

Step One for Mr. Soros was to begin making friends in Washington, and throwing large sums of his ill-gotten gains at the Democratic Party—for they shared his vaguely anti-American, socialist beliefs, and they were, historically, more easily compromised.

His vehicle for tossing cash at Democrats was the Open Society Institute—so named because with a little more "openness" the world would be a better place, right? He thought so. All those old goosebumpy patriotic tidings were such a bother—away with them, he announced. All that nationalist fervor was so antiquated and, well, provincial and the world was changing, Mr. Soros decreed, and he offered himself and his riches as compass and lantern of the new enlightenment. Most importantly, in his view, all those old financial regulations had to go—they were nothing more than cumbersome artifacts of dinosaur times, standing astride the historical tide, gumming up the march of progress.

Mr. Soros made these very arguments to all who would listen.

He wrote book after book laying out his theories of "reflexivity," ideas so patently obvious they wouldn't get him through Economics 101. But he was a successful investor, in that he had made billions. So people listened to him and read his books. And since he would generously slather his wealth on any Democrat who lent an ear, his parlor was always full of sycophants and fools. Men of conscience would cut him a wide path, but a conscience is such a liability in politics, especially Democratic politics, so Mr. Soros got traction.

He was ready for Step Two. This was trickier—but he was up to the task. He needed to be more than the Democratic Party slush fund; he needed to be its kingmaker. That way, everyone in the party would be beholden to him. He could call the president anytime it suited him and talk about the inherent reflexivity of the markets, and other such hokum. He could exert a powerful influence over the political opinions of about half the people in America. He liked that.

DID "DEREGULATION" CONTRIBUTE TO THE PANIC?

It's popular in liberal circles to blame "Republican-led deregulation" for the Great Financial Panic of 2008. Is this correct, or twice wrong— in that deregulation wasn't the culprit and Republicans didn't lead it?

The biggest piece of banking deregulation was the Gramm-Leach-Bliley Act of 1999, initiated by Republicans in Congress and signed into law by President Clinton. This legislation repealed part of the Great Depression–era Glass-Steagall Act, and it allowed banks, securities companies, and insurance companies to all live and profit happily together in what's called a Financial Services Holding Company.

In defense of his bill, former Senator Phil Gramm has insisted that the impact of financial deregulation "has been greatly exaggerated." He says regulators had all the whistle-blowing resources and authority they needed to bust the wrongdoers, but they "seemed unalarmed as the crisis grew."[27] "Unalarmed" is one word for it; another is "intimidated." As we'll see, the regulators were sometimes unaware of brewing problems, but at other times were quite aware, though cowed into silence by their superiors in government. (This should be a cautionary tale for President Obama as he seeks to revamp the government's regulatory system.)

So is Mr. Gramm credible?

Following eight years in the House of Representatives—five as a Democrat, three as a Republican—then seventeen years in the Senate, which included a run for the presidency in 1996, Mr. Gramm landed squarely in the position of vice chairman of UBS Investment Bank. UBS is a Swiss powerhouse that's now holding billions in assets that had been in the accounts of hardworking Americans.

But Mr. Gramm also asks an interesting question. If his bill was the problem, he says, "The crisis would have been expected to have originated in Europe where they never had Glass-Steagall requirements to begin with." [28] This is true, as far as the logic goes. Left unsaid is that the European banking system was not in the crosshairs of the Killionaires. American banks and the American-led system of capitalism was the bull's-eye. In the words of George Soros: "I am not so optimistic about capitalism; it is built on false foundations . . . The main obstacle to a stable and just world order is the United States . . . We must puncture the bubble of American supremacy."

As Mr. Soros saw it, the puncturing would evolve over three steps:

1. The larger and clumsier American banks became,
2. The more vulnerable they'd be in a severe downturn,
3. The sweeter prizes they'd make when toppled and then picked up in turnaround for pennies on the dollar.

That was the real end-game for long-term plotters like Mr. Soros and fellow Killionaires.

MAKING MONEY FREE AND UNINHIBITED

You can't strip people of their money unless they've got money. So it was that in early 2001, Federal Reserve Chairman Alan Greenspan set on a determined course to lower interest rates and make money much less expensive. Mr. Greenspan began with a series of appearances on Capitol Hill to assure legislators that on matters of high finance, well, he was brilliant and they needn't worry. He put it like this to the Senate Banking, Housing, and Urban Affairs Committee:

. . . Because the advanced supply-chain management and flexible manufacturing technologies may have quickened the pace of adjustment in production and incomes and correspondingly increased the stress on confidence, the Federal Reserve has seen the need to respond more aggressively than had been our wont in earlier decades. Economic policymaking could not, and should not, remain unaltered in the face of major changes in the speed of economic processes. Fortunately, the very advances in technology that have quickened economic adjustments have also enhanced our capacity for real-time surveillance. . . . [29]

Seated up on their dias listening to Mr. Greenspan, the senators were clearly not having a V-8 moment. They probably had no idea what the good Chairman was saying—but it sounded brilliant! So the senators thanked Mr. Greenspan for being so brilliant and then kicked their feet up to watch in awe as Mr. Greenspan made money appear out of nowhere—an easy feat for a man as brilliant as he. His game plan was a cloud of dust and four yards simple: Each time something spooked the economy, he lowered the cost of borrowing money.

The federal funds rate, which is the basic interest rate we agree to pay for borrowing money, was at 6.5 percent in early 2001. When technology investors finally figured out that sock puppets are not business plans, the tech bubble exploded and $5 trillion of so-called shareholder value vanished into thin air. Moving swiftly, Mr. Greenspan slashed the federal funds rate all the way to 3.75 percent—making money far cheaper, but still a ways from free. Then 9/11 hit, and the nation was in shock. Mr. Greenspan responded this time by taking interest rates all the way to 1.0 percent—making money *almost* free. Another year would pass before the federal funds rate would be lowered to less than the inflation rate. When that happened, what was the effect?

Few of the talking heads on cable news had any acceptable explanations. But the Killionaires knew the effect. They had helped to create a classic Chinese crisis, or *weiji*, correctly read as "an opportunity for danger." If money was free—genuinely free, in that it was available at less than the rate of inflation—then what value did all the starched shirts on Wall Street bring to the table? How long could they get away with charging big fat commissions to their clients when money was not only free, but also as a result it was generating no real return on investment? From such a dangerous situation, opportunity emerged.

These institutional investors had trillions of dollars of other people's money invested in Treasury bills. Yields on these bills were down to nothing. That was a problem. How could these big-time money managers justify their $2 million a year salaries for taking $1 and turning it into $1? They needed a twenty-first century solution, some magical new product (or even a dusty old product) that nobody truly understood.

They needed mortgage-backed securities.

What could be better than a piece of paper guaranteeing a cut of the appreciation in a home? That sounded enticing—almost magical! Of course, there were thick gobs of fine print that nobody dared read. But the players all knew the nature of the game. They knew that the Mensa boys at Goldman Sachs, Morgan Stanley, and the like were suiting up for the game, so they were, too. When asked what they were investing in, they had their ad-libbed lines well rehearsed, along the lines of . . . "Oh, it's quite simple really. We acquire the value of homes all across the country—thousands of them—and we then bundle all these mortgages into a single security, or bond, or piece of paper, if you will. Then we sell it!"

Left unmentioned by these money managers, at least in their conversations with clients, was the fat commissions they were paid to bundle up the paper and sell it. In private and in industry journals such as *The Deal* they would wax eloquent on the qualities of this magical paper: "It makes like Peter Pan; here, there, everywhere . . . like pixie dust . . . metamoney with aphrodisiacal properties."[30]

And oh how intoxicating it was! In the first years of the decade, mortgage loan originations increased an amazing 56 percent a year—from $1.05 trillion in 2000 to $3.95 trillion in 2003.[31] Almost all of these mortgages were turned into pixie dust. Yes, magic was afoot and the gods of money were dancing on Wall Street.

FOOLING GOVERNMENT FOR FUN AND PROFIT

While the investment houses in the Northern Offices busily passed their magical pieces of paper back and forth to each other and grabbed billions of dollars in commissions for their labors, their brethren running the Southern Offices of Fannie Mae and Freddie Mac were busy picking America's pockets on an even grander scale.

Congress had created Fannie Mae in 1938 and Freddie Mac in 1970 for the purpose of pumping money into the housing market, making it cheaper and easier for people to buy homes. Fannie and Freddie would buy mortgage certificates from banks, bundle these pieces of paper into mortgage-backed securities, and sell them to investors. For their efforts, Fannie and Freddie kept a cut of the action. And it was a lot of action.

During the 1990s boom times, Fannie and Freddie became darlings of Wall Street for two reasons. One, they posted steady earnings. Two, they came with implicit guarantees that if anything ever went wrong, Washington would ride to the rescue. As an investor, it's hard to top that one-two combo. If you invested in Fannie in 1995, you were up 400 percent by 2001. Your investment in Freddie was up 500 percent by 2004. But not everything was on the up and up.

In June 2003, auditors were doing a routine review of the finances of Fannie and Freddie when they uncovered certain "accounting irregularities." A small panic rippled across Washington and made its way into the Oval Office. Wasting no time, President Bush put Fannie and Freddie under Treasury Department oversight and ordered them to behave responsibly. Presumably that meant to stop with the inflated earnings, the overpaid executives, and the risk-taking with other people's money. But if the President was serious in his admonitions, none of his subordinates were. Months passed without any corrective action being taken. Soon reports of irregularities were upgraded to evidence of "extensive financial fraud."[32]

Turns out that Fannie's chairman, Franklin Raines, had been cooking the books to help himself to an estimated $90 million in bonuses during his tenure. His accomplice in the scam? None other than Goldman Sachs, headed at the time by Henry Paulson, who would go on, years later, to run the Treasury Department and engineer the 2008 bailout of all his Wall Street friends. But we're getting ahead of the story.

Despite clear proof of a scandal so monstrous and damaging to the nation it made Watergate look like child's play and Teapot Dome a college prank, nothing happened. Trillions of dollars of home equity was in jeopardy because of bad dealings at Fannie and Freddie, but the principles walked with hardly a wrist slap. How could that have happened?

Was it because Fannie Mae Chairman Mr. Raines was an old pro at gaming the system? Was it because he had been the budget director under President Clinton? This isn't rocket science.

In any case, Mr. Raines had played a central role in the asset-stripping of America. And he was unrepentant. He wasn't about to give it back. He started calling in favors. He got plenty of help in his fight from a woman who had been vice chairman at Fannie Mae, Jamie Gorelick. She had previously served as deputy attorney general under Mr. Clinton, and was connected. (An aside: Ms. Gorelick was also the person most responsible for sabotaging U.S. intelligence agency efforts to stop 9/11, as documented in the movie *FahrenHYPE 9/11*).

With Ms. Gorelick and Mr. Raines calling in chits across Washington, and because the White House was taking a powder, the cover-up was soon complete. To put a bow on it, the senior Democrat on the House Financial Services Committee, Barney Frank, trotted out before the cameras and, guileless as a schoolboy, announced: "These two entities—Fannie Mae and Freddie Mac—are not facing any kind of financial crisis. The more people exaggerate these problems, the more pressure there is on these companies, the less we will see in terms of affordable housing."[33]

As Democrats lined up to hide their culpability in the biggest financial disaster in American history, the housing crisis deepened. It was just as the Killionaires wished. All part of the plan. The more people bought homes they couldn't afford, the more chaos was bottled for later exploitation.

And a lot of homeowners were in over their heads.

By the time the housing market collapsed, 56 percent of Fannie's and Freddie's home loans had gone to folks with below-average incomes, 27 percent of their loans had gone to folks who couldn't afford rent, much less a mortgage, and 35 percent of their loans had gone to folks in the "underserved areas" (read: wherever the Democrats needed to buy more votes to win).[34] The results?

Back when the housing bubble was but a gleam in the Killionaires' eyes, circa 1994, only about 4 percent of all home mortgages were subprime, with 31 percent of those subprime loans being turned into securities. By 2006, just over 20 percent of the mortgage market was subprime, and 81 percent of those loans had been turned into now toxic securities.[35] Former Senator Phil Gramm noted: "If this crisis proves nothing else, it proves you cannot help people by lending them more money than they can pay back."[36]

While true, his comments were but *official* window dressing. What the crisis proved, in our view, was that the Killionaires were prepared to go to incredible lengths to undermine the economy and amass their criminal fortunes.

THE FOUL DEED IS CONSUMMATED

By 2006, anyone on the right page of the script knew the score. Certainly the people who'd produced and directed the elaborate wealth grab knew. They had almost completed Act One—the creation of a crisis. Their work had been masterful and would come to a climax in late 2008.

We had warned as much in *Obama Unmasked*, writing that Mr. Soros would deliver an "October Surprise" that would simultaneously crash the U.S. markets, discredit the Republicans, and ensure victory for his handpicked candidate for president, Barack Obama:

> Enter George Soros and a conspiracy of Asian and European currency traders, all hitting the currency markets on the same day, and crashing the dollar, sending Wall Street into a panic. The Dow could drop another 500 to 700 points with investors fearing the end is here and believing the economy is going into a complete tailspin, with the whole mess blamed on President Bush and the Republicans.[37]

In fact, the "surprise" came on September 19, when the Dow plummeted 600 points in one day and then continued falling. Readers of our book found themselves in fine position to protect their investment portfolios. Some did, we've since learned. But having issued an accurate and actionable prediction lent only meager solace. For as we joined with everyone—bruised, poorer, shaking our heads in frustration and anger as the financial markets ground to a halt and the clock stopped on western civilization, the Killionaires moved on to Act Two.

This required little of the Killionaires, since people were bent on revenge and reaching for their pitchforks.

Fed Chairman Greenspan, the man who kept interest rates too low, too long, took the lion's share of attacks. Once he had been the most popular man in America. He had written a bestselling book and was awarded the Presidential Medal of Freedom, Knight Commander of the British Empire, and Commander of the French Légion d'honneur. But by the end of 2008, few disagreed with Italy's finance minister Giulio Tremonti when he portrayed Mr. Greenspan as second only to Osama bin Laden in hurting America the most.[38]

Was Mr. Greenspan fairly treated? Trying to anticipate future events and gauge the effect they'll have on a current-day economy is as much art as it is science. That is certain. Was he but a scapegoat for our collective anger—someone easily attacked? He was that. But was he also carrying water for Killionaires? We aim to find out.

Interestingly, two tweaks to the nation's financial accounting rules might have halted the carnage. As Michael Flynn wrote in *Reason*:

> Suspending mark-to-market accounting rules (using a five-year rolling average valuation instead, for example) would have helped shore up the balance sheets of some banks. And a temporary easing of capital requirements would have given banks the breathing room to sort out the mortgage-backed security mess. Although it is hard to fix an exact price for these securities in this market, given that 98 percent of underlying mortgages are sound, they clearly aren't worth zero.[39]

But there was no intention of halting the carnage. Just the opposite. The summer of 2008 was the target date that the Killionaires had slotted at least four years prior: the date for mortgage-backed securities to go toxic. It was an ideal confluence, in their view. Markets would be near to bursting with all the subprime loans resetting, and that would create widespread financial panic. That panic could then be harnessed to discredit Republicans and grease the chances of the Democrats. Those Democrats, having been elected with over a billion dollars in Killionaire money, could then be relied upon to protect the Killionaires' winnings.

A few years from now, there will be a magazine cover story on the folks who swooped in after the carnage and picked up mortgage-backed securities and other crazy financial products for pennies on the dollar, on the correct assumption that they'd be worth a whole lot when the initial panic subsided. Good chance these folks will be the ones we're profiling here, along with others we didn't suss out. Our hope is that in identifying their names and shenanigans, we'll contribute to their eventual demise.

CROOKED CULTURE FEEDS THESE KILLIONAIRES

Our earth is degenerate in these latter days;
bribery and corruption are common; children no longer obey their
parents; and the end of the world is evidently approaching.
—Assyrian clay tablet, 2800 B.C.

IN THE "TWO scripts" concept we advanced in Chapter 2, there were the *Traditionalists* and the *Revisionists* with dang clear differences in the behavior that comes naturally to each.

We generalize, but *Traditionalists* try to live by a code, whether Christian commandments, or Semper Fi, or even the way of the Ronin. There is an expectation that honesty pays, hard work will be rewarded, and the Golden Rules are worth their weight in, well, gold.

Revisionists dismiss all this as naïve backwoods sentimentality. They get a thrill out of breaking every rule that will bend, exploring the dark recesses of the soul, betraying principle because they can.

Neither script has a lock on goodness. But one script, the former, has guided the course and character of the greatest democracy the world has ever known. The other script is tearing it all back down. We will take a look at that "tearing down" in this chapter, but first an important caveat.

We're not pessimists by nature. We've never seen the glass as half empty or half full—we've gone looking for a larger glass. When we see old farts shaking their fists at today's youth and insisting that America's best days are over, we take them to a high school science class and watch miracles unfold. And when confronted with radical professors or Che Guevara T-shirted students agreeing with Osama bin Laden that America is Satan's spawn, we're more likely to burst out laughing at them. We are optimists. We are hopeful of joining with like-minded individuals in celebrating an American future that is again full of promise and good cheer. We are, in a number of ways, dedicated to making that happen.

But right now our hearts are broken, because a small but seriously powerful group of *Revisionists* are having their way with our culture. They've turned that culture upside down so that the stinking underbelly of mankind is somehow in widespread public favor.

This "anything goes" crookedness plays right into the hands of the Killionaires. Indeed, it is often a plan and product of their own hands.

HOLLYWOOD MOCKING TRADITIONAL FAMILY VALUES

As we chronicled in *Obama Unmasked*,[40] and Dick Morris wrote more eloquently in *Off With Their Heads*, the creative talents of Hollywood had long stood for wholesome entertainment, pro-American imagery, and profit—all good things. But steadily since the 1960s, the *Revisionist* script has captured the imagination of producers and creatives. And now they revel in feeding misogynist, disgusting, and foul programs into our living rooms. And far too many parents look the other way, go along to get along, or drift off into their daydreams or drugs of choice. The net effect is like an acid drip on society, not so different from the acid trips of the 1960s that gave birth to it all.

Just look at the rapper known as Akon. He's celebrated for tossing young girls down on stage at concerts and humping them as the young teen crowd roars its approval.

Just look at ABC's primetime show *Cougar Town*. It's disguised as a comedy that "dares to tell the truth about dating after divorce." But its star, former good girl Courteney Cox, is a prowling sex fiend more concerned with her desires than her duties as a mother.

Just look at MTV's *16 and Pregnant*. This "reality show" follows pregnant teens to term, showing how "cool" teen pregnancy can be. Not much chance the producers will mention findings from the National Campaign to Prevent Teen and Unplanned Pregnancy. The killjoys at that nonprofit group report that 40 percent of teenage mothers do not graduate from high school; two-thirds of families begun by an unmarried teen mother are poor; and most of the increase in child poverty is a result of nonmarital childbearing. So that's cool?

In this culture of indifference and exploitation, it's no wonder late-night TV host David Letterman was surprised at the uproar caused by his crude sexual jokes about Alaska Governor Sarah Palin looking like a "slutty flight attendant," and her fourteen-year-old daughter being "knocked up" by a professional baseball player. In Letterman's world, being young and pregnant is just grist for the joke mill.

TV execs cling to the tired cliché that their programs are not real, just escapist fantasy. They know better, of course, but in their dark hearts they enjoy cheating even truth (or else they leave the profession). TV has become a crash course in getting divorced, having affairs, covering up crimes, getting addicted to drugs and alcohol, cheating, stealing, and manipulating in every imaginable way.

Audiences become desensitized. The line separating right from wrong is blurred. More of America is converted to the *Revisionist* script.

Meanwhile, good parents express shock that a majority of teenagers are regularly having sexual encounters with strangers met online, drinking themselves into nightly stupors, experimenting with mind-scrambling drugs, and cynically tuning out on a world that doesn't understand why they act the way they act.

What's next from Hollywood's finest? A show named *Sexting*, featuring young hotties receiving text messages from the viewing audience while having sex? Surely some enterprising screenwriter has already pitched the idea.

If there is a core problem in Hollywood, it's how it has become a one-party town, politically speaking. Absent is the old give-and-take and clash of opposing views that lends perspective and meaning to dramatic programming. Those with conservative political views either zip it, or they don't work. Liberals make most programming decisions. And they are beyond shame, beyond perspective—so much so that most of them don't even realize that (1) the main way that millions overseas learn about America is through TV, and (2) they see the non-stop menu of depravity and violence, and (3) think that's what every street in America is like, and (4) they want nothing to do with it. Hollywood's movies, more than the local oil derrick guarded by U.S. soldiers, are a major cause of discontent around the world. Hollywood liberals will contemplatively ask, "Why do they hate us?" and then answer their own question with one word: "Bush!" or "Cheney!" They should look in their *Revisionist* mirrors for an answer.

PROFESSORS UNDERMINING
THE PRINCIPLES OF HIGHER EDUCATION

College professors hewing to the *Revisionist* script are the cerebral counterparts to Hollywood producers, but they've gone a step further. They've created a responsibility-free zone, a kind of cocoon that guarantees lifetime employment with zero accountability. With fewer restraints on them than Keebler has on elves, this professional class spends their days cheerfully rewriting history and befouling young minds, steadily undermining a liberal arts tradition that had once elevated American universities into the envy of the world.

Perhaps the nastiest scoundrel to ever to be given tenure was Ward Churchill. This professor of Ethnic Studies at the University of Colorado sleazed to national recognition by praising al-Qaeda terrorists for their "gallant sacrifices" on 9/11 and calling the victims "little Eichmanns." How anybody, especially so many Jewish professors, could support Mr. Churchill's comparison of the victims in the World Trade Center to the architect of the Holocaust is beyond our comprehension. But support him they did, in droves. And feeling enabled, he clarified his warped views in a 2004 interview: "I want the state gone: transform the situation to U.S. out of North America . . . U.S. off the planet. Out of existence altogether."[41]

Mr. Churchill's contempt for his country was already well known to those unfortunate enough to find themselves in his classroom. In numerous rants he labeled America "a genocidal nation" for actions dating back 200 years. He felt so resolute in that position that he lied on his job application and checked the box for American Indian, earning an affirmative action set-aside. In any workplace except academia, he would have been summarily dismissed and labeled a fraud. But at Colorado's finest he was encouraged by his "distinguished" colleagues. Only after a concerted national campaign by leading conservatives such as David Horowitz did the truth finally out: Mr. Churchill had plagiarized most of his published writings; unable to think on his own, he had the audacity to grade down students who disagreed with his poisoned views. It took Colorado's ivory tower narcoleptics until 2007 before giving Mr. Churchill his long-overdue pink slip.[42]

If Churchill was just one bad apple, he could be overlooked. But across the nation, from our grade schools through our universities, those in positions of responsibility have decided that their own personal political views trump an open-minded liberal arts education. Rosalyn Kahn, a professor at Citrus College in Glendora, California, asked her Speech 106 students to write letters to President Bush about the war. This was 2003. Some students wrote letters professing their support for the president, the country, and the troops. They were denied credit for their work.[43]

In the last election, it was difficult to find one liberal arts college student who was given an assignment to write a critical essay on the Democratic candidates. But not so the Republican candidates. Andrew Hallam, professor of English at Metro State College in Denver, directed students to write an essay that "undermines, criticizes and contradicts" the fairy tale image of Palin which "Republicans may wish . . . the American people to believe." Students were shocked, but fearing for their grades, they complied. One brave student filed a complaint, which led to the discovery of a long pattern of bias and abuse. Apparently, Mr. Hallam would single out conservative students and chuckle while liberal students hurled verbal insults at them. He thought it was "cute."[44]

The talented cartoonist Bruce Tinsley captured this blatant bias best in a Mallard Fillmore strip showing a journalism school professor lecturing ". . . when reporting on protesters, it's important to distinguish between, say, those carrying funny, clever pictures of

Bush with a Hitler mustache . . . and those with hateful, racist pictures of Obama with a Hitler mustache."[45]

This matters because by some estimates liberal professors outnumber conservative professors ten to one on American campuses. The net effect of this overwhelmingly liberal view on students was characterized by Accuracy in Academia in this way:

> Today's colleges and universities are not, to use the current buzzword, "diverse" places. Quite the opposite: They are virtual one-party states, ideological monopolies, badly unbalanced ecosystems. They are utterly flightless birds with only one wing to flap. They do not, when it comes to political and cultural ideas, look like America.[46]

Today's political science departments offer little in the way of Edmund Burke, Adam Smith, Friedrich Hayek, and Milton Friedman. But there's a Chinese menu of *Revisionist* tracts for students to choose from. Pick up a syllabus of a number of colleges today and you'll be treated to courses on neo-Marxist redistribution (legislate away wealth), black liberation theology (shame away wealth), and radical feminist liberation (just castrate men). Let's look briefly at each of these . . .

Of all these radical fringe ideologies, black liberation theology is the most worrisome because Barack Obama spent twenty years soaking it up at Trinity United Church in Chicago. As we wrote in *Obama Unmasked*:

> In these teachings, there is a God who commands people to rise up and demand that government (1) create subsidized jobs for them, (2) guarantee health care and education by putting government in control of both, and (3) achieve economic equality by redistributing wealth through massive taxes on the affluent and generous entitlements for the poor . . .
>
> As described by its founder, James Cone of New York's Union Theological Seminary, "Black Liberation Theology . . . refuses to accept a God who is not identified totally with the goals of the black community. If God is not for us and against white people, then he is a murderer, and we had better kill him. The task of black theology is to kill Gods who do not belong to the black community. . . ."[47]

You could be forgiven for thinking we made this up. But sadly, truth is stranger than fiction here. We wrote previously that you could visit Trinity United's website and read the angry entries from the pastor's pen. But they've since cleansed this bit of ethnic hate, no doubt to spare Mr. Obama any more embarrassment and ridicule. But Mr. Obama was there in that church for some twenty years, soaking in this drivel. Did it have any effect on him? How could it *not*?

And how could it *not* leave a lasting impression on many students who are told this is the way to think, and graded up for thinking this way?

Ken Blackwell of the Family Research Council explains how this corrosive ideology was brought into contemporary society:

It was often offered up by Marxists regimes that knew they could not uproot the church, so they tried to weaken the doctrine of the church. So it is an alternative doctrine of the church that embraces "big government," it advances a collectivist ideal and idea, and it says the state, not the individual, is central to society.[48]

Most disturbing is how black liberation theology, as taught in churches and schools, promotes hatred toward all whites, without distinction. It is an explicitly racist movement justified by the racism of others long since condemned to history. It stands athwart history, holding us back. It contradicts the teaching of genuine black leaders such as Martin Luther King, and that is more than disturbing, it is tragic.

Many of Mr. King's liberal sisters failed him as well. In the model of black liberationists and neo-Marxists, radical feminists have sought to characterize the traditional family unit (you know: mom, dad, the kids) as the root cause of all oppression.

Some feminist groups advocate mere separation from men, while others teach superiority over men. One such group is SCUM—the Society for Cutting Up Men. (Again, we're not making this up!) In her original *SCUM Manifesto,* group founder Valerie Solanas declared for male "gendercide" and the creation of a new world order:

Life in this society being, at best, an utter bore and no aspect of society being at all relevant to women, there remains to civic-minded, responsible, thrill-seeking females only to overthrow the government, eliminate the money system, institute complete automation and destroy the male sex.[49]

How did liberal academics and fair-minded pundits respond to the release of Ms. Solanas' book?

> *"SCUM Manifesto* is a chic little object."
> —CLAIRE DEDERER, *The Nation*[50]

> "Recent world events suggest the book's time has come."
> —A.S. HAMRAH, *Boston Globe*

> "Her anger is a raw, seductive call to arms for
> any woman scorned."
> —RACHEL KRAMER BUSSEL, *The Village Voice*

Does the *SCUM Manifesto* and similar books from groups such as W.I.T.C.H. (Women's International Terrorist Conspiracy from Hell, in case you didn't guess the acronym) make it onto the reading lists in our universities?

Absolutely.

Want to know what your daughter, or son for that matter, will be treated to in a typical "women's studies" class? Here's the agenda that the "Radical Women" organization foists on those it cultivates for leadership roles in our schools and social welfare offices:

The Radical Women Manifesto: Socialist Feminist Theory, Program and Organizational Structure defines Radical Women's purpose and ideology as follows: Radical Women is dedicated to exposing, resisting, and eliminating the inequities of women's existence. To accomplish this task of insuring survival for an entire sex, we must simultaneously address ourselves to the social and material source of sexism: the capitalist form of production and distribution of products, characterized by intrinsic class, race, sex, and caste oppression. When we work for the revolutionary transformation of capitalism into a socialist society, we work for a world in which all people may enjoy the right of full humanity and freedom from poverty, war, racism, sexism, homophobia, anti-Semitism, and repression.[51]

We should be able to rely on universities to offer a comprehensive range of viewpoints, not just the marginal or deranged. It shouldn't be that hard to encourage free and open-minded thinking in the classical liberal arts tradition. But apparently it is.

Apparently we don't need Muslim extremists to "raise" a generation of American haters—we have all those *Revisionist* academics and Hollywood polemics already doing a bang-up job of it.

Just as the Killionaires want it.

LAWYERS SHREDDING THE FABRIC OF FREEDOM

From the Founders' intent through a Civil War, flirtations with a Socialist government, two World Wars and a Cold War, right up to the 1960s rebel years, the American experiment in democratic freedom was on a steady march forward, improving by the year. There was a general consensus that folks should be free to pursue their dreams and make their own choices within the context of the greater good. Always the greater good. An entire society not without its problems and grievances but with everyone executing on the old Musketeer's slogan, "one for all, and all for one." But then the radicals of the 1960s took their grievances from the streets to the courthouses, where they began a slow killing of freedom. It was a death by a thousand cuts, as chronicled adeptly by Philip Howard, author of *Life Without Lawyers*:

Americans don't feel free to reach inside themselves and make a difference. The growth of litigation and regulation has injected a paralyzing uncertainty into everyday choices. All around us are warnings and legal risks. The modern credo is not "Yes We Can" but "No You Can't." Our sense of powerlessness is pervasive. Those who deal with the public are the most discouraged. Most doctors say they wouldn't advise their children to go into medicine. Government service is seen as a bureaucratic morass, not a noble calling. Make a difference? You can't even show basic human kindness for fear of legal action. Teachers across America are instructed never to put an arm around a crying child . . .

Here we stand, facing the worst economy since the Great Depression, and Americans no longer feel free to do anything about it . . .

All this law, we're told, is just the price of making sure society is in working order. But society is not working.[52]

Expect society to work even less effectively in coming years. With Democrats back in charge, lawyers are in the political pole position because as a special interest lobby, lawyers have thrown in with the Democratic Party.

Federal Election Commission figures from October 2009 showed lawyers sweeping past health care, real estate, and financial firms in total campaign contributions—officially donating $140 million to federal campaigns.[53] Of that money, 73 percent went to pet Democratic causes to ensure that phone calls get answered, demands met, freedom destroyed. Call it the Lawyer Full Employment measure. Call it the Killionaire Pay-To-Sue racket. It will thrive again under Democratic rule in Washington. And the easiest targets of all the litigation are, as we'll see, small business owners and investors.

There are nearly one million lawyers in America, or three for every thousand people. In England there's one lawyer per thousand people. In France, it's a half a lawyer per thousand people. What does this mean? That there's an attorney out there somewhere looking to sue you? Probably.

Apologists for the legal profession will huff indignantly if you dare to suggest that liberal access to the law leads to:

- The filing of thousands of frivolous lawsuits that accomplish nothing except gumming up the wheels of justice
- The exodus of thousands of good doctors from the profession because of exorbitant malpractice insurance costs

- U.S. exports losing their competitive edge because of costly safety features that are required
- Dozens of additional injuries to societal equity, which we'll revisit in Chapter 11.

These apologists are quick to trot out statistics on how tort lawsuits are actually decreasing. One author claims these suits are down 9 percent since 1992.[54] His source? The American Bar Association. Now there's a reliable source of information on the grave societal costs of legal disorder.

Here's some numbers that are credible—to the extent that any are. The National Center for State Courts, which simply services the judicial system and has no pony in this race, reports that the number of litigation filings for contract disputes shot up 21 percent over the decade since 1993.[55]

There is, in short, one new lawsuit filed every 1.9 seconds.

Kansas led the pack, with lawsuits up a staggering 77 percent and rising. Lawsuits and liability insurance cost small businesses $88 billion a year. Legal costs for actual litigation range from $3,000 to $150,000, with the average case costing the small business owner about $10,000. Trials last from eight months to twenty, distracting the company's senior team during the entire trial. Small businesses bear 68 percent of the nation's tort liability costs, though responsible for 25 percent of business revenue.

The steady escalation of lawsuits nationally would be higher than 21 percent were it not for Texas. Lawmakers there took a stand against BS lawsuits, and drove plaintiffs' lawyers back into the holes they crawled out of. This is great news for Texan entrepreneurs and for others thinking of Texas as a future destination (more on this promising idea later).

For anyone who believes the increase in lawsuits is the price of modernity, it's useful to note that lawyers are not allowed to run amuck anywhere else as much as they do in the United States.

No group of people is better trained for outright thievery. And under an Obama administration, lawyers will be given the entire license they desire. Fighting back will get costlier.

We'll return to the ways and means of sending lawyers back from whence they came.

NEWS MEDIA REPLACING TRUTH WITH TITILLATION

Does anyone still believe in the so-called objectivity and editorial independence of the news media? If so, call the Guinness book. Only the partisan-impaired still fight the old media bias battle.

The media, biased?

That is so 1990s, back when liberals concealed the truth of their advantage in the media. Want a real definition of "torture"? Force today's students to bear some windbag sociology professor holding forth on the mainstream media. Mainstream? Rip any kid away from his iPod, and he'll tell you there is no mainstream media, not on a national scale anyway.

Today we have a Leftstream and a Rightstream. The Leftstream media exists to sell the political ideas of liberals and pander to the prejudices and glaring, mind-numbing stupidity of liberal activists. The Rightstream exists to sell the political ideas of conservatives. Those are the business plans. And both streams know the rules.

Rule No. 1: Never admit bias.
Rule No. 2: See Rule 1.

There are other rules about how to fabricate sources and stretch the truth. But at some point they all refer back to Rule No. 1. Anyone caught betraying the rules is sacked, a million-dollar salary forfeited. The only guys daring to confront the obvious truth are the comics. As Conan O'Brien quipped on his late show:

> Former President George Bush Sr. celebrated his 85th birthday today by skydiving with CNN anchor Robin Meade. Fox News reported the story as, "Liberal media pushes old man out of airplane."

In the old days, back when most Americans still believed in an "objective" media, one of the popular news shows was called *Meet the Press*. Today it ought to be called *Beat the Press (Seriously, Beat Them)*.

Liberal journalists have only themselves to blame for losing monopoly control over news reporting. By tacking so far to the left even when there was no value in doing so, they created a giant vacuum. That great whooshing sound Ross Perot once referred to? NAFTA, schmafta. It was the sound of smart businessmen rushing into a wide open media landscape. First to rush in was talk radio, then Fox News, then bloggers and citizen journalists reporting over the Internet directly.

Despite the great whooshing, the chattering class still tacks much more to the "left" in their political views. This is partly because being good at the trade requires a certain adversarial liberal mindset, partly because they've been educated by adversarial liberals, and they've taken that adversarial liberal product out into the world.

Every year, the respected Pew Research Center asks reporters about their political affiliations and choices. Turns out that while 36 percent of America identify as conservatives, only 8 percent of journalists do. By huge margins, journalists backed the Democratic candidate in every presidential election since 1964, including landslide losers George McGovern, Walter Mondale, and Michael Dukakis. In 2004, journalists backed John Kerry by a two-to-one margin. In 2008, Barack Obama enjoyed an even greater margin over John McCain.[56]

Of course, a journalist's personal politics need not influence his or her reporting. But journalists are by nature a hot-blooded group, and as the British politician William Gladstone reminded, "Men are apt to mistake the strength of their feeling for the strength of their argument. The heated mind resents the chill touch and relentless scrutiny of logic."[57] It's just plain common sense that who we are affects how we view the world. The diarist Anaïs Nin put it even clearer: "We don't see things as they are; we see things as we are."[58] So when a majority of those in the news business lean left, even if there are two streams, we know which way the news leans in any default situation.

Leftstream attacks on Sarah Palin in the 2008 election went beyond the pale. There was no mention of the fact that she made fewer gaffes and missteps in her first six weeks on the national stage than another relative newcomer, Barack Obama, made in his first six weeks. The Leftstream leaped beyond mere bias in a concerted effort to destroy Mrs. Palin because, as an attractive conservative female, she was a threat to the liberal machine that wanted desperately to run America.

The 2008 election saw the Leftstream move from bias to advocacy. While the *New York Times* published a report alleging that John McCain had an affair with a lobbyist and questioned whether he was eligible to be president because he was born on a military base, they ignored questions about Barack Obama's own eligibility and his extreme inexperience.

Rather than talk about the issues, the Leftstream was busy ogling a shirtless Obama and elevating him as the world's newest celebrity. Chris Matthews even reported that Obama gave him a tingly feeling in his leg.

In an interview special with NBC's Brian Williams, not a single substantial question was asked of the recently inaugurated President Obama. Two things did happen in this big news event, though. Mr. Obama gave a plug to new *Tonight Show* host Conan O'Brien. And Mr. Williams formally "bowed" to Mr. Obama as they parted ways. If we hadn't seen it ourselves, we wouldn't have believed it.

Newsweek editor Evan Thomas called Ronald Reagan "parochial, chauvinistic and provincial," and by comparison "Obama is standing above the nation, above the world . . . he is sort of God." This is the same Evan Thomas who in 2007 stated unequivocally, "Our job is to bash the president. That's what we do." Evidently, they only bash the president if he is a Republican.[59]

In June 2009, Mr. Obama made a show of claiming that his stimulus bill had created or saved over 150,000 jobs and would do the same for 600,000 jobs by end of summer. This claim was as empty as a gourd. Fact is, employers cut 467,000 jobs in June, the unemployment rate rose to 9.5 percent, and hourly earnings stagnated. There was no evidence the Obama stimulus package had any effect on the labor market. "This will be another jobless recovery," predicted John Silvia, chief economist at Wachovia.[60] But the Leftstream dutifully parroted Mr. Obama's claims and reported that—*shazam!*—jobs had been created!

Did President Bush ever walk all over these journalists so easily?

Certainly it is unfair to hold Mr. Obama personally responsible for not turning the economy around *overnight*. But that's no excuse for the media to take a powder in their reporting.

As the Obama presidency unfolds, we expect the Rightstream to tack toward the ideological middle in a savvy attempt to increase market share. But as of now, the media's fist-fighting in the pursuit of ratings points and advertiser dollars is doing great harm to our nation, We all know that unbiased information is critical for an informed citizenry—not only in the political arena, but in the financial as well. The Great Financial Panic of 2008 was proof of that. But don't expect anyone in the media or the Obama administration to confront these uncomfortable truths.

Again, that's just the way the Killionaires want it.

POLITICAL OPERATIVES STEALTHILY STEALING ELECTIONS

How about a quick round of *Jeopardy*? The answer is:

Hey man, you don't gotta pay taxes and they just give you food and the police can't touch you or else you sue their asses and best of all you don't gotta learn no stinkin' English. All you gotta do is vote the Democratic Party ticket, man.

So what is the question? Would you believe . . .

What is the script used by left-wing political organizers working border towns and skid rows, signing up recent arrivals to vote for the Democratic Party?

No way, you say? Total farce? Maybe in isolated cases, but not as a rule? Sorry, but wrong, wrong, wrong.

This is a fabricated script—*yes*. But only because we don't have an actual recording of the tactics used by these left-wing organizers, as reported by former employees turned whistleblowers. What we do have is corroborating evidence. A tree full.

We are speaking of the activities of ACORN—short for the Association of Community Organizations for Reform Now. ACORN is one of those public-private partnerships that exist in the hazy afternoon shadows of political life. That is, it is supposed to register voters and lend assistance in impoverished communities—nothing wrong with those goals. It receives funding from the government and from private organizations—and that's where the problems begin. Because almost all of those "private" donations come from liberal donors with an agenda in tow.

That agenda is to herd masses of people, by any means necessary, into voting for liberal candidates.

ACORN sends paid activists out into areas where immigrants are most likely to be found, where the homeless huddle, where economic conditions are wretched. These activists are paid a bounty for each person they register to vote. Then, on Election Day, they often go back into the neighborhoods and deliver their charges to the polling places with instructions on how to vote.

They've delivered 1.3 million new voters to date—but many of those voters don't even exist. They were invented. For several presidential elections now, ACORN has been out there committing fraud on a grand scale.

And they got away with it, why?

They have powerful benefactors in one political party on Capitol Hill. The Democratic Party benefits handsomely from all these new voters— real or not—and so the Democrats provide cover, cynically pretending that ACORN is in fact a do-gooder group this country needs.

All of this came to light when longtime ACORN workers, so repulsed by what they saw happening, turned into whistleblowers. They went public with documents proving a long history of criminal behavior, including fraud and embezzlement.[61]

More than $1 million was embezzled by the brother of ACORN founder Wade Rathke, and yet this was covered up for almost a decade.

The ACORN whistleblower also went public with private correspondence between ACORN's political director, George Soros, and the Service Employees International Union in which these parties discussed the need for additional funding to achieve their shared political goals. The document talked about the great opportunity in the 2008 election:[62]

The election of 2008 will be the most important national election in a generation and presents an unmatched opportunity for progressives to win the White House, build a progressive majority in the House and Senate, pave the way for the post 2010 redistricting struggle . . .

If this was a Democratic National Committee document, more power to them. But this was ACORN management, whose paycheck is signed by taxpayers, actively campaigning for Democratic—that is, progressive—candidates. That makes this behavior a serious violation of campaign finance law.

ACORN's dirty history has become such an embarrassment that even *Democrats* at the state and local levels are taking action against them. Nevada's attorney general, Democrat Catherine Cortez Masto, has filed a criminal complaint against ACORN saying that its training manuals "clearly detail, condone and . . . require illegal acts," such as forcing its workers to meet strict voter-registration targets to keep their jobs. ACORN spokesman Scott Levenson dismissed the complaint as "political grandstanding" and insisted the problems were the work of one bad apple.[63]

Nevada election officials disagreed when, for example, their offices received *two* registration cards for one Roberta Casteel. For her part, Ms. Casteel was rather surprised when she received a rejection letter for an application she never made. Both of her applications had been submitted by ACORN, one as an "Independent" and the other as a "Democrat." Not surprisingly, neither of the signatures matched Ms. Casteel's own.

Connecticut officials disagreed when they found O'jahnae Smith registered to vote by ACORN. The girl was seven years old at the time. [64]

Illinois officials disagreed when they suspected ACORN vote canvassers of pulling names and addresses from telephone books and forging signatures. How did they suspect this? One registration was for a fast-food chain. Another for a man who died years earlier. Large numbers of registration forms bore signatures all in the same handwriting style.[65]

John Fund of the *Wall Street Journal* writes a column on voting fraud and has summed up some of the juicier acts of outright fraud perpetrated over the last two election cycles:

> [In May 2009] Nevada officials charged ACORN, its regional director and its Las Vegas field director with submitting thousands of fraudulent voter registration forms last year. Larry Lomax, the registrar of voters in Las Vegas, says he believes 48% of ACORN's forms "are clearly fraudulent" . . .

> [P]rosecutors in Pittsburgh, Pa., also charged seven Acorn employees with filing hundreds of fraudulent voter registrations before last year's general election. . . .

> . . . Fred Voight, deputy election commissioner in Philadelphia, protested after ACORN (according to the registrar of voters and his own investigation) submitted at least 1,500 fraudulent registrations last fall. . . .

> . . . St. Louis Democrat Matthew Potter, the city's deputy elections director, had similar complaints. . . .

> . . . Washington state prosecutors fined ACORN $25,000 after several employees were convicted of voter registration fraud in 2007. . . .

> . . . in the 2008 election, ACORN's practices led to investigations, some ongoing, in 14 other states. . . .

> . . . ACORN canvassers in Washington state and Missouri admitted to falsifying voter registrations. . . .

> . . . Lake County, Indiana, found more than 2,100 bogus applications among the 5,000 ACORN dumped right before the deadline. All the signatures looked exactly the same. . . .

> . . . Houston had rejected or put on hold about 40% of the 27,000 registration cards submitted. . . .

. . . [I]n 2004, four ACORN employees were indicted in Ohio for submitting false voter registrations . . . in 2005, two Colorado ACORN workers were found to have submitted false registrations . . . four ACORN Missouri employees were indicted in 2006 . . . five were found guilty in Washington state in 2007 for filling out registration forms with names from a phone book . . . .

[T]he IRS has filed a number of tax liens totaling almost $1 million against ACORN.[66]

You would expect this litany of fraud and abuse to raise some eyebrows on Capitol Hill. After all, a politician can only plunge his head into the sand for so long before coming up for air. In fact, Congressman John Conyers of Michigan chairs the Judiciary Committee, and he felt it necessary to hold hearings on ACORN. But even before his gavel hit walnut even once, Mr. Conyers released a statement saying that apparently he had been mistaken—all was hunky-dory at ACORN. Democratic sources on the Hill later told reporter John Fund that the leadership had strong-armed Mr. Conyers into shutting his trap.

No wonder, ACORN is on a first name basis with all the right people, beginning with Barack. During his campaign, Mr. Obama paid $832,000 to Citizens Consulting Inc., a front group for ACORN that had been tied to the embezzlement scheme. In its required filings with the Federal Election Commission, the Obama campaign detailed the payments as being for "staging, sound, lighting," only correcting them after reporters from the *Pittsburgh Tribune-Review* exposed their true nature—registering every possible derelict or felon they could find, and instructing them to vote the Democratic Party ticket.[67]

Mr. Obama got his start as a community organizer at ACORN's side. And importantly, in 1995 Mr. Obama represented ACORN in a key case upholding the new Motor Voter Act—the very law ACORN workers use to flood election offices with bogus registrations. While Mr. Obama and Mr. Soros served as hired guns and beneficiaries of ACORN, its workers were out in communities registering voters fifteen times over; canvassing the graveyards for potential voters;

registering Mickey Mouse in Florida, Batman in New Mexico, and Dallas Cowboys players in Nevada.

During a campaign debate when the question of ACORN was raised, Mr. Obama pulled a forgetting act. At first he denied knowing the first thing about ACORN. Once reminded that (1) ACORN's own newsletter says Obama attended their leadership training sessions for years, (2) he served as general counsel for ACORN in Illinois, (3) he was executive director of ACORN's voter-registration arm, Project Vote, in 1992, and (4) his campaign had written a check to them for nearly a million dollars, he adjusted his story a bit to suggest that his ties with ACORN were "insignificant" and that he was being attacked with "naked lies." His website decried the "vile Republican pattern of mockery and viciousness" that had "absolutely no basis in fact."[68]

We wonder why Mr. Obama protests so loudly?

If all the state's evidence is nothing more than a vast right-wing conspiracy run amuck—if that's really true—then why grace it with a response at all?

Why distance himself from ACORN just as he had previously distanced himself from other longtime friends such as terrorist William Ayers, the hatemongering Rev. Wright, racketeering artist Tony Rezko, and Jew-hating Louis Farrakhan?

Is he trying to stonewall in hopes that a lovestruck media won't call him to account for his role in criminal activities?

Could it be that Mr. Obama is a clever attorney who has learned a lot from Hillary Clinton? Perhaps he worries that an indictment that is working its way through the Justice Department may eventually drag him into the muck, and he's doing his best to insulate himself from any criminality and create conditions of plausible deniability.

We don't know. But we will, soon. As this book goes off to press, ACORN finally made such a terrible public blunder that even their friends on Capitol Hill and in the White House turned their backs. ACORN is finally being taken down, good riddance. What's not yet known is whether Mr. Obama will be taken down with ACORN.

Meanwhile, the Killionaires watching the action from their sky boxes are most entertained. They've paid good money to watch the partisans hurl their nasty charges and countercharges back and forth. While the partisan foment goes on and both sides gird for another "what did he know, when did he know it" game, they miss the bigger picture.

CONGRESS SPENDING LIKE AN ENTIRE DRUNKEN NAVY

Any conversation about fixing our government begins, as it must, with Congress. There is no more dysfunctional institution in the country. But sadly, no good argument can be made for tossing out our elected representatives and replacing them with direct citizen participation. Just spend a few minutes on an online political blog to get an idea of the wild and insane rabbit hole a genuinely democratic system of governance would lead us down.

For years now, through Republican and Democratic rule, the budget process in Washington has been a responsibility-free spendathon. Early in 2009, President Obama made a big public show of "convincing" lawmakers that they should pass his $787 billion economic-stimulus bill and not lard it up with earmarks (those last-minute spending projects designed to curry favor back in the home district). Mr. Obama took the high ground and said that earmark-infested budgets were Republican creations—that kind of irresponsible spending had to stop, and his budgets would "mark an end to the old way of doing business."[69] Making himself perfectly clear, he insisted that his Administration would "operate in a transparent fashion so that taxpayers know this money is not being wasted on a bunch of boondoggles."[70]

Democrats in Congress heard their president.

They let two whole weeks pass after the stimulus bill before voting for an additional $410 billion spending bill laced with thousands of wasteful earmarks. Their restraint was impressive! A few of those earmarks tell the story of all of them:

- A sizeable $74 million went to the storing of peanuts (a vital need, we're sure, in hard economic times).
- Pigs smell, but unconvinced of that, $1.7 million was earmarked for pig odor research ('nuf said).[71]

- Former gang members in California got $200,000 for the removal of tattoos (a two-fer, attacking both crime and dwindling sales at tattoo parlors).[72]
- Las Vegas took home $951,000 to tell the world they exist (apparently not everybody knows) and another $143,000 for a museum on the natural history of Las Vegas (seventy years ago it was desert, end of tour).
- The Buffalo Bill Historical Center in Wyoming received $190,000 to digitize the collection (now they're angry for not requesting more, and scalpings are planned).
- In Utah they have a "Mormon cricket" problem. That's the bug's name, oddly, and $1 million was earmarked to fight infestations (though the bug is quite resilient and cannot be killed off).[73]

Wild out-of-control spending used to be the Democrat swine flu; now both parties are infected equally. And with so much competition to spend, it's just a matter of time before scandal erupts. Republicans lost control of Congress in 2006 because of out-of-control spending and the corruption scandal of Jack Abramoff, among others. The Democrats at the time were spending just as much of your taxpayer money as the Republicans, but their scandals were more subdued for a change.

Look at House Speaker Nancy Pelosi, for example. Set aside the fact that our third most powerful politician represents a district where sexually transmitted disease is the primary industry. Her district of San Francisco is also the headquarters of StarKist Tuna, a major employer in American Samoa and responsible for the jobs of 75 percent of the Samoan workforce. In January 2007, the Congress increased the minimum wage from $5.15 to $7.25. Ms. Pelosi led the charge. But she had American Samoa exempted from the increase so that StarKist wouldn't have to pay the higher wage. This action certainly qualifies as crony favoritism and unprincipled hypocrisy, though it stops short of outright corruption.

But now Ms. Pelosi has her own Abramoff-type scandal brewing, and she's trying to force fellow Democrats to go down with her.

Here's the story.

There's an outfit named PMA Group that some 100 members of Congress have used over the years as an "intermediary" to exchange lucrative earmarks for campaign contributions.[74] PMA Group was set up by an aide to Democratic Congressman John Murtha, and Mr. Murtha himself directed some $78 million in earmark dollars through the PMA "money laundering operation." In this circle of Democratic political life, taxpayer money was funneled by Democratic congressmen into PMA Group, which then paid it out to selected recipients in the form of government contracts, and those recipients showed their gratefulness by making generous campaign contributions to the Democratic congressmen.

Shouldn't this kind of thing be illegal?

Yes. Which is why federal investigators raided PMA Group in November 2008 and have since subpoenaed a number of Democratic congressmen. As we write, the water is nearing boil. Several of the subpoenaed congressmen have defied Ms. Pelosi's orders to button their lips and remain at their posts. They're jumping ship like so many rats who know something about the nature of the ship's hull.

Congressman Jeff Flake has introduced nine resolutions calling for an ethics committee investigation into PMA. Yes, nine. Each time Ms. Pelosi has shut him down. But each time he picks up a few more Democrats who won their seats screaming loudly about Republican sleaze and are not at all eager to go out the way they came in. Representative Flake is winning other converts by making a convincing case that the Democrats' earmark corruption makes the old Republicans look like pikers. Earmarks used to be about bringing home the bacon; now they're fundraising tools—a way to reward companies who funnel cash into the campaign coffers.

A Justice Department investigation may be public as you read this. Mrs. Pelosi may be a private citizen again.

After studying the ways of Congress and walking the halls of the Congressional office buildings, it is easy to be struck by an altogether uncomfortable realization. There's some kind of mold growing on the walls of those buildings. Painting crews can often be spied, like Tom Sawyer in the summertime, pretending to whitewash the walls while the congressmen pretend to reform their wicked ways. At one point, perhaps unbidden, a question bubbles up from the depths and it becomes hard to ignore, like bile filling the throat. Ken Connor begged that very question admirably in a recent Townhall column:

> Politicians are elected by the people. And since ours is a "representative" government perhaps it's time we asked ourselves whether the character of our leaders is representative of the character of our nation? Americans have grown accustomed to a culture characterized by moral relativism and individualism. We have mocked Judeo-Christian values—humility, virtue, honor—and in the process, eroded restraints on social conduct. The results have become painfully obvious in the business arena and are becoming increasingly obvious in the political arena. When we do not demand honor, virtue, and accountability from ourselves, can we really expect more from our leaders? Have we merely gotten the leaders we deserve?[75]

Have we? What a question! Are the basic values that once defined our character as a nation and our promise as a people now lost like a river flowing into an unknown sea? Have we become the worst possible versions of ourselves—so incapable of decency, so confused in our values, so lost to a lackadaisical culture that we've gone from the label "The Greatest Generation" to an opposite label "The Worstest Generation"?

THE WORSTEST GENERATION?

According to unscientific polling (twenty passersby on Main Street in Boise one sunny autumn afternoon), only one in ten Americans is aware that our nation has an official creed. Written in 1917 and adopted by Congress, *The American's Creed* reads as follows:

> I believe in the United States of America, as a government of the people, by the people, for the people; whose just powers are derived from the consent of the governed; a democracy in a republic; a sovereign Nation of many sovereign States; a perfect union, one and

inseparable; established upon those principles of freedom, equality, justice, and humanity for which American patriots sacrificed their lives and fortunes. I therefore believe it is my duty to my country to love it, to support its Constitution, to obey its laws, to respect its flag, and to defend it against all enemies.[76]

This creed captured the deep patriotic pride and nationalist fervor of turn-of-the-century America. Today such a creed, if even known about, would be regularly mocked or dismissed as an anachronism of a jingoist past. If the *Revisionists* had their way with the creed today, and they were expressing their core beliefs, the creed would read something like this:

I believe in myself as a sovereign individual willing to consent to the dictates of the United States of America if and when it suits my interests; I recognize in this nation deeply flawed concepts of freedom, equality, and justice for which innocent soldiers have sacrificed their lives while a permanent war machine profits obscenely. I therefore believe it is my duty to my country to tolerate its shortcomings, shirk its laws, burn its flag from time to time, and work for unilateral disarmament to make the world safer.

Now this is a creed the *Revisionists* could support, unlike that "old rag" of a creed. Interestingly, the years circa 1917 would give birth to men and women who survived a far worse depression than today's, who faced and conquered far worse adversaries militarily, who built the mightiest engine of prosperity this world has ever known and rightfully earned the moniker *The Greatest Generation*. Just a generation or two later, a group of *Revisionists* would reject all this tradition and devolve from *greatest* to *worstest*.

Back in the 1960s, these *Revisionists* took to the streets chanting the functional equivalent of *"I want what I want and I want it now."* They would age, but hardly mature, and would continue taking little or no responsibility for their actions. Instead they've run up outrageous bills and passed the burden of payment on to the next generation. They've turned against God and taken to worshipping the false idols of celebrity or crusading for strictly environmental convictions. They've engorged on a junk diet of superficial thrills and created a health crisis in the process. They will go to their graves wanting what they want.

High on the list of the *worstest* is Oprah Winfrey.

Surprised? Ms. Winfrey is truly a great American story, having overcome a dreadful childhood to become one of the wealthiest entertainers in Hollywood, with a power base that is truly impressive. She has been generous to her fans. Her charitable works are many. In every way, Ms. Winfrey appears to be golden. She's surely unaware of the devastating impact she's had on modern culture.

She invites people onto her daytime TV show to talk about the hard knocks they've endured. She listens empathically, genuinely caring. Then she leads a studio audience and millions of viewers through a celebration of her guest's misfortunes. Ms. Winfrey insists she's trying to lift these poor, wretched souls out of their misery. But she might as well be peddling heroin.

Her drug is "victimhood," and people itch to get it.

Folks line up outside her studios for days, or cling to their televisions, to group-emote with Oprah. "We're all victims, honey" is the message gonged into their heads.

Ms. Winfrey's sizeable pocketbook and her $50 million Santa Barbara home have come from hooking these millions—mostly women—on the drug of victimhood. Her ratings would tank if she delivered a more conscientious message, such as "Life's not fair, honey, deal with it!" But Ms. Winfrey is too smart a businesswoman, and too dedicated to the *Revisionist* script, to deliver such a responsible message.

Equally *worstest* is the filmmaker Michael Moore. He's something of a Falstaff—a lying tub of lard, vainglorious and cowardly, but entertaining and often insightful. His targets are almost exclusively Republicans, and he skewers with such zest that it's easy to laugh. Mr. Moore has made himself a very rich man by catering to an apparently insatiable liberal desire to live the lie.

In his film *Fahrenheit 9/11*, there were a total of fifty-nine deceits, fabrications, and distortions, according to Dave Kopel of the Independence

Institute and our own analysis.[77] That's almost one lie every two minutes—not easy to do. So how did Mr. Moore deal with this?

He came half-clean with interviewers like Lou Dobbs, cleverly admitting that his agitprop was a comedy and "how can there be inaccuracy in comedy?"[78] Meanwhile, on his website Mr. Moore insisted that every detail was patently true, backed by extensive supporting documentation, carefully constructed so that the casual visitor could totally believe. Millions of deep thinkers still believe the film was totally accurate through to the credits, and Mr. Moore does little to dissuade them. This makes him no less a fraud than those he's targeting in his latest film, *Capitalism: A Love Story*. Mr. Moore has given a teaser:

> The movie is not going to be an economics lesson; it's going to be more like a vampire movie. Instead of the main characters feasting on the blood of their victims, they feast on the money. And they never seem to get enough of it.[79]

The film was only just released as we wrapped up our writing. If you haven't seen the film, save your money and skip the show. We can give you the storyline without seeing five minutes of the film. It will go like this: Years and years of Republicans deregulating the Republican-controlled financial markets allowed greedy Republicans to steal billions and billions from hard-working Democrats. Oh, Mr. Moore will blame a handful of Democrats, such as Timothy Geithner, Larry Summers, and Robert Rubin. How can he not? But his storyline will be head-spinning in its inaccuracy—exactly how the *Revisionists* like it.

A big fan of Mr. Moore and Ms. Winfrey, we suspect, is Peggy Joseph. She got her fifteen minutes after listening to the future president at a campaign event in Sarasota, Florida. She became known as "Peggy the Moocher" when recalling the event for a Florida reporter:

> I never thought this day would ever happen. I won't have to worry about putting gas in my car. I won't have to worry about paying my mortgage. You know, if I help [Obama], he's gonna help me.

Peggy's got it all figured out, hasn't she? Columnist Michelle Malkin did a wonderful job of capturing the thought processes of Peggy and similar moochers nationwide:

> Can't blame Peggy the Moocher for viewing Obama as the superior Santa Claus. With a relentless messianic campaign, a grievance-mongering wife touting him as the country's soul fixer and a national infomercial promising to take care of every need from night classes to medical bills to rent and fuel-efficient cars . . . Peggy sees government as her salvation and the president as her subsidizer-in-chief. She voted with the expectation that the Spreader of Wealth will reward her with payback.[80]

By creating an even wider gap between people and responsibility in America, Mr. Obama perpetuates the *Revisionist* views that undermine our culture and reward Killionaires.

When Mr. Obama has sought to play the role of all-knowing and caring father figure, the results have been mixed and suspect, at best. In the heat of the financial panic, there was tremendous populist anger rightly directed at bloated CEOs for taking million-dollar bonuses while their companies were being bailed out with taxpayer dollars. With Wall Street down, President Obama was quick to kick them, as well. He labeled as "shameful" and the "height of irresponsibility" the Wall Street honchos who took $18 billion in bonuses in 2008.

He was right—it was shameful.

But he may well have been a Saturday night sinner scolding the Sunday morning choir. He didn't care a whit about the demon fleecers of Wall Street; he cared only about whipping up the passions of unthinking liberal voters. We know this to be true by comparing his words ("shameful . . . height of irresponsibility") with his actions both before and after the fact.

The before: You can search the Congressional Record and not find a single instance of Senator Obama decrying the shamefulness of executive bonuses back in 2006 or 2007 when those bonuses totaled $62 billion—three times higher than the 2008 tipping point.

The after: Nine months and a trillion dollars in bailouts into his presidency, Mr. Obama had said nothing or done nothing, but the folks on Wall Street had. Major banks and securities firms were on track to pay their employees $140 billion in 2009—a *record* high, higher than the scandalous year of 2007, much of it funneled directly from taxpayers through the bailout funds to the folks on Wall Street.[81]

As the old saying goes, fool you once, shame on me; fool you twice, shame on you.

There's more than enough shame to go around, it must be noted. While a nation gets all flustered about the fat paychecks of corporate executives, what about sports stars and movie stars? The best athletes and actors make millions of dollars for providing a few minutes of entertainment. Their value in the big financial scheme of things is practically nonexistent. These entertainers fetch such princely salaries because millions of people of this country would rather worship a celebrity than God. Celebrity worship is a growth industry, and has been for some time. Journalist Neal Gabler has tried to explain how America climbed onto this slippery slope:

> In the 1980s, a new virus of celebrity infected the country, one feature of which was the "celebritization" of wealth. In a society where celebrity was suddenly considered the most exalted state one could achieve, the rich discovered that a large fortune and an extravagant lifestyle would bring media attention—witness that TV paragon of 1980s overindulgence, "Lifestyles of the Rich and Famous." Now that celebrity had become a source of power, previously obscure titans of industry, from Lee Iacocca to Donald Trump, began bidding for stardom, too. In fact, the business world practically demanded it . . .
>
> Not so long ago executives served their companies. Now the companies served the executives. . . . [82]

What makes Gabler's chronicles of life in the wealth lane so interesting and relevant to us here is that he does not paint our modern CEOs as demons and scoundrels. He traces the problem deep to the heart of modern American culture. If this is correct, and we believe it is, then our national economy faces a far bigger problem than any president can solve. For no amount of government regulation, criminal proceedings, or public shaming sessions are going to change the corporate culture if it is merely an extension of our national character.

The more honest we are as a nation in confronting the corruption that has taken root all around, the better prepared we'll be in defending ourselves in the years ahead.

And no group will require a more robust defense system than the entrepreneur. That's because under the Killionaires' high-stakes gambit, the rich get the sugar, the poor get the sugar, and the entrepreneur gets the shaft—as we see next.

4

THE SUGAR/SUGAR/SHAFT STRATEGY

*Our electoral strategy was really quite simple: rich donors got the
sugar; poor voters got the sugar; small business owners got the shaft.*
—BARACK OBAMA, speaking honestly, many years from now

IF THE KILLIONAIRES had a code name for their trillion-dollar heist, it
might have been the sugar/sugar/shaft strategy. In some ways it was
far easier to execute than a bank holdup, or even a purse snatch. All it
required was a deep seething contempt for their fellow man, and an
execution on three levels:

Level One: Cozy up to elected officials in both parties and earn a
voice in the legislation-crafting process, slowly and artfully removing
the controls that had guided capitalism successfully for a great many
years.

Level Two: Underwrite the campaign of a completely untested but
wildly charismatic candidate for the presidency, and then keep close
to the "trophy" president to ensure that his various departments (and
especially his attorney general) never convene a grand jury or issue an
indictment alleging anything illegal—no matter how obviously so.

Level Three: Keep your trophy president popular with the people
so he remains in office. And how? Well, one good way is to have your
president tell the rich they'll be taxed through the nose (they know

it won't happen, so they won't worry much) and tell the poor they won't be taxed at all (they will believe whatever you tell them). Ideas such as these may subvert the Republic, but they will keep a president ensconced in the Oval and provide cover to ensure that the thievery continues on, unchecked.

And what happens when the national treasury has been thoroughly looted? Government simply cranks up the taxes on entrepreneur investors who have no protection and, historically, no options.

But can entrepreneur investors be relied upon this time? Sure, we're accustomed to taking hits and being slammed to the canvas, over and over. That's what we do. We're fighters. We push back to our feet—weakened, dizzy, disoriented, and uncertain about our prospects. But back on our feet. As chief cook and bottle washer for our businesses, we seldom finish Monday before Tuesday and can hardly afford Wednesday. How we ever make it to Thursday is one of the enduring mysteries—like the disappearance of socks into the dryer or women into the bathroom. We are constantly told by the politicians that our efforts drive the U.S. economy, that our grit and gumption keeps half the nation in gainful employment while creating as many as eight in ten *new* jobs every year. But do we feel like the "driver"?

As an entrepreneur investor in today's political environment, you may feel more like the mechanic leaning over the hood of the vehicle, trying to coax a little more oomph out it. Growing a small business from an upstart into a great "lifestyle" company or even an IPO prospect is a tricky business. The odds are stacked brutally against us, and success is so elusive. We wouldn't choose the entrepreneurial life, probably, if we had a choice. But it seems to be hard-wired into the DNA. Like a primal motivation. For actors it is "fame," for politicians "power," and so for entrepreneurs it must be "freedom" we need more than anything. The freedom to choose our own path, make our own decisions, succeed or fail on our own terms. And we wouldn't have it any other way. But the difficulties in growing a business now have increased by an order of magnitude.

In tight times, as revenues shrink, small businesses don't have the cash reserves larger companies have. And there are fewer ways to cut costs without also cutting essential pieces of the company. So our small businesses can be forced into starvation mode and selective amputation at the same time—an always unhealthy combination.

That's why many of us cannot be relied upon this time to cough up the revenues Mr. Obama is expecting from us. That's also why many of us got fighting mad when the Obama administration released its financial rescue package. The American Recovery and Reinvestment Act of 2009, or ARRA, bailed out banks and large companies but left entrepreneur investors to fend for ourselves. Says Margot Dorfman, chief executive of the U.S. Women's Chamber of Commerce: "Our members are angry that the federal government is giving taxpayer money to big companies that have been horribly irresponsible while small businesses are not getting the money they need to keep their doors open."[83]

But the Obama administration knew what it was doing. It was carrying out the sugar/sugar/shaft strategy developed long ago. It knew that at the core of the entrepreneurial experience is a fierce independence and a desire—practically pathologic—to go it alone. Some entrepreneurs wouldn't accept bailout money even if it was forced on them. We would feel cheapened by it. And we have no illusions about who, ultimately, will be footing the bill for the bailout funds.

Entrepreneurs would rather play by the old rules—developing products people want, borrowing money to build up inventory, selling at a profit, paying off loans, expenses, and taxes, and pocketing the remainder. Mr. Obama understood this. He expected little opposition to his plan from entrepreneurs—or at least little organized opposition. What Mr. Obama may have miscalculated was how far entrepreneurs have been pushed. And how few options we now have, except to fight back on our own terms.

MAJOR COMPANIES CATCH COLD . . .

The Financial Panic of 2008 saw $8 trillion in "wealth" change hands practically overnight. First people lost their mortgages, then their credit cards, then their student loans. Then companies lost their commercial real estate holdings and began defaulting on bonds at rates last seen in 1933, according to Moody's Investors Service. Big companies are expected to default on $500 billion in corporate bonds and bank loans by 2010. Importantly, this is not the end of the default chain. The debt held by states and municipalities across the nation is larger than all the others (mortgages, credit cards, student loans, corporate paper) combined. When this last kink in the chain breaks, we could see an unprecedented $25 trillion transfer of wealth.

According to the folks at Standard & Poors, the health of big business in 2009 was every bit as bad as portrayed in nightly news programs. The operative word was "junk." By comparison, back in the early 1990s the recession took the credit rating of one in three companies from "investment grade" to "junk." In the recession of 2001, 50 percent of all companies went to "junk." In 2009, 66 percent of the companies in America were not creditworthy by traditional standards. "This is the most toxic mix of U.S. corporate ratings we've seen," S&P's Diana Vazza reported. And it is still sliding for the worse. S&P singled out media, travel, entertainment, auto makers, and retailers as "distressed" sectors and estimated that 90 percent of the nation's top companies would see their credit rating drop to "junk" within a few years. [84]

Name-brand companies seeking bankruptcy protection or reorganization in 2009 included Charter Communications—the giant cable network; Muzak—the elevator music king; Sirius-XM Radio— the leader in satellite radio; General Growth Properties—the nation's largest mall owner; Circuit City—the once dominant electronics store; Nortel—maker of communications products; Tribune Company— one proud newspaper leader; Pilgrim's Pride—poultry producer; Six Flags—the amusement park chain; Chrysler—the third-largest automaker; Fortunoff—owner of jewelry, home, and furniture stores; and Eddie Bauer—the outdoor apparel retailer.

As one major company after another goes into receivership, reorganization, or restructuring, they cut out the lavish offices and shutter the storefronts. The effect on commercial real estate is devastating. The Real Estate Roundtable has put the value of commercial real estate in the United States at approximately $6.5 trillion, financed by about $3.1 trillion in debt. This debt is very dangerous to the financial system because of its sheer size. What happens when this debt becomes due? By 2012, over $500 billion in commercial mortgages held by U.S. banks and thrifts are expected to come due, and will require refinancing. Half of them don't qualify for refinancing because the loan exceeds 90 percent of the property's value, and lenders are not wise to loan over 65 percent of a commercial property's value.[85]

Most of this commercial real estate lives or dies based on occupancy rates and delinquency rates. As long as tenant companies continue to fail and break leases, renegotiate the terms of their leases, or just plain pay late, the owners of those commercial properties will be in deep trouble. The current real estate slump has already surpassed that of the late 1980s, when bad commercial-property debt helped collapse 1,256 banks between 1985 and 1992.

How many banks will fail? We know about the big-name failures, but how widespread will the carnage be before it bottoms out?

The death count in the first ten months of 2009 was 109 banks—a still small number compared to the massive and widespread S&L failures of the late 1980s. And while some analysts such as those at CreditSights expect more than 1,100 banks to fail between 2008 and 2011,[86] that number could just as easily be limited to a few hundred as the government steps in again and again to keep its banking friends' heads above water. There will be an ever greater price to pay for all this government intervention, as we will see, but in the near term the banking industry will appear superficially stable.

When the big banks fail, what happens?

A case in point is Florida's BankUnited—one of the most costly failures of 2009. The government, through the Federal Deposit Insurance Corp. (FDIC), stepped in and guaranteed $4.9 billion in BankUnited assets. Then the FDIC sold off the company's banking operations to a private-equity team headed by John Kanas—for $900 million.[87] So what does this mean? It means that a group of Killionaires first helped to crash the banking system, making a fortune in the process. Then they got the government to make good, resuscitating the banks back to life. Then they stepped in and "offered" to buy back the banks at dimes on the dollar. Literally. BankUnited was bought for $900 million and is now potentially worth $5 billion.

If this drama had been played out in a Miami back alley, the thug would have beat you bloody, stolen your car and taken it on a crime spree, then returned to force you to pay to have your car back, conveniently disappearing as the police arrive on a tip that a car matching your description had been involved in criminal activity. That is why the actions of these Killionaires are so vicious and unpardonable—they helped engineer the crisis that produced cheap assets for the picking.

. . . SMALL BUSINESS ENDS UP WITH PNEUMONIA

When the federal government began bailing out big companies, a signal was sent. Big companies were again good credit risks in the eyes of lenders because, well, if anything went wrong, the government could be relied upon to step in and make good on the debt. No such implied warranty was extended to small business owners.

In fact, the opposite message was sent.

The largest national lender to small- and medium-sized businesses and franchises with over 100 years of experience was CIT Group. This Fortune 500 lender had extended $60 billion in credit to thousands of businesses when the Great Financial Panic of 2008 hit. They were slammed just as hard as companies such as Citibank, Bear Stearns, and General Motors, which received hundreds of billions in bailout money. So how much did CIT receive? It got a relatively paltry $2.3 billion in TARP money in December 2008, but was then cut off and allowed to twist in the political winds for months before finally declaring bankruptcy. This company that was so vital to the functioning of thousands of businesses across America, and certainly as vital to the U.S. economy as one of the Wall Street name brands, got the equivalent of a bitch slap. And why?

Because CIT focused on smaller businesses, and the Killionaires directing traffic at the control towers in New York and Washington had no need for them. Small businesses and entrepreneur investors had to be made to pay if the sugar/sugar/shaft strategy was going to work.

And so the credit sources for small businesses have dried up one after another. In May 2009, for instance, packaging producer UniFoil Corp. went shopping for a loan to purchase new equipment the company needed to boost sales. They were a solid, long-successful company doing about $35 million a year in revenue and as creditworthy as any business can be. But they were unable to secure a $2 million loan from any of the major lenders. J.P. Morgan Chase, which received $25 billion in bailout funds courtesy of the U.S. taxpayer, was one of the banks that turned down the UniFoil application. J.P. Morgan spokesman Tom Kelly insisted that his bank was in fact making loans using "disciplined and sound lending standards." Translation: The bailout money he and his pals received could not be lent to small companies creating legitimate products and providing real jobs; it could only be used to pay executives' deserved salaries and most-noble bonuses.[88]

Many small businesses spent 2009 in this credit crunch. Over their morning coffee they read in the papers how banks were given billions of dollars in taxpayer money for the express purpose of jumpstarting the American engine, and yet they couldn't get so much as a push-start from a banker. An April 2009 Federal Reserve survey of bank loan officers found that 40 percent of U.S. banks had tightened their lending standards; 70 percent had raised interest rates on credit lines; only a handful of banks had eased loan qualifying terms. [89]

Since it was carefree lending that got the country into such a pickle, the banks would be wise to price risk more rationally. But when the banks then took taxpayer money, the game changed. The market was no longer in charge; government was. If government was going to skew the credit markets and create new winners and losers, then it made no sense for big business to be the winner and small business the loser.

With tight credit at banks, entrepreneurs have historically been able to turn to angel investors and early-stage venture funds for start-up capital, bridge loans, factored financing, and the like. But that went away in 2008 as well.

The financial crisis brutally winnowed the number of venture capital firms. At the start of 2007 there had been 1,019 firms; by 2008 only 882; by 2010 the number is expected to be 30 percent less than when the crisis erupted. The reason for the shrinkage was evident in the raw numbers: Venture-capital funds sunk $29.7 billion into start-ups in 2008, and took out only $24.9 billion from IPOs and the sale of start-up firms. They lost about 20 percent on their money after expenses—that doesn't work when you're billing yourself as the smartest investors in the land.[90]

Add it up—the collapse of markets, the tightening of credit, the loss of investment sources—and entrepreneurs faced a stiff uphill slog in 2009. That fit the pattern of the Killionaire plan. For they had no use for entrepreneurs and their little entrepreneur dreams. Out of the way, they harrumphed. In their view, the big plum companies of America were available for easy pickings, and cheap. Every transaction government secured. But there was more work to be done. Once obtained, these companies had to be nurtured back into performing shape so that profits could again be generated. And that would take credit . . . from banks.

BAILOUTS ARE HOW KILLIONAIRES USE GOVERNMENT

As a truly gifted orator and politician, President Obama is very good at saying the right thing and knowing that most people will judge him only by what he says, not by what he does. And so Mr. Obama strode onto the stage at George Mason University in January 2009, and then Georgetown University three months later, to deliver what were billed as his "house upon a rock" speeches. Together these speeches were to lay out his vision for America. Several excerpts from the speeches are worth a closer look:

> Wall Street executives made imprudent and dangerous decisions, seeking profits with too little regard for risk, too little regulatory scrutiny, and too little accountability. Banks made loans without concern for whether borrowers could repay them, and some borrowers took advantage of cheap credit to take on debt they couldn't afford. Politicians spent taxpayer money without wisdom or discipline, and too often focused on scoring political points instead of the problems they were sent here to solve. The result has been a devastating loss of trust and confidence in our economy, our financial markets, and our government. . . .

Now, the very fact that this crisis is largely of our own making means that it is not beyond our ability to solve. Our problems are rooted in past mistakes, not our capacity for future greatness. It will take time, perhaps many years, but we can rebuild that lost trust and confidence . . .

It is true that we cannot depend on government alone to create jobs or long-term growth, but at this particular moment, only government can provide the short-term boost necessary to lift us from a recession this deep and severe. . . .

Instead of politicians doling out money behind a veil of secrecy, decisions about where we invest will be made transparently, and informed by independent experts wherever possible. Every American will be able to hold Washington accountable for these decisions by going online to see how and where their tax dollars are being spent. . . . [91]

There's a parable at the end of the Sermon on the Mount that tells the story of two men. The first built his house on a pile of sand, and it was soon destroyed when a storm hit. But the second is known as the wise man, for when "the rain descended, and the floods came, and the winds blew, and beat upon that house, it fell not: for it was founded upon a rock." . . .

We must build our house upon a rock. We must lay a new foundation for growth and prosperity. . . . [92]

Fine words, uplifting and inspired. Who could argue with them? Certainly not us, not if they were indicative of the actions the Obama administration intended to pursue.

So let's see.

President Obama insisted that the bailout money was desperately needed to keep the ship of state afloat. He claimed that every economist from the left and right agreed with him. Yet there had been nothing in the way of debate in Congress. No townhall meetings in cities across America. None of the open transparency and spirited bipartisanship that Mr. Obama had trumpeted as being essential to the enterprise of government. Seemingly overnight, the decision was made to spend a staggering $1.7 trillion, and to spend it fast—in a few short months.

So if there was another way to keep the ship of state afloat—and there was; if there were plenty of economists who disagreed with him—and there were; if public debate and town hall meetings and Congressional debates would have offered insight into the best solution—and they might have—oh well! Mr. Obama pushed forward, believing that despite his lofty rhetoric to the contrary, his electoral mandate entitled him to do whatever he damn well pleased.

To an extent, his mandate did just that. But his decision to spend a staggering sum—$1.7 trillion—in just a few months was entirely unprecedented. Not even Franklin Roosevelt attempted anything so radical, and he faced far worse economic conditions.

Unprecedented, yes. And practically inconceivable from a strictly logical point of view. Mr. Obama proposed to spend at a rate of almost $19 billion a day without so much as a floor debate in Congress. $19 billion a day; $792 million an hour; $13 million a minute; $220,000 a second. How could he spend that fast? It boggles the mind.

Most of the cash, it turned out, went straight to Mr. Obama's big business supporters in troubled sectors like banking and auto manufacturing—they got the sugar. Some of the cash went to Mr. Obama's organizers in poorer communities, though most of the sugar that'll be delivered into those communities to buy votes will come in the form of tax breaks. Not one billion found its way to the small businesses that create, oh yes, we remember, 80 percent of the new jobs in America. Small business got the shaft.

To make matters worse, the number of loans backed by the Small Business Administration (SBA) dropped dramatically in Mr. Obama's first year. SBA-guaranteed loans are likely to total $10 billion in 2009—or about half the inflation-adjusted average volume of previous years. Small business owners' reaction to the bailout lopsidedness and SBA lending siesta was summed up well by Raymond Keating, chief economist at the Small Business and Entrepreneurship Council:

Rather than fiddling with various government programs, the Obama administration would accomplish much more in terms of boosting confidence and getting the economy moving by, at the very least, moving away from imposing higher personal income, capital gains, dividend and estate taxes on investors and business owners.[93]

It's important to understand the politics at work here: Mr. Obama ripped into big business on the campaign trail for his true believers to lap up, but liberals have something of a love-hate relationship with big business. Think about it. Who else can liberals rely on to deliver huge corporate tax checks to the IRS, or buy into exorbitant labor contracts, if not big business?

Under Mr. Obama, big business gets the sugar with a capital S.

For example, Mr. Obama publicly rips Detroit for its "appalling" inability to build a fuel-efficient car. Unsaid is a truth Mr. Obama surely knows: Detroit is quite capable of building high-MPG cars—they've been doing it in their overseas subsidiaries for decades. It was equal parts onerous federal laws, union extortion tactics, and mismanagement in Detroit that turned the Big 3 into the Munchkin Men.

Twisting the old tale to this situation, by forcing the automakers to travel to Washington (Oz) and grapple with Congress (scary monkeys) along the way, the Obama administration could pretend to be all-powerful and munificent. In this sense, Mr. Obama's speeches would have been more honest if they used a "nightmare on a Kansas farm" metaphor, since that is the effect his policies will have, and coincidentally, that is where he spent his formative years with his white grandparents. But he chose "house upon stone" as his vision, and he told a nation that it wouldn't be easy rebuilding that house since we had "lost trust and confidence" after years of Republican misrule. He's right. It won't be easy, the way things are going. As reported nicely by Conn Carol of BeyondBailouts.org:

Don't worry, President Barack Obama and his Treasury Secretary Tim Geithner are on the case. Just yesterday they enacted new guidelines aimed at eliminating the influence of lobbyists on bailout funds. Feel better? Then you'll love this news. On the very same day Geithner announced his anti-lobbyist rules he hired Goldman Sachs lobbyist Mark Patterson as his Chief of Staff.[94]

Yes, it may take a long time to rebuild that lost trust.

TRICKLE OF RELIEF COMING FROM GOVERNMENT

In fairness to the Obama administration, they have offered a few token gestures of assistance to entrepreneur investors. The president's 2009 plan included a tax break for businesses with receipts of $15 million. The big plus was the change to the provision known as "carryback." This lets you take operating losses on tax bills going back five years and use them to offset past tax liabilities. The tax code already lets you apply current losses to reduce taxes on future profits. The change lets you use those current losses to offset tax on past profits, and file for a refund.

There are also some new write-offs in the works. Plus, if you hold your investments in your small business for five years, 75 percent of your capital gains will remain untaxed. It's not a lot, but it's something. And we're going to need every scrap we get tossed in coming years. Because first Mr. Bush and now Mr. Obama have landed serious blows on the entrepreneur in a 1-2 KO. And there's more hurt ahead. Our judgment is that on the economic front, we're in for a long "rolling stall."

5

PRESIDENT OBAMA'S ECONOMIC BRINKMANSHIP—STIMULUS OR DEPRESSANT?

Our enemies are innovative and resourceful, and so are we.
They never stop thinking about new ways to harm our country and
our people, and neither do we.
—GEORGE W. BUSH, August 5, 2004
(a gaffe, yes, but a prophetic one?)

NOBODY WILL EVER accuse Barack Obama of dallying. Within hours of taking office, he took to the airwaves to enlist America's support in facing down a "profound economic emergency" with an economic stimulus plan designed to "save or create up to four million jobs." His words were powerful and sober. He is a great communicator, especially when he's got a teleprompter in front of him. He was careful to boil down the many complexities and contrivances of governance into one effortless line: "The federal government is the only entity left with the resources to jolt our economy back into life."[95]

Watching the new President perform in his first prime-time press conference, we were struck by the sincerity of his delivery. Mr. Obama appeared to deeply believe what he was saying. If there had been any doubt about the approach he would take, it was dispelled on that day. Those four words—*"Only the federal government"*—would become the mantra, the money line, the end-game. Everything else was just noise.

Elsewhere in his speech and with grand rhetorical flourishes, Mr. Obama would warn that failure to act boldly could lead to the kind of economic stagnation that ravaged Japan in the 1990s and resulted in "a lost decade." But the end-game was clearly understood by all who were listening: *"Only the federal government . . . "*

Of course, there was never any doubt about the direction Mr. Obama would take the country once in office. He had campaigned as a centrist—because that was the only way he could get elected. But once in office and with a compliant Congress, he was free to pursue his real leftist aims. White House Chief of Staff Rahm Emanuel gave the first hint of the intense passion behind those aims soon after the November victory: "Never let a serious crisis go to waste. What I mean by that is it's an opportunity to do things you couldn't do before."[96]

Some have wondered if Mr. Emanuel, a well-educated man, was aware that he was parroting the revolutionary motto of Vladimir Lenin ("the worse, the better"). One of the first people to answer that question for certain was Senator Judd Gregg. He was tapped by Mr. Obama to be Commerce Secretary. As a Republican and a legendary budget cutter, Mr. Gregg was a big "get" for Team Obama. It was proof the Democrats were willing to reach across the aisle. But two weeks after being tapped, Mr. Gregg withdrew his nomination and publicly admitted to being rather naïve about the new administration's plans:

> [They are] really capable, dedicated, smart, sharp people with an agenda that they intend to pursue aggressively. . . . They are going to grow this government. . . . If you look at the Obama budget, it projects on average about a $1 trillion deficit [per year] over the next 10 years.[97]

The Obama Strategy was indeed "revolutionary." They would shock the system hard and fast, in a way not so different from Ronald Reagan's first budget, which sharply increased defense spending while holding the line on domestic spending. The stimulus plan thus became a tool for transforming the economy during the financial crisis so that if or when the crisis finally passed, a new country would emerge. Americans were so angry and frustrated that we were willing, at least for awhile, to accept something of a velvet glove revolution. Mr. Obama was only too happy to oblige:

It's more than just a budget; it's a blueprint for our economic future. It's a vision of what the Democratic Party stands for—that boldly and wisely makes the choices we as a nation have been putting off for too long. [98]

So what were these choices we'd been "putting off"?

We quickly found out when Mr. Obama unveiled a two-year, $787 billion stimulus package and a $3.6 trillion federal budget within weeks of each other. In his own words, he aimed to create jobs with the stimulus package and use the budget process to push the new priorities: push caps on greenhouse gases, pour more federal money into education, take over health coverage. It became an article of faith within the administration that all three initiatives could move forward simultaneously while also solving the financial crisis and fighting two major wars in far-off countries. So no dallying, and no lack of ambition.

Early 2009 gave America the most "revolutionary" legislative changes since Ronald Reagan in 1981, Lyndon Johnson in 1964, and Franklin Roosevelt in the early years of the Great Depression.

Back in his 1935 State of the Union speech, Mr. Roosevelt sought only to replace relief checks with genuine jobs. People wanted to work and not accept handouts, Mr. Roosevelt believed, and so he aimed to help. But much to his dismay, the economic crisis radically altered the relationship between the people and their government. A dependency was created and made permanent—and it would corrode the work ethic of America steadily with each passing decade. Ultimately, another Democrat would use that dependency as a baseline, and build from there.

That Democrat was Barack Obama.

At public appearances throughout 2009, Mr. Obama reiterated his firm conviction that the stupendous sums he was spending in hurry-hurry style were intended solely to "revive our flagging economy," and nothing else. You be the judge.

STIMULUS AS "HELPING HAND" OR "TROJAN HORSE"?

As presented and promoted to the American people, the Obama Stimulus Package had one goal: put people to work to revive the economy. Odd, then, that most of the money went into sectors of the economy where unemployment was historically low and economic cycles nonexistent. The December 2008 unemployment rate for government workers was 2.3 percent; for education and health workers it was 3.8 percent. To set that in context, the unemployment rate for the manufacturing sector was 8.3 percent, and for the construction industry 15.2 percent. Yet well over half of the stimulus spending went to government, education, and health care. [99] If the intent was to fight unemployment, why focus on the sectors where there was none?

Only $70 billion, or less than 10 percent of the total package, went to fixing highways, roads, bridges, airports, clean water projects, electric grid, and broadband development. These are more worthwhile uses of taxpayer money, and they put people to work, but they represented only ten cents on each dollar of spending. What of that other 90 percent—was any of it stimulating?

Well, the federal government needed stimulating, according to the Obama administration, and what better way than by giving them more cars to tour around in? Yes, the federal fleet of 600,000 vehicles costing $3 billion a year was apparently inadequate. So another $600 million was set aside for more cars. And $7 billion was added to modernize federal buildings. That sounds stimulating!

There was also Amtrak—the government-subsidized railroad that hasn't turned a profit in forty years and won't for another forty. Amtrak and similar transit systems are vital pieces of our nation's transportation infrastructure, but they are often so poorly managed that fares cover less than half the costs. And it's not like there's no alternative. A number of entrepreneurs have been trying for decades to buy Amtrak, and they come with impressive plans to turn it profitable—with zero need for taxpayer underwriting. But the folks who operate Amtrak belong to public-employee unions. These unions contribute heavily, and exclusively, to the Democratic Party. So "change" ain't gonna happen, especially when the Democrats are running things. They'll keep pumping good money after bad into Amtrak. They spent $1 billion in the 2009 stimulus to keep the union conductors in suspenders— though that buys only a few months of subsidies.

One of the biggest chunks of the stimulus package, $252 billion, went straight into income-transfer programs. These were not investments in job creation or business development. These were cash payments or handouts made to folks for just being alive and living in the United States.

Some $83 billion went to "earned income credits," otherwise known as tax breaks for having kids.

Another $81 billion went to Medicaid, covering medical bills for the deserving and undeserving alike.

For those suddenly out of work, a full $36 billion was allocated—an understandable move given that unemployment was at 5.8 percent when Mr. Obama took office, and sure to rise above 10 percent in 2010.

Also understandable was $20 billion set aside for food stamps. Already, some 28.4 million Americans receive food stamps, according to the USDA, and at least half of all children will be on food stamps by the end of Mr. Obama's term. This will ensure that future generations are tied to the Democratic Party, no doubt. In the near term, however, there was an argument to be made for helping less fortunate Americans through the tough economic downturn.

That said, absolutely no case could be made for job creation or economy stimulation.

Of the income-transfer programs, some $2 billion went to child-care subsidies. Perhaps the economy was stimulated a bit by these funds, since a lot of mothers could leave their child-rearing responsibilities and go looking for jobs in the workforce. Oh, that's right, *looking for* a job doesn't much stimulate the economy.

Another big winner in the stimulus lottery was the Department of Education. They received a $66 billion bump in their budget, a bump that was larger than the entire budget of the department just a decade ago. Has all the money thrown at the Education Department accomplished anything valuable, such as improving student test scores? No, it's too early to assess improvements in scores. But there have been promising reports from the department's $4.3 billion "Race to the Top" program. The idea of this program is for states to compete for federal funds by enacting genuine reform.[100] It's the kind of program that may yield genuine results—and we are hopeful.

There is every reason to believe the teachers' unions will subvert

Mr. Obama's efforts. They will certainly try. But if Mr. Obama is able to demonstrate to the American people that there is an important connection between teacher pay and student performance, then he will have used his bully pulpit well. He will not have stimulated the economy any, but the effect on students' minds will pay dividends.

Another major thrust of the stimulus was for (1) global-warming research, (2) carbon-capture demonstration projects, and (3) renewable energy projects. These R&D projects captured about $11 billion of the stimulus pie. The idea behind each of these, as we'll investigate in greater depth later, is to drive up the cost of fossil fuels so high that a desperate America will stop driving their cars, heating their houses, or carrying their groceries home in plastic bags.

We don't see how the economy will be stimulated or jobs created by (1) funding questionable and certainly partisan scientists, (2) figuring out how to suck a little of the damaging CO_2 out of the air, and (3) building bigger and more exciting windmills out on the fruited plains. But maybe we missed something. So we turned an ear to what nonpartisan scientists were saying. One of them, Nobel laureate Gary Becker, had this comment about the $11 billion spent on R&D:

> Much of it doesn't have any short-term stimulus. If you raise research and development, I don't see how it's going to short-run stimulate the economy. You don't have excess unemployed labor in the scientific community, in the research community, or in the wind power creation community, or in the health sector. So I don't see that this will stimulate the economy, but it will raise the debt and lead to inefficient spending and a lot of problems.[101]

Moving on to other powerful stimulants the Obama administration built into their rescue page, we find that $650 million was set aside to make it easier for people to watch TV. Seriously. The government had already spent several billion to pay for digital TV conversion coupons. But apparently many millions more would help people get jobs by sitting on their couches watching, what, *The Biggest Loser*?

Then there is that powerful engine of job creation, the National Endowment for the Arts. They landed $50 million to keep a couple of hundred bureaucrats and possibly a few artists off the streets. Nice stimulus, if you can get it.

Think the stimulus couldn't get sillier? How about sending $150 million across the Washington Mall to the curators at the Smithsonian? Yes, $150 million. Now, we're big fans of the Smithsonian, as surely you are. But we're a bit confused as to how the museum's talented curators plan to create millions of jobs and turn around the economy.

Of all the stimulus spending, the "cash for clunkers" program got the most press—probably because it's the only one average folks could understand. It was hailed as a phenomenal success by one and all. Proof that the Administration was "on the right track." Well, let's see.

The first person to publicly question cash-for-clunkers was Peter Kornafel of CARQUEST. His back-of-napkin analysis found that the average trade-in clunker had been getting 15 MPG and its shiny new replacement 25 MPG. That trade-in would use 800 gallons of gas a year, assuming normal driving. The replacement would use just 480 gallons to drive as far. So the average clunker transaction reduced gas consumption by 320 gallons per year. Now figure into the equation that 700,000 vehicles were reportedly traded in, equaling a savings of 224 million gallons of gas a year, or 5 million barrels of oil, or about $350 million at current oil prices. So the taxpayers spent $3 billion to save $350 million. We join Mr. Kornafel in asking, "How will more government spending like this get us out of the hole?"

But wait, there's more! Randy Fardal next came along and in an *American Thinker* article, dug a little deeper.[102] Turns out that the Obama administration pulled the 700,000 new car sales figure out of a murky pit of tar. Two weeks after blanketing the media with the 700,000 figure, the president's Council of Economic Advisors quietly reported the actual number of sales was closer to 330,000.

That means we taxpayers forked over $9,000 to underwrite the cost of each new car sale—what a deal we got!

Oh, but there's still more. Mr. Fardal then factored in the normal increases in car sales we would have expected between June and January without the clunkers program. Turns out, the clunkers program generated only 56,000 additional sales—not the 700,000-unit gain widely reported.

Yes, $3 billion is a lot of taxpayer money to stimulate sales of just 56,000 cars. That translates into about $50,000 per car. As is so often the case with government spending, we got the loud quacking goose but no golden egg.

The only conclusion we can take from all this? The $787 billion stimulus succeeded on the level it was intended to—it was the most extravagant *political* stimulant in history. Every pet project of the Democrats and their unseen Killionaire benefactors got some sugar, and the real job creators of this country got the *you know what*.

Want further proof? A study done by *USA Today* found that the 872 counties that supported Mr. Obama averaged about $69 in stimulus money per person, while the 2,234 that supported McCain averaged about $34 per person.[103] As the good folks at *Human Events* said, "Liberals don't call that vote-buying—but we do."

Political analysts Dick Morris and Eileen McGann agreed that the stimulus package was vote-buying—yes, but it was more than that. It was the ultimate political Trojan Horse:

> At most, his stimulus will act as methadone while we withdraw from our debt addiction, mitigating the pain, smoothing over the trauma, and soothing our system. But Obama's strategy is to hide inside the Trojan Horse of stimulus an army of radical measures to change America permanently. [104]

We are already seeing Mr. Obama's strategies take deep root in Washington and across bail-me-out America. This is as planned. Recall . . . *"only the federal government."* The stimulus spending of 2009 created a budget deficit topping $1 trillion. This deficit will become permanent—there is no way it cannot, and it will stop conservatives in future years from cutting taxes. That, too, is part of the plan. As Mr. Obama funds the pet spending projects that have been piling up in liberal backrooms for forty years, he is turning the public sector into the largest sector.

HOW DO WE PAY FOR THIS ENTIRE STIMULUS?

Mr. Obama campaigned as a big supporter of "responsible fiscal policies." In his acceptance speech at the convention, he pledged to "go through the federal budget line by line, eliminating programs that no longer work." Even in office, he continued to insist that he would cut the deficit in half by the end of his first term. He would do this, he insisted, by "rooting out waste and abuse" wherever he found it. But his words and his actions bore absolutely no resemblance to each other. So much for hope and honesty you can believe in. Or as comedian Dennis Miller observed, "Washington is to lying what Wisconsin is to cheese."

That Mr. Obama inherited a financial crisis and a soaring budget deficit is well known. That he was required to improvise and think up solutions fast is granted to him. Every reasonable citizen knows he faced tough decisions with disagreeable options. He was owed some of that "patriotic grace" that Peggy Noonan wrote so beautifully about. He was owed a little patience, and a measure of time sufficient to make good on the promise of his presidency. But when month after month he continued to insist publicly that he could balance the budget in four years when in fact he was taking the federal government's share of GDP to levels not seen since World War Two, he entered the realm of the incredulous. He gave the lie to his every public utterance.

And it became obvious to every independent observer that Mr. Obama was not trying to merely "revive the economy," as he insisted so strenuously. His spending bonanza was intended to become the annual budget baseline that Congress would begin with. So with a new baseline of $3 trillion, the next budget request would be 10 percent higher or 15 percent higher. What was billed as temporary, emergency spending would become permanent spending increases of 10 percent to 15 percent per year.

This is a risky game Mr. Obama plays. He knows that there is no way he can pay for his mountains of spending without (1) defaulting on the government's debt obligations and declaring bankruptcy, or (2) heaping new taxes on the 95 percent of American taxpayers he vowed repeatedly in his campaign to exempt from taxes. We presume he's not eager to take the former path. But the latter path could cost him a second term when angry moochers turn on him for not making their lives free. So how will Mr. Obama cross the huge chasm between his promises and the realities of governance? One observer, the talented Gerald Seib, took a crack at an answer:

> His read-my-lips moment was that no family with an income under $250,000 will pay a "single dime" in new taxes to support the construction of this new federal skyscraper. If that's still true in 2015, Mr. Obama will be walking back and forth across the Potomac River.[105]

WE WERE ASKED TO SPEND $646,214 TO CREATE ONE JOB

Recall that Mr. Obama had initially insisted that his stimulus bill would create or save three or four million jobs in two years, with many of those jobs being in government. How did he arrive at these job numbers? Alan Reynolds, a senior fellow at the Cato Institute and author of *Income and Wealth*, went poking in the pudding.

It turns out that Mr. Obama's Council of Economic Advisers lifted some economic forecasts from Mark Zandi of Moody's (the people who told us all those banks were doing just fine in 2008). Mr. Zandi had crunched the numbers and concluded that the stimulus would create 330,400 new government jobs over two years.

This was found pleasing by the Obama people, and they plugged those numbers into their own spreadsheets. Since about $215 billion was then slotted for creating government jobs, and 330,400 was the forecast of new jobs that would be created, that meant taxpayers were spending $646,214 per new job created.

Such a deal! Only the federal government could give you that kind of deal. *"Only the federal government."*

And what about "creating" jobs in the private sector? As we wrote in Chapter 3, Mr. Obama claimed that his stimulus bill would create or save some 600,000 jobs overall by Fall 2009. So, did it?

Not surprisingly, no.

There's no surprise in this because government can't create jobs;

only the private sector can. Government can take from the most productive in the private sector to "create" jobs for the least productive among us. *That* government can do. So government can destroy some jobs to create other jobs. Political outcomes can be achieved. But net jobs creation cannot—not by government.

And in fact, while Mr. Obama was claiming victory in the fight to create jobs, the unemployment rate was stubbornly pushing above 10 percent in some states, and millions of jobs were disappearing, perhaps forever.

Mr. Obama cannot rightfully be blamed for structural changes in the global job market. But if he's going to spend billions of dollars of our money to "create or save" jobs, we hope he at least succeeds in the short term so that the wealth that has been taken from taxpayers is not entirely frittered away. Reports in November dashed our hopes.

Instead of a job total of 600,000, apparently the official number was only 30,000 (5 percent of the promise) but even that figure was inflated. The Associated Press reviewed the program's first report card and found that Team Obama wildly inflated (or passed along wildly inflated) job creation estimates.[106]

One Colorado company said they created 4,231 jobs with the help of stimulus money, but they created fewer than 1,000.

A child-care center in Florida claimed 129 new jobs, but they used the stimulus money to give pay raises to existing employees.

AP reviewed hundreds of contracts and found that in some cases, the job counts were five to ten times less than reported publicly.

If your kids tell you they did all of their homework but they only did a quarter of it, you know it's a lie. So what is Team Obama doing? You can be the judge of that.

Even giving Team Obama credit for good intentions, they still spent $787 billion to create or save only a few thousand jobs. That's bad governance in anybody's book.

USING FUZZY MATH TO CONFUSE AND CONFISCATE

Back in the 1980s, when your authors were young toilers in the Reagan administration, we were continually amazed at the vitriol the media would hurl at Mr. Reagan's economic policies. Commentators called it "voodoo economics," borrowing a line George Bush had tossed out in the heat of the campaign. The voodoo was the supply-side view that by cutting the income taxes of the most productive members of society they would increase their output, open up new markets, employ people in need of jobs, and even increase overall tax receipts.

That the "voodoo" somehow managed to lower the crucial prime rate from a choking 20 percent to a more manageable 9 percent by the time Mr. Reagan left office was appeared lost on his detractors.

Was supply-side economics some kind of nirvana pill? Certainly not. But it did set the stage for the great prosperity the nation enjoyed in the 1990s. Though less than perfect, the financial structure that grew out of the 1980s *somehow* resulted in the creation of the 20 million new jobs that President Clinton would take credit for in the 1990s.

Liberals see it differently. They maintain that the 20 million new jobs and economic prosperity occurred at the precise hour a newly elected President Clinton began setting policy. They insist that it was Mr. Clinton's rejection of supply-side economics that resulted in a virtual overnight creation of 20 million jobs. And this blue-sky thinking is back in vogue.

Instead of supply-side magic, we have demand-side magic. Team Obama is promising us that every $1 the government spends will turn into $1.50 in economic activity . . . somehow. They call this the "multiplier" effect. How do they do it? For answers we consulted Robert J. Barro, economics professor at Harvard, senior fellow at Stanford's Hoover Institution, and author of *Macroeconomics: A Modern Approach*:

> First assume that the multiplier was 1.0. In this case, an increase by one unit in government purchases and, thereby, in the aggregate demand for goods would lead to an increase by one unit in real gross domestic product (GDP). Thus, the added public goods are essentially free to society. If the government buys another airplane or bridge, the economy's total output expands by enough to create the airplane or bridge without requiring a cut in anyone's consumption or investment. The explanation for this magic is that idle resources—unemployed labor and capital—are put to work to produce the added goods and services. . . .

If the multiplier is greater than 1.0, as is apparently assumed by Team Obama, the process is even more wonderful. In this case, real GDP rises by more than the increase in government purchases. Thus, in addition to the free airplane or bridge, we also have more goods and services left over to raise private consumption or investment. In this scenario, the added government spending is a good idea even if the bridge goes to nowhere, or if public employees are just filling useless holes. Of course, if this mechanism is genuine, one might ask why the government should stop with only $1 trillion of added purchases. . . .[107]

Yes, why not spend $10 trillion to make $15 trillion—that would be the kind of boon our economy could surely use!

Professor Barro has done extensive studies of the massive run-up in federal spending that peaked in the war years of 1943–1944. He estimated that the United States spent $540 billion on the war effort (in 1996 dollars). He then estimated that the war increased the nation's gross domestic product by $430 billion per year. So the "multiplier" was 0.8—every dollar spent created 80 cents in jobs and output, effectively. When he tried to estimate what the "multiplier" would be for government expenditures made in peacetime, that 0.8 dropped to nearly 0.0. He found no benefit to people out of work, or businesses strapped for credit, from government purchases made in "normal" times.

Another student of the "multiplier" and World War Two is economist Mancur Olson. He focused on the economies of Germany and Japan, and he concluded that those two nations gained a lot by losing that war. They were able to restructure their economies and become commercial powerhouses on a global level in just a few decades.

So which of these scholars has the ear of Team Obama?

It appears that Mr. Obama and his economic advisors are big fans of Mr. Olson, as reported by David Leonhardt in the *New York Times*:

Once governments finally decide to use the enormous resources at their disposal, they have typically been able to shock an economy back to life. They can put to work the people, money and equipment sitting idle, until the private sector is willing to begin using them again. The prescription developed almost a century ago by John Maynard Keynes does appear to work.[108]

Oh really? For a bit more astute analysis of the differences between post-war Germany and Japan, and the United States today, we turned to our friend Bill Bonner writing in *The Daily Reckoning*:

> The Germans did not fix their system. Neither did the Japanese. Instead, WWII fixed them both. Their industry and their government were destroyed—by bombs, artillery, tanks and aircraft. Olson noticed what comes after destruction: Renaissance. America is a long way from that. Its politicians and opinion mongers—such as Leonhardt— are still in their bunkers, still directing what is left of their troops. Still raising money. Still taxing. Still spending. Still fixing. They hope to save the system, not rebuild on the ruins. [109]

The working assumption of the Democratic leadership appears to be *the bigger the government action, the better the outcome—deficits be damned.* Watching Congress approve the largest expenditure in history with nary an afternoon's deliberation was Niall Ferguson, the author of *The Ascent of Money,* a book that traces the history and impact of money on society. There was melancholy in his observations:

> There is something desperate about the way economists are clinging to their dog-eared copies of Keynes' *General Theory*. Uneasily aware that their discipline almost entirely failed to anticipate the current crisis, they seem to be regressing to macroeconomic childhood, clutching the Keynesian "multiplier effect" . . . like an old teddy bear. They need to grow up and face the harsh reality: The Western world is suffering a crisis of excessive indebtedness. Governments, corporations and households are groaning under unprecedented debt burdens. . . .

> The delusion that a crisis of excess debt can be solved by creating more debt is at the heart of the Great Repression. Yet that is precisely what most governments propose to do. . . .

The born-again Keynesians seem to have forgotten that their prescription stood the best chance of working in a more or less closed economy. But this is a globalized world, where uncoordinated profligacy by national governments is more likely to generate bond-market and currency-market volatility than a return to growth.[110]

A CONCERTED EFFORT TO DESTABILIZE U.S. BANKS

When the news broke in early January 2009 that the Obama administration would spend more than $2 trillion restoring America's banks to health, it became painfully clear that the inmates were in control of the asylum. The chiselers, frauds, and cheats who had used America's big banks as tools to strip American investors and then destabilized those banks so that they would fail in the first financial downturn were now screaming the loudest about the financial Armageddon that surely awaited if immediate actions were not taken to refill their coffers.

So it was that the loudest shouters were handed $2 trillion with a slap on the wrist and a stern—or was it *very* stern?—warning to be better custodians of the public purse this go around.

The Obama administration carried out its part of the plan. They handed over the $2 trillion to the Killionaires in private meetings, while at the same time stoking a very public debate about how best to reform those arrogant, rapacious bankers.

Their conclusions on how best to proceed with "reform" were as predictable as a donkey headed back to its barn: affix blame for the entire mess on the Republicans. That the perpetrators of the financial crisis had ties to both political parties, and if anything were more present in the Obama administration than in the previous Bush administration, mattered not to the storyline. A compliant media and pitchfork-wielding public were eager to demonize somebody—it was those Bushies, those Chenies, those Rovies, get 'em! Everyone piled on. Mr. Obama's genius at speechmaking was gravy—the people needed a scapegoat, and Mr. Obama was happy to oblige.

But there was still work to do for Team Obama. The banks had to be loudly reformed in a convincing public spectacle. With an especially vengeful public drubbing of the banks, the people would feel that justice was being properly meted out.

So Team Obama divided into two camps to debate the future of banking as an industry. One camp was led by Paul "The Asperger's Kid" Krugman—seasoned economist, childlike politics. He argued that the federal government should nationalize all the banks for good. Turn them into something similar to the DMV, free of private sector meddling and administered by public servants who seek only to attain the highest coefficient of societal equity. Since the top ten banks in the country control 75 percent of all our national cash, pensions, and investments, he argued, they needed to be controlled.

Opposing the Krugman crew were the folks aligned with National Economics Council director Larry Summers. These guys worried that any big restructuring or nationalizing of the banks might backfire and collapse the entire financial system. Instead, the Summers team wanted to turn banks into something similar to local electric or water utilities—heavily regulated, but still calling all the unimportant shots.

The Krugman-Summers argument raged through 2009, delighting observers in the Rightstream media, for they thought they had raw meat—dissension within Team Obama, warring factions, trillions on the line.

But it was mostly for show, to feed the beast of public spectacle.

Behind the curtain, the real business was being conducted—all the promise of "change" and accountability was being papered over to the benefit of the Killionaires. According to a special PBS *Frontline* show "The Warning," Larry Summers personally stepped in and blocked attempts to properly regulate the secretive, multitrillion-dollar derivatives market that was at the core of the 2008 meltdown. Brooksley Born, head of the Commodity Futures Trading Commission, correctly called derivatives a "dark market" lacking the transparency of a genuine capitalist market. She tried to clean it up—but was blocked, and so the abuses pre-Obama continue post-Obama.[111]

Free from official scrutiny, the Killionaires could continue their looting and fleecing. Their next big decision in the chronology of wealth killing was to determine which pieces of the bankrupt and begging capitalist landscape they most wanted to buy back for less than book value, with their purchases being warranted by taxpayers.

So many bankrupt companies, so little time.

They had to act fast, because the Obama administration would only be able to provide cover for so long before the public caught on. Simon Johnson caught the flavor of this private raid on the public treasury in a May 2009 article in *The Atlantic*:

[The government's latest Financial Stability Plan] is likely to provide cheap loans to hedge funds and others so that they can buy distressed bank assets at relatively high prices—has been heavily influenced by the financial sector, and Treasury has made no secret of that. As Neel Kashkari, a senior Treasury official under both Henry Paulson and Tim Geithner (and a Goldman alum) told Congress in March, "We had received inbound unsolicited proposals from people in the private sector saying, 'We have capital on the sidelines; we want to go after [distressed bank] assets.' And the plan lets them do just that: By marrying government capital—taxpayer capital—with private-sector capital and providing financing, you can enable those investors to then go after those assets at a price that makes sense for the investors and at a price that makes sense for the banks." Kashkari didn't mention anything about what makes sense for the third group involved: the taxpayers.[112]

It remains to be seen which side in the Obama administration battle will prevail—Krugman or Summers. But it doesn't matter, really. The entire financial system in America has been completely destabilized. The Killionaires are free to have their way with it.

6

FAST-PATCHING OR EURO-TRASHING AMERICA?

I love America today. I've seen the first black president in America. I'm sure the world is going to change. [113]
—Reaction to Barack Obama's victory from AHMED KELIFI, a Frenchman

Victory for the hysterical Oprah Winfrey, the mad racist preacher Jeremiah Wright, the US mainstream media who abandoned any sense of objectivity long ago, Europeans who despise America largely because they depend on her. . . .

Victory for the cult of the cult. A man who has done little with his life but has written about his achievements as if he had found the cure for cancer in between winning a marathon and building a nuclear reactor with his teeth. Victory for style over substance, hyperbole over history, rabble-raising over reality. . . .

Victory for those who believe the state is better qualified to raise children than the family, for those who prefer teachers' unions to teaching and for those who are naïvely convinced that if the West is sufficiently weak towards its enemies, war and terror will dissolve as quickly as the tears on the face of a leftist celebrity. . . .

Victory for social democracy even after most of Europe has come to the painful conclusion that social democracy leads to mediocrity, failure, unemployment, inflation, higher taxes and economic stagnation. . . . [114]

—Reaction from the *Daily Mail*, a British newspaper

I T IS WIDELY believed that the world loathed our forty-third president and loves our forty-fourth. Like most generalizations, it is both truthful and misleading.

Politically passionate Europeans do feel a kinship with American liberals because they view the world similarly—with a wide-eyed sense of all that is possible, though unrealistic. And on the European streets, there is a long lurking contempt for the Yanks, owing to the simple fact that we're so fabulously successful. And we strut. When we show up at the party we're hotter, louder, richer, ornerier, fatter, bolder, and yes, even wiser, if you agree with Winston Churchill that "Americans will always do the right thing . . . after they've exhausted all the alternatives."[115]

But the main reason that Europeans are so loathing is not because of Mr. Bush, but because of a deep dependency on us. Like the welfare bums who whine about the system while cashing their monthly checks, these Europeans don't enjoy playing second fiddle to U.S. economic prowess.

There are reasons we've enjoyed financial success over our European cousins. It is *largely* a result of different paths taken. America chose the path of "opportunity" that resulted in more of a free market democracy. Europe chose the path of "equality" which gave them more of a social democracy. On each continent there has long been an abundant love of both opportunity and equality; America just leaned one way, Europe the other. That is reversing, even now, and so there is value to both Europe and America in comparing the two paths taken.

How much better do folks live on one continent or the other? How much more they can afford? How much leisure time do they have? How many more opportunities will their children have? These are "quality of life" measures best represented in the gross domestic product *per capita* in a country. The following chart shows the difference between the United States and France since 1960 (Table 6.1):[116]

GROSS DOMESTIC PRODUCT PER CAPITA		
	USA	France
1960	$14,960	$9,803
1970	$19,879	$15,164
1980	$24,500	$19,787
1990	$30,729	$23,932
2000	$37,572	$27,643
2008	$46,859	$34,208
		Source: IMF

Table 6.1 Gross Domestic Product per Capita

Going back a half century, the average Frenchman has enjoyed only two-thirds the standard of living of the average American. Now, as the French president himself, Nicolas Sarkozy, has pointed out recently, GDP is an imperfect measure of a nation's well-being, but it is still the best overall measure that the world's democracies have all agreed on for the last fifty years. And by that measure, the French and other similar European countries have come up short on the prosperity meter.

Think about how your life would be if the European model prevailed in the States. What would you choose to forfeit if a third of your annual income was erased? A night out a week at a restaurant? A second car? A second vacation, or even a first? A college education for the kids? Major sacrifices would have to be made.

So what is the attraction of American liberals to the European social welfare state? Why the pining for a system in which the standard of living is one-third lower than ours? Why is the Obama administration marching us, perhaps now irreversibly, toward a European-style social welfare state with its long history of relative economic stagnation? And how will this new lower standard of living look in your day-to-day life?

TWO STEPS LEFT, ONE STEP RIGHT

It bears repeating here and often that Mr. Obama stepped into the Oval Office at a particularly difficult time, facing what Peggy Noonan has called "an almost daily parade of horribles." [117] His colleagues in Washington and New York had nothing useful to offer in the way of solutions to the intractable political and economic crisis gripping the nation. As for the political parties, they had had long since slipped their moorings. Into that mess Mr. Obama strode with a youthful confidence that America thought it needed. That he came without a resume was of little concern.

Look what the resumes had given us.

For this reason, many Americans extended an extra measure of goodwill to the new president, and wisely so. Each new president deserves our respect, and Mr. Obama deserved patience, as well.

Our view of Mr. Obama is straightforward: he is a idealist with a strong belief in the power of government as a force for bettering people's lives. At the same time he is a realist; he recognized that without the support of the Killionaires, he would never have risen to the highest office in the land. So now he is stuck with both—the angel on one shoulder and the devil on the other, if you will.

Perhaps that is why we've so often seen Mr. Obama take two steps left for every step right. Throw in some fancy head fakes and stutter steps and you see why he once wisecracked, "I'm LaBron, baby!" His innate athleticism and eagerness to cover a lot of ground, and even play all the positions at once, is something to be prized in the gym, less so in the Oval. And if he keeps pulling these head fakes, pretty soon he'll be lining up far left.

Mr. Obama's first big move left came as a surprise to anyone who took him at his word during the campaign. He promised a change from the old politics. No more spin. He was "turning the page" on old-style politics. No more unsustainable budget deficits, he promised. He would get our fiscal house in order—that was his solemn vow. But not ten minutes into his presidency, he began spending taxpayer money on a scale not seen since the pharaohs. He'd sniffed at Mr. Bush's bloated budget deficits during the campaign. America "cannot and will not sustain" deficits like Mr. Bush's, he intoned. That wouldn't happen with his team in charge, he said, with an easy smile, and so many wanted to believe.

Then wham! A budget blueprint with record-setting deficits topping

$4.9 trillion for his first term, $7.4 trillion if given a second term. He will double the national debt in five years and triple it in ten. When pressed for a rationale for all this spending, White House budget director Peter Orszag claimed that the president had "inherited" the deficits, and that the earmark-laden spending bill was "last year's business."[118] He was half right. Mr. Obama inherited a mess, requiring action. But the runaway spending which happened on Mr. Obama's watch was not the fault of his predecessor. Mr. Bush ran $2.9 trillion in deficits after being hit with 9/11 and Katrina, and choosing to fight two difficult wars. Mr. Obama had an economic downturn to deal with. Sure, it was a mean one. But downturns are regular occurrences in economic life, and there are options for dealing with them. Mr. Obama chose to spend and then spend and then spend some more. His first twenty months of budgets included more spending than Mr. Bush's nearly 100 months.

Mr. Obama is spending $5 for every $1 Mr. Bush spent.

Mr. Obama's budget adds more to the debt than all previous presidents combined. But the budget is only the beginning. There was also the stimulus package, and the 8,500 earmarks added to the budget, and all the new money printing and make-good pledges from the Federal Reserve. When all of the "money going out" was added up at one point early in the going, heads shook in complete disbelief. In all, the U.S. government had spent or lent $12.8 trillion.

A pause to let that sink in.

$12.8 trillion. Equal to the value of everything the United States produced last year. Equal to the nation's gross domestic product. Within his first few months, Mr. Obama had transformed the public sector into just about the same size as the private sector.

Of course, there's a difference between the public and private sectors, isn't there? The private sector comprises 5 million companies and 115 million employees, while the public sector comprises 89,000 taxing authorities and 20 million public servants. Private sector employees earned an average of $49,935 in 2008, while federal civilian employees earned 50 percent more—$79,197 for the same kind of work.[119] On the private sector side, there are sellers and buyers matching up in a kind of equilibrium known as the free market. In theory, then, the free market is truly free—it costs nothing to run. Not so the public sector. It is almost entirely funded by . . . the private sector.

The price tag for Mr. Obama's spending now totals $168,420 a year for a family of four. That is how much each family would have to pay for the nation to meet its bills. Less than 1 in 100 taxpaying families could realistically afford to pay such taxes if there was any honest attempt to pay the bills we're racking up.

Mr. Obama has dramatically altered the relationship between the government and the people, the public and the private sectors, the economy and society. Oklahoma Senator Tom Coburn has offered a succinct explanation for what Mr. Obama has accomplished:

> President Obama is not merely part of some "clean-up crew" but, as President of the United States, has offered a sweeping and bold budget. I believe President Obama has proposed the most significant shift toward collectivism and away from capitalism in the history of our republic. I believe his budget aspires to not merely promote economic recovery but to lay the groundwork for sweeping expansions of government authority. . . . [120]

DISTORTING THE RELATIONSHIP BETWEEN PUBLIC AND PRIVATE

The "sweeping expansion" that Senator Coburn referred to went well beyond the mind-blowing spending spree Mr. Obama undertook. Far more impactful long-term is the machinery the President has put into place to wrestle power away from the private sector. Without preamble, the Obama administration physically took over companies—whether they liked it or not. Other companies were allowed to remain private—no matter how desperate their financial plight. There was no rhyming or decent timing to the takeovers. There was also no public discussion. Late-night deals were cooked up on the backs of napkins over dinner in dark restaurants and made material in the morning light by executive order. The lack of consistency and heavy-handedness in dealings forced the business world to follow the lead of the White House, as an orchestra follows its conductor, for direction on every movement.

We've seen Team Obama's affinity for big sweeping org charts, rule books, and action agendas. We haven't personally seen the org chart that's pinned up in Rahm Emanuel's office, but we've heard enough to know that the White House chief of staff has ambitious plans for the country—perhaps something along the lines of Figure 6.1?!

THE GOVERNMENT OF THE UNITED STATES

THE ~~CONSTITUTION~~   Who cares about that old rag?

LEGISLATIVE BRANCH   EXECUTIVE BRANCH   JUDICIAL BRANCH

EXECUTIVE OFFICES ←   THE PRESIDENT   Formerly
                                           INDEPENDENT
Muzzle!   ESTABLISHMENTS
VICE PRESIDENT ←   & GOVERNMENT
                  THE CZARS   CORPORATIONS

Fun new industries   Keep happy   Boring old
                            at all costs!   departments

AIRLINES	BANKING	REAL ESTATE		LABOR	EDUCATION	AGRICULTURE
HEALTHCARE	APPROX. 38 STATES			TREASURY	INTERIOR	COMMERCE
APPROX. 3,400 COUNTIES	AUTOMOTIVE			TRANSPORTATION	DEFENSE	JUSTICE
TELECOMMUNICATIONS	RETAIL APPAREL			ENERGY	HEALTH & HUMAN SERVICES	
CONSTRUCTION	CARGO & SHIPPING			HOUSING & URBAN DEVELOPMENT	STATE	
TRAVEL	INTERNET	DRY CLEANING		VETERANS AFFAIRS	HOMELAND SECURITY	

Figure 6.1 The Government of the United States

Government bailouts have gone to financial services companies, the airlines and automobile industries, and many more. In the months ahead, we'll see continued encroachment of government into the private sector and into states unable to pay their bills. In the chart above we only half-jokingly list some of the industries that Team Obama wants to nationalize. We would not be surprised to see several industries—yes, even dry cleaning!—suddenly become wards of the state before Mr. Obama is finished.

Indeed, we would not be surprised if Team Obama is already hard at work rejiggering our nation's currency so it's no longer "In God We Trust" but now "In Gov We Trust."

Within the ranks of Team Obama, there is a deep belief in their infallibility as public servants. As products of the "entitled" generation, they can look at themselves in the mirror and affirm that they're smart enough, they're strong enough, and gosh darn it, they're good enough to run this country. So into the deep end they dove and before even surfacing for air began issuing grandiloquent proclamations about the urgent "fixes" the economy needed. They said things such as "we must marshal government resources to ensure we don't suffer a Japanese-style lost decade of wealth."

Okay.

But we wonder if they are even aware that Japanese economic woes are a *direct* result of well-meaning but disastrous government intervention?

Japan's government ran their economy into the ground using the very command-and-control style Team Obama favors. They tried to control the output of the nation and decided that mainframe computers would be big, laptops not so much. Oops. Then they added insult to injury by allowing their own corporate scoundrels to dictate the terms of the economic recovery, stunting the nation for two long decades and still going. Now America is facing a similar situation, and Team Obama tells us with straight faces that government knows best?

It makes you wonder if there's more going on than meets the eye. Look at the folks Mr. Obama has chosen for posts in his administration. A large number of them spent years contributing to our economic problems; this might make them uniquely qualified to solve those problems, but we tend to be more circumspect. Much of the nasty wealth-stripping of the last two decades was done with the explicit help of career government workers who have again weaseled their way back into senior posts in the Obama administration. Senior Obama officials have for the most part spent their entire adult lives in politics, public administration, or academia. They are public sector types. They know little of the business world they seek to command and control.

There is the president himself, who has never held a private sector job—except for a brief stint as a lawyer, which hardly counts.

Then there's Tim Geithner and Larry Summers, who wield power over our financial health. No private sector experience there either.

Run through the senior administration posts—the EPA director, Commerce Secretary, Transportation Secretary, Agriculture Secretary—they're all bureaucrats, technocrats, and hack Democrats.

How can a businessman's daily struggles be anything more than abstract case studies for this group?

What do they know of risk capital and sweat equity, of shoestring marketing and line extension strategies? They know org charts and feasibility studies; they know how to decipher the impenetrable gobbledygook of government memoranda (such as this memo, received by one of the authors back in his government days, titled: "Elimination of the magnitude of diminishing increases in overlapping factual cohesiveness").

They get this stuff . . . because they're public sector people. Boy, are they.

THE "FOOT IN THE DOOR" GAMBIT OF OBAMAHOMES

By committing the U.S. government to $12.8 trillion in bailouts in just a few months of furious-paced decisions in 2009, Mr. Obama broadened his job description to include CEO of Bailout Nation with subsidiaries ObamaHomes, ObamaBank, ObamaAir, ObamaCare, and soon, ObamaCalifornia, ObamaNewYork, and on downward.

The housing collapse was widely believed to be the principal cause of the financial crisis, so it became a big focus of Barack Obama, CEO. When he took office, plummeting real estate values had put an estimated 13.8 million homeowners, or about 27 percent of all mortgage holders, in hot water.[121] They owed the bank more than the house was worth. So at his CEO's behest, Secretary Geithner donned his cape and flew into the heart of the crisis, declaring that the government would rescue as many as 9 million homeowners who faced difficulties with their mortgage payments. The plan would help one and all:

It is imperative that we continue to move with speed to help make housing more affordable and help arrest the damaging spiral in our housing markets, just as we work to stabilize our financial system, create jobs and help businesses thrive.[122]

If we follow Mr. Geithner correctly, there was a "connection" between houses being "affordable" and a downward "spiral" in housing. So if houses could be made more affordable, then the housing crisis would go away, the economy would mend, jobs would return, businesses would flourish. That's the apparent logic of his statement, and we're at a loss to understand how he got there.

We know Mr. Geithner to be a learned man. So why did he ignore the obvious—that helping people buy homes they couldn't afford was the biggest root cause of the housing crisis, not the opposite as he suggested? Why was he treating the symptoms and ignoring the disease? Surely he knew that at least one of the roots of the mortgage meltdown—if not the taproot—was the government's obsession with putting people in homes they couldn't afford. Mark Calabria of the Cato Institute has offered insight into Mr. Geithner's backward thinking:

> The administration can't confront the basic fact that the most important mortgage indicator is the borrower's equity: How much of its own money a household puts into the home tells us far more about probable default than whether the loan was adjustable-rate or has a prepayment penalty. Admitting these facts, of course, would mean admitting that programs like the Federal Housing Administration have been at the forefront of pushing unsustainable mortgage lending. In short, the Obama team has once again put politics ahead of policy, offering "answers" that will sound good to the uninformed without threatening any of the vested Washington interests that played so large a role in creating the current crisis.[123]

It was pure and simple "politics" that twisted the logic of Mr. Geithner's public statements. ObamaHomes was political calculus. So how did that ObamaHomes rescue plan actually work out? May 2009 was the first real chance to evaluate the effectiveness of the program. A study by Alan M. White of Valparaiso Law School found that in the period leading up to May, 15 percent of all subprime mortgages fell into foreclosure, and 6 percent were modified. Of those 6 percent that were modified, 11,200 homeowners received a lower monthly payment. A larger number actually had their loan modified in the opposite direction—*increasing* their monthly payment! Since Mr. Geithner had promised to save 9 million homeowners, the helping of 11,200 appeared to fall short of the mark.

Why were so few helped?

At least two reasons. For one, the mortgage rescue plan quickly became a typical government creation—long on restrictions and short on common sense. People couldn't qualify if they had lost their job, or owed more than 5 percent above the house's value, or had been making all their payments faithfully, or were already in default, or didn't have a mortgage backed by Fannie Mae or Freddie Mac, or had a mortgage over $759,000, or had some other suitable financial problem necessitating a rescue. As Dick Morris and Eileen McGann wrote in the prelude of *Catastrophe*: "The number of beleaguered homeowners who can slip through the eye of this particular needle and qualify for a mortgage modification is tiny."[124]

Morris and McGann tell us that a genuinely workable solution to the mortgage meltdown does exist. We need only look to the Swedish government's solution of the 1990s: go into the banks, buy up their sour mortgages, work with the homeowners to get to terms they can afford; when the economy recovers, the homeowner pays back the government or gets his home taken away. This clever plan costs the taxpayers nothing, and even stands to make a profit as the economy comes back. So knowing that this program was a success in Sweden, why didn't Team Obama give it a try? Because a Democratic administration could never "throw people out of their homes. Better to let them default and make the big, bad bank do the dirty work."

And the second reason the rescue plan failed: It was meant to. When Mr. Geithner announced that 9 million homeowners would be helped, he had to be working extra hard to keep a straight face. There wasn't a snowman's chance of it happening. But the very act of announcing such a bold solution made it real in the adoring eyes of Obamaphiles everyone. Their man was on the job. Change was happening. Go Blue!

On that level, the Obama administration accomplished all that they wished for. Plus, and more importantly in their view, they got a foot in the door of the mortgage market, setting themselves up for a big walkthrough of the American housing market down the road. That's how big change happens—first with a foot in the door, then barrel through.

COMING TO A NEIGHBORHOOD NEAR YOU: OBAMABANK

How catastrophic will the losses on toxic loans be when all the books are finally cleaned up and the taxpayers foot the bill for all the Killionaires that stripped our assets and then ducked for cover?

The economists at Goldman Sachs, who should know better than anyone since their boys led the looting, have estimated that the total losses will exceed $2 trillion worldwide. They figure $1.1 trillion in mortgages will be lost—$390 billion in corporate loans and bonds, $234 billion in commercial real estate, $226 billion in credit cards, $133 billion in auto loans, and lesser assorted billions for student loans and the like.[125]

It was no secret what was required for the floundering zombie banks to get back on their feet in 2009. They needed to get all the toxic assets out of their vaults and into broad daylight, figure out what those assets were actually worth, then write them down so that loan officers could get on with business. Martin Feldstein, who headed the Council of Economic Advisors under President Reagan, returned to Capitol Hill during the crisis to say as much to lawmakers:

> You can't solve the overall economic problem if you can't get the financial institutions lending again . . . and you can't do that as long as they don't know what the value [of their troubled assets] is, particularly the residential mortgage-backed securities and derivatives based on them.[126]

Mr. Feldstein's advice, echoed by many thoughtful economists, fell on deaf ears at the White House. Team Obama didn't want public disclosures of how financially insolvent the nation's banking system really was. Such a disclosure could cause a run on the banks, mass hysteria, who knows what. At the minimum, it might sidetrack his plans to push through the most sweeping financial reform regulations since 1933. Team Obama was not about to be sidetracked by a little reality. And besides, they reasoned, their benefactors on Wall Street were being taken care of; their voting blocs across America were taken care of; entrepreneurs would pay dearly as precious credit resources clamped tight, but oh well! That was the cold political calculus of the sugar/sugar/shaft strategy.

But as 2009 unfolded and bankers could see no bottom to the hole they'd dug into, it became increasingly apparent that half measures would no longer suffice. The Obama administration began laying the foundation for a wholesale nationalization of 75 percent of the U.S. banking industry. Such a draconian move was probably *not* part of the original Killionaire plan, but it had become so.

What had begun as a nation top-heavy with banks that were too big to fail had degenerated into a nation teetering from the weight of banks that had become even-bigger-to-fail. Bank of America had swallowed Countrywide and then Merrill Lynch. J.P. Morgan had taken over Bear Stearns and Washington Mutual. Wells Fargo now owned Wachovia. It was foolish madness. As banking guru Nouriel Roubini observed: "You can't take two zombie banks, put them together, and make a strong bank. It's like having two drunks trying to keep each other standing."[127]

For their part, the Republican minority in Congress was in no position to dress down the Obama administration's apparent lack of coherent policy. Back in 2008 when the crisis erupted, the Bush administration was quick to leap across the banking Rubicon, interfering with the industry deeply and apparently with caprice. Why was the failed investment house Bear Stearns bailed out, but Lehman Brothers not? The failure of each was of equal threat to the global system of finance. But no good explanation was ever offered for that bit of financial manipulation. The whole thing smacked of fast-and-loose double dealing, or callous disregard, or both.

Net net, you can expect more than half of the banking system in America to be nationalized by 2011. The six largest banks that together hold or represent 75 percent of America's capital base will become even more dependent wards of the state, with federal bureaucrats posted at the branches, overseeing financial transactions large and small. These banks will be slotted into the same club as Fannie Mae, Freddie Mac, AIG, GM, and Chrysler.

Already the string of ObamaBank affiliates is receiving loan guarantees, liquidity support, and direct capital infusions to the tune of $7 trillion to $9 trillion. In every sense but a legal one, the government is already the nation's banker. Key financial leaders have given their blessing to a nationalization of the major banks. Former Fed Chairman Alan Greenspan and Senate Finance Committee member Lindsey Graham have thrown their support behind the notion.

Mr. Obama has repeatedly insisted that he doesn't want to be in the banking business, and that he'll return the banks to private control as soon as possible. If he means it, he will find it easier said than done. As senior administration officials hastily crafted their bank nationalization strategy in 2009, a few insiders let slip that they have no exit strategy, no endgame. There is no way, they've admitted candidly off the record, that such a strategy could even be conceptualized, given all the unknowns and imponderables. That is not encouraging, and leaves us with little but hope that ObamaBank does not become ObamaQuagmire.

As for the 8,000 smaller independent banks across America, they should remain independent in the main. They'll carve out niches in their communities, struggling mightily to compete against the big boys. But they should in fact thrive by offering the local touch, lines of credit that can actually be tapped, and a warm voice at the end of the line rather than a lifeless and demeaning computer phone tree—all things the big banks will not be offering.

Whether nationalized or independent, banks will be subjected to a tight-fitting straightjacket of new regulations. Secretary Geithner has crafted a plan that gives the government top-to-bottom authority over every kind of financial product sold to consumers. This revamping of financial market oversight will ripple through the economy, in ways known and unknowable, touching everything from bankers, to consumer protection, to mortgages and credit cards.

There was certainly a need for a financial makeover. The old system of regulations was the dumb blonde joke of the financial world. The system looked good, but was incapable of keeping tabs on all the moving parts in modern finance. As a result, bankers could shop around among the alphabet soup of regulators to find the one offering the least intrusive oversight. Mr. Geithner hopes to address the old problems by giving the Federal Reserve more power in monitoring and addressing potential systemic risks such as the 2008 crisis.

Also promised is greater transparency in capital flows, tougher reserve requirements for big banks, and a consolidated policing force to better protect consumers. All of these reforms are well-intentioned, but are just as likely to make future financial crises more likely and more costly. That is because of the Obama administration's foolhardy insistence on assembling a list of banks that are "too big to fail." In so doing, they are sending a clear signal to the markets that these fortunate few companies will be bailed out should they fail. This kind of reverse Darwinism means we'll have fewer banks, but larger ones that are insulated from market pressures. However weak they are, they'll stay in business crowding out stronger, but less-connected banks. This makes banking bailouts a permanent feature of our regulatory landscape. Of course, Team Obama insists that they know what they're doing. They seem oblivious to the irony of their claim, but Cato Institute's Mark Calabria is not: "The administration tells us that bailouts won't be needed—because the same regulators who missed the signs of the current crisis will get added powers to prevent the next one."[128]

HOW FAR WILL WE BEND OVER FOR OBAMACARE?

Every president since Franklin Roosevelt has tried on some level to tackle the "health care problem" in America, and every one has failed. It's probably our nation's most obstinate problem. Somehow we are capable of the most astonishing medical breakthroughs and yet incapable of inexpensively slapping a Band-Aid on a needy child. As a nation, sadly, we are no longer the healthiest on the planet. Indeed, we are far from any goal of national health that should be considered the minimum acceptable by elected leaders of either political party.

With such a history of health policy overtures, can Mr. Obama succeed where others have failed? Let's see.

In 2009 Mr. Obama barnstormed the nation, whipping up support for the Affordable Health Choices Act (ACHA), which had been drafted by the late Senator Edward Kennedy's staff. Mr. Obama then orchestrated a photo-op which, if nothing else, surely made Hillary Clinton jealous: he gathered into the Rose Garden before clicking cameras the heads of drug companies, hospital administrators, insurance company execs, medical device manufacturers, labor union leaders, and prominent doctors. All these health honchos sheathed daggers and announced their unqualified support for Mr. Obama's lofty goal: slashing $1.7 trillion in health costs over the next decade and finally fixing the system. It was a big moment.

Mr. Obama next exhorted every American to contact his or her elected representative and demand swift approval of the legislation. But something happened along the way. People out in the real world, far removed from all the manufactured hoopla of Washington but closely attached to their own sad medical stories, said "Whoa!"

Everyone knows health care needs fixing. But they can also smell a rat. And if the President publicly claims that $1.7 trillion can be saved while opening up health care to all comers, something's not right. Fixing health care is bound to be difficult, and costly. It's about one-sixth of the U.S. economy. Perhaps, the people said, there's wisdom in approaching the issue as if it were a life-and-death issue. After all, it is.

With more time to study Mr. Obama's plan, the Congressional Budget Office released an analysis saying the plan would jack the federal deficit by $1.6 trillion over the decade. Not only that, but it wouldn't get around to treating all those uninsured Mr. Obama was hoping to help.

So much for saving $1.7 trillion. Seemed the opposite would happen. People began to wonder if Mr. Obama had any kind of a coherent plan, or if we were seeing just another HillaryCare boondoggle.

So Mr. Obama pulled in his horns, and instructed his brain trust to rethink strategy. As we write a new plan has come out of the Democratic Congress and it's quite similar to the ACHA plan, though we'll soon be calling it the ACHOO plan!

We're not joking. A blogger at the Huffington Post website apparently felt similarly when writing:

Let me get this straight. We're going to pass a health care plan written by a committee whose head says he doesn't understand it, passed by a Congress that hasn't read it but exempts themselves from it, signed by a president that also hasn't read it, and who smokes, with funding administered by a treasury chief who didn't pay his taxes, overseen by a surgeon general who is obese, and financed by a country that's nearly broke. What possibly could go wrong?[129]

What we're likely to end up with will be something like the Holy Roman Empire, which was neither holy, nor Roman, nor much of an empire. Health care reform won't improve our health, or the level of care we receive, and it doesn't reform what truly needs reforming.

We'll see Americans of all income levels herded in mass into stingy health plans with rigid, HMO-style controls that put cost containment before disease containment.

We'll see the beginning of medical care rationing. Quantity will be valued over quality. To even begin providing universal coverage for some 50 million uninsured Americans and aliens, the new ObamaCare plan will have no choice but to cut care.

In public hearings, the ObamaCare promoters have said that rationing will begin with diagnostic imaging tests such as MRIs and CAT scans. Such tests are being abused now, and so getting them in the future will be very difficult. We'll also see sharply reduced use of antibiotics, far fewer Caesarean sections, and a nixing of treatment programs for chronic back pain sufferers.

This is how it will begin, but with health care spending running out of control, the government will look for other ways to ration care. The decisions will have to be made on a financial basis, not a medical basis.

We'll all have to learn to live with our aches and pains. Better that a greater number of people have access to worse care, the Obama logic goes, than fewer people have access to better care.

The eventual success of ObamaCare will depend on how people feel about cutting care to the old folks so the young folks can get more. Will an aging baby boomer population feel all warm and fuzzy knowing they have to wait three months for a life-saving procedure because that procedure is expensive and the funds could be "better spent" on folks who don't work for a living, or are living here illegally?

We suspect that the support Mr. Obama enjoys now for his health care plan is a mile wide and an inch deep. When folks in coffee shops and town halls across the country begin batting around the idea of "rationing" and ponder the hard ethical questions such as who lives, who dies, and who decides . . . all bets are off. As a people, we've never had to confront these kind of medical issues. We've been in denial. But Mr. Obama wants us to have those discussions.

He could pay dearly for forcing these discussions on people, because few among us are eager to confront end-of-life concerns.

The most interesting innovation in ObamaCare is the incentives-based approach to medicine. Mr. Obama believes that the way to afford universal care and not go broke in the process is to enlist doctors in a "pay for performance" system that rewards them for spending less.

Interesting.

Actually, for our part, when it comes to incentive programs, we're rather fond of the old Chinese method: the doctor gets paid *only* if the patient gets better! But since that would never fly in the land of the free and the home of the brave, we're stuck with government turning doctors into "care police." In the president's words: "If doctors have incentives to provide the best care, instead of more care, we can help Americans avoid unnecessary hospital stays, treatments and tests that drive up costs."[130]

Sounds good in theory, but what of practice? What does a doctor do when he or she doesn't quite know your ailment, and one more test might do the trick? Is the test ordered, or not? We went looking for less abstract explanations. That is, we went to real doctors who wrestle with real medical problems.

Dr. Lee Hieb is a veteran surgeon practicing in Yuma, Arizona.[131] Almost all of her patients, 97 percent of them by her count, are on Medicare or the state-run medical program. For that reason she deals with federal and state health officials and regulations on a constant basis. Yuma is the third-fastest-growing community in America, and has a shortage of physicians. There are also an unusually large number of "uninsured" because of folks hopping the border. Some are legal, some not, but almost all have made a conscious economic decision about health care.

They've figured out that they can spend their money on other things—cars, motorcycles, or just plain food—and not worry about getting insurance. Why should they bother, they figure, when they know the government will take care of them? They need to simply show up at the emergency room, and they'll receive first-rate care.

Because health care is basically free in Yuma, it is not valued. It's simple human nature to attach a lower value to things we don't work for and to distort the decisions we make.

For example, a woman was brought to the emergency room by ambulance for a sprained foot. Dr. Hieb was on call, and attended to her. In talking with the woman, Dr. Hieb learned that earlier that day the woman had walked into the emergency room—the sprain was a minor one, apparently—but she was told there was a six-hour waiting list. So the woman drove home and called an ambulance. The ambulance brought her in and she went to the head of the line. Who do you suppose paid for that wasteful and totally unnecessary ambulance ride?

Yes, taxpayers.

That is one example; there are thousands more. And the thread running through each of them in the same: People abuse health care when it's free or nearly so. Not only that, but as more people try to access the same system, we'll see shortages and rationing.

Why is the breast cancer death rate higher in England and Canada than the United States? Because in England and Canada the average wait for treatment after your biopsy is two months. In that time, serious complications can arise.

Medical care is free in Russia as well. Yet people regularly book Aeroflot to get their care in America. They simply can't count on *timely* treatment under universal care. Sure, it's free—but at what price?

Up in Canada, that marquee provider of health care according to liberal thought leader Michael Moore, folks must wait an average of ten weeks to get an MRI—just to find out what is wrong with them. Ten weeks, during which time a lot of bad things can happen. If surgery is then prescribed, 27 percent of the people will have to wait up to four months. In the United States, by comparison, only 5 percent have to wait that long.[132] Sure, the cost of getting medical care is much cheaper in Canada. But is cost the only criteria?

In Massachusetts, there is a preview of the health care program we get if Mr. Obama gets his way. In 2006, Governor Mitt Romney unleashed a reform plan that covered most residents. Folks were required to either buy into the health insurance plan, or opt out and pay a fine for doing so. The plan became the model for the Democratic ACHA plan, so any federal plan is likely to resemble that of Massachusetts.

Turns out, the clever people of Massachusetts were quick to figure out new and exciting ways to game the reform plan. Administrators at the community-based health plan, Harvard-Pilgrim, report that people buy health coverage for a few months, run up the medical bills, then dump the policy after government has paid all their bills:

> Between April 2008 and March 2009, about 40% of its new enrollees stayed with it for fewer than five months and on average incurred about $2,400 per person in monthly medical expenses. That's about 600% higher than Harvard-Pilgrim would have otherwise expected . . . The penalty for not having coverage is only about $900, so people seem to be gaming the Massachusetts system. [133]

Harvard-Pilgrim's CEO, Charlie Baker, offered an assessment of the reform plan: "It is raising the prices paid by individuals and small businesses who are doing the right thing by purchasing twelve months of health insurance, and it's turning the whole notion of shared responsibility on its ear."[134]

So maybe the Massachusetts plan isn't yet perfected, and maybe it can be improved upon at the federal level. Time will tell. As for now, we do have enough information to judge the medical cost savings the plan generated.

Governor Romney had budgeted $472 million for the plan's first year, but spending came in at $628 million. Estimates for 2010 costs could top $880 million—about double the original estimate after only a couple years.

If this kind of "cost containment" becomes a feature of the federal ObamaCare, we could see the federal budget for Massachusetts-style health care begin at $6 trillion a year—or half of our nation's GDP, or

$80,000 a year for a family of four. Without jumping to conclusions, that may just be unworkable.

Importantly, just as the United States is plunging headlong into European-style social medicine, Europe is in fast retreat. Years of inadequate care have the people there in rebellion. There has been a clamoring for private hospitals, doctors, and clinics because government-run programs don't work, the lines are too long, and you can't get the drugs you need.

In response, England's Gordon Brown recently imposed sweeping new rules designed to shorten waiting lists. And when the medical gatekeepers find that those lists cannot be shortened, then residents are allowed to end-run government care and go to a private doctor or alternative solution.

Over in France, President Nicolas Sarkozy is trying to kick-start that nation's social democracy into the twenty-first century with tax cuts, more competition, and less government. It would appear that the United States wants to roll back to twentieth-century Europe, while Europe wants to be the United States of the twenty-first century.

Almost entirely lost in the public debate about health care is the doctor, the lone fellow or lady working down in the trenches. How will they be affected by ObamaCare's reforms?

Marc Siegel, an internist and associate professor of medicine at NYU, doesn't see how Mr. Obama can reconcile his promises with bottom-line medical realities:

> None of the current plans, government or private, provide my patients with the care they need. And the care that is provided is increasingly expensive and requires a big battle for approvals. Of course, we're promised by the Obama administration that universal health insurance will avoid all these problems. But how is that possible when you consider that the medical turnstiles will be the same as they are now, only they will be clogged with more and more patients? The doctors that remain in this expanded system will be even more overwhelmed than now. I wouldn't want to be a patient when that happens.[135]

What makes Dr. Siegel's rather dour observations all the more interesting is that he's not a partisan taking sides. He accepts that the health care crisis is every bit as debilitating as the economic crisis. But he also knows that an estimated 131 million people will be moved onto ObamaCare—that's 131 million people cueing up to the turnstiles.[136]

The current crop of doctors cannot meet such a caseload.

What's more, doctors will be getting Medicare-style payment for their services. This means their take-home pay will decline by about 20 percent, depending on their specialty.

To salt the wound, doctors will be hit with even more government red tape to hack through. There are already more than 100,000 pages of regulations that doctors are supposed to understand and follow. And with ObamaCare, there will be entire new layers of regulations and rules. Any doctor will tell you: government sabotages medicine by forcing too much time with paperwork and too little time with patients. With the plans we see coming, it will only get worse.

If the situation is bad for established doctors, it's even worse for those aspiring to the profession. To become an orthopedic surgeon, for example, a young person must slog through four years of college, four years of medical school, five years of residency, and often another two years in a specialty fellowship and even a year of research. That's a lot of slogging, and it comes with debts topping $200,000. How many people will endure this knowing that they'll enter a system in which they're paid only slightly above sanitation workers, in which their every move is prescribed by a faceless Washington medical bureaucracy, in which their patients increasingly come to despise them because they're the human face of a unworkable system?

When all physicians become employees of the state and have their right to practice medicine decreed by a bunch of bureaucrats who have never even taken an anatomy course, probably a bunch of sociology majors fresh out of school, the willingness to practice medicine will erode away. We'll have a shortage of good doctors. Good ones will go elsewhere.

Behind the human face of American medicine, there is another equally impressive face about to be slashed. We speak of the medical technology leadership of America that still astounds the world. A Columbia University economist, Frank Lichtenberg, did a study of medical advances made in the 1980s and 1990s alone. He estimated that 40 percent of the actual *increase* in our life expectancy could be attributed directly to "new medicines."[137] These improvements in the human condition had been expected to accelerate in years ahead, especially with the opening of the human genome yielding daily clues into the origins of disease and giving fresh insights into new medicines.

But most of these advances were being funded by big medicine. Though often maligned, and deservedly so in some cases ("erectile dysfunction" advertisements on TV during family hour is reprehensible in our view), big pharma invests about $50 billion a year on R&D, and without this investment, few of these new lifesaving drugs would ever make it into people's hands.

What happens when the government, in sincere efforts to cut costs, forces doctors to prescribe only generic drugs and clamps down on the expensive drugs? It's a good bet that big outfits like Merck, Roche, and Lilly will pare back research—in fact, they'll have no choice. They won't be able to invest the billions required to develop breakthrough drugs if they cannot hope to recoup their investment many times over. Advances we've seen in quality of life will stop.

Other things will stop, as well. All those good-hearted celebrities who actively supported candidate Obama will find that their pet causes are plum out of money. If an actor wants to make a TV spot asking viewers to donate to Parkinson's research, he may have to turn to Bollywood or learn Mandarin to appeal to funding sources in India or China.

We received a solicitation recently from the National Foundation for Cancer Research with this catchy headline: "What date will go down in history as the day we cured cancer?" What a wonderful question! The solicitation continued:

> "Many Americans remember April 12, 1955, as the day polio was conquered through the research of Dr. Jonas Salk. Like polio, smallpox, and other once-dreaded diseases, cancer can be cured . . . But how soon? What date we will all remember?"

If the Obama administration succeeds in cutting the quality of care so more can have care, then funding for cancer research and some 300 other diseases will wither and die. Not overnight, but not slowly either.

If in trying to fix a broken system, Mr. Obama bleeds away the vitality of a market-based health care system, where will folks go for the best care? There has to be a place where people can go for the best. If it's not going to be America, where will it be? India? China?

Probably.

Finally, we've seen that ACHA under Mr. Obama will affect small business owners in ways known and not. The legislation is banging around in Congress as we write, but we know certain things. We know that doctors who enjoy having their own practices will be up the creek. Many will be driven into big-practice behemoths set up to work the massive Washington bureaucracy. Many will be driven out of business, no longer willing to face the daily frustrations for paltry payments.

It won't be pretty for doctors or patients, so we think it won't be pretty for Mr. Obama either.

ENTREPRENEURS GET THE SHAFT

By all accounts, it looks like war. Federal armies are amassing to dictate how businesses should operate. Thousands of pages of new rules and regulations will spew forth—all intended to "end" the abuses of the free enterprise system that were created from the last bunch of rules and regulations that were spewed. Businesses will be scrutinized down to detail as granular as our articles of incorporation. Washington thinks it knows what's best for us. Let's sum up what's in store:

- Political agendas now define the relationship between government and business, and in the process, spoil what does work in free markets.
- With the federal budget doubling the national debt in five years and tripling it in ten, federal borrowing will crowd out the small borrower, or drive interest rates to untenable levels, or both.

- Stupendous tax hikes will slash into the funds entrepreneurs would otherwise use to create great new products.
- Coming in the mail soon will be rule books thick with mandates and dictates. Government is now in the health business, the auto business, the energy business, the banking business, and more. In each of these industries it will be government and not the market that decides the winners and losers.
- Massive new lobbying flotillas will land on Washington to suck up to the bigger public teat. With ever greater government largess, entrepreneurs will spend more time and talent chasing handouts subject to bureaucratic whims, not the needs of the marketplace or the desires of consumers.

It's not a pretty picture, obviously. But there are a few pieces of Mr. Obama's agenda that should benefit entrepreneurs. We expect a permanent indexing of the alternative minimum tax and other tax reduction benefits. We'll look at these in coming chapters.

And we can thank God that America isn't in worse shape. We're up against hard financial times. But absent are the guns of revolution or demonstrations in the streets. Things are stable, for now. Several more state governments will topple into bankruptcy, and bailout funds will be shoveled in. People are dealing with debt problems, paying down credit cards, and slashing spending; whether by necessity or choice, it is happening. The consumer balance sheet will emerge in overall good shape. Even when unemployment tops 10 percent, we're still a long way from the unemployment levels of the Great Depression, and there will be federal relief for the truly needy. Our nation's household net worth has taken a beating, but is still running at $45 trillion as we write.

These are the times that, in theory anyway, entrepreneurs live and long for. Everything is tossed and upset, cracked and broken. The old order has all but crumbled, and a new order is still uncertain.

In this sense it is a yeasty time, a time when the mixing of the right ingredients can result in things new and wonderful.

In times such as these, it is more important than ever to remain alert and humble, accepting of the unknown properties, which like yeast itself can give rise to prosperous new possibilities.

Of all the entrepreneurial skills that will be needed now, an eagle eye will be most essential. Just as a speck of yeast is small and easily missed even when right in front of you, the seed of a renewed prosperity will not be easily spotted. But it will be there, you'll see.

SWEET LUCRE FOR THE KILLIONAIRES

We've talked about the central strategy the Killionaires have executed: First underwrite the campaigns of ambitious men and women seeking higher office and ensure that they are properly beholden. Next, drive up the price of valuable assets such as real estate and commercial equities. Then forcibly kick the floor out from beneath the markets for these assets. All work and no play is boring, so kick back and enjoy the fireworks while a nation panics and action is demanded. Then loudly insist that a government populated by your front men step in and guarantee your repurchase of those assets at pennies on the dollar.

That is the thumbnail of the events that began for a few like George Soros in 1994 and culminated for many Killionaires like him in 2010. We have now seen as much. Those who might line up to charge us with inventing convenient conspiracies to suit our needs will fall into at least one of three groups:

- Those unwilling to accept this great swath of evidence
- Those blindly naïve to how the world really works
- Those happy to be manipulated by their partisan leaders

Both political parties have been co-opted, with some of the people we used to call "elites" rolling over easier than others. But along the way, as the years passed, more and more of our national leadership at the political, corporate, and social levels all gave up and decided, *"to hell with everyone else, I'm getting mine."*

So now that the avarice of these Killionaires is so widely known, why does the asset-stripping continue? Why is it not stopped? There are many reasons why, as we will see in coming chapters, but understand that it is not easily halted. It is endemic now. The fleecers have elevated their practice to a most impossibly complex level. Like the mentalist who bends the spoon or the magician who makes the pretty girl disappear, we know there's a trick in there somewhere; we just can't see it occur.

That is how we felt on March 4, 2009, reading the *Wall Street Journal*. The headline was clear: The Obama administration was launching a program to finance up to $1 trillion in new lending to consumers and businesses, "in an ambitious attempt to jump-start credit for everything from car loans to equipment leases."[138] That sounded like a hopeful sign—something good from the government, perhaps.

The program would be called TALF (for Term Asset-Backed Securities Loan Facility) to complement the ever-changing and interconnected and rather puzzling Scrabble game's worth of acronymic lending and insurance programs including but not limited to PPIP (for Public-Private Partnership Investment Program) AIFP (for Automotive Industry Financing Program), and TIP (for Targeted Investment Program)—and, of course, TARP (for Troubled Asset Relief Program). That's when we ran into MEGO (Mine Eyes Glaze Over). It was all too complex, and we hadn't gotten to the fine print yet. Still, we pressed on.

We were determined to figure out how our government intended to spend a trillion dollars to help business. We knew from experience that 10 percent would be wasted, lost, or embezzled. Government handouts have historically tithed 10 percent to the crooked class. But what of the rest?

What we learned can be summarized, and made much clearer, through a simulation of a car-buying outing. Let's say that you really want a car, but can't afford it. What do you do?

You go to the car dealership (there are only half as many now—but still more than enough) and pick out your favorite car with a financing package built in (your credit rating is too low—but that's not a problem thanks to Uncle Sam), and the lender bundles your loan in with other car loans, and boat loans, and skateboard loans, and calls this bundle a "security" (isn't that the practice that got us into trouble in the first place?); then the lender sells this security to investors (who pay for this security with money borrowed from the Fed at a really, really low interest rate), and the investors hope this security appreciates in value (but if it doesn't, no matter, the contract with the Fed ensures that any losses will be covered).

If you followed that, congratulations! The whole process is a bit complex, like the magician's trick, by design. But if we could film the process with one of those fancy 100-frames-a-second cameras, and then study each frame, we'd see how the illusion was created. We'd find that about fifteen months after the global financial meltdown, the government was again doing the same thing that got us into the mess. Big hedge funds and private-equity firms were being given cheap credit from the Fed, and they were using that money to purchase all kinds of securities at cheap prices. And should those securities lose money for some reason, the government will step in and cover the losses. Yes, it's the same practice that got us into the mess.

They're doing it again, pretending otherwise!

Mr. Obama and the Democratic leadership is counting on the glazed eyes of the public to miss the whole thing. And what do the Democrats get for abetting this continued looting of the national treasury? Let's see . . .

CREATING A PERMANENT SUBCLASS OF FREELOADERS

Any attempt to game the American system of free enterprise and strip its assets would have fallen flat on its face if the politicians cared one whit. But they had been bought off, each to their weakness. Republicans were easily bought. They needed only be told that free market principles were being advanced. Who were they to argue with such assurances, especially when coupled with timely campaign contributions? Democrats were a tougher nut to crack. Having no real understanding of or trust in free enterprise, they had to be approached from an entirely different angle. In the 1990s, one such angle presented itself.

The Reagan Revolution of the 1980s had so thoroughly discredited the term "liberal" that Democrats were on the ropes as a national political organization. Sure, Bill Clinton could get elected—but in all likelihood it was *only* because independent candidate Ross Perot peeled away 19 percent of the vote from incumbent George H.W.

Bush. Democrats were on the retreat in a nation that traditionally leaned center-right anyway. They needed to reboot.

The *Revisionist* script provided them with just such a plan. Democrats would, with funding assistance from Killionaires, hand out "care packages" to those subclasses who felt left behind by the Reagan Revolution. And who were those classes?

Illegal aliens were eager for handouts, and could be signed at the "work walls" to vote Democratic, legalities be damned. Those who refuse to work could be coaxed into soup kitchens, and then signed up. Those who were disabled and convinced they were owed something special could be promised the moon and then signed. On and on through the underbelly of American society the Democratic Party rummaged for votes. Along the way they institutionalized the sign-up process with ACORN and got taxpayers to foot the bill on that one—such a hoot!

The cherry on the plan was the 2008 election. The Killionaires' candidate for president had the audacity to declare that under his administration, half the nation would *not* have to pay taxes. Oh the mendacious triumph of that! Convincing people that they really could have something for nothing—that would ensure their vote and Democratic Party victories for generations to come.

In another time, a snarling mainstream media would have jumped on such a cynical corruption of democracy and chewed it into disrepute. But the 2009 Leftstream media heralded the tax scheme as "brilliant statesmanship," convincing liberal voters that their president was doing the right—er, left thing. The Rightstream media was quick to blast the giveaway, though not a peep escaped the echo box on the right, so nothing came of the warnings of respected economists such as Michael Boskin:

> New and expanded refundable tax credits would raise the fraction of taxpayers paying no income taxes to almost 50% from 38%. This is potentially the most pernicious feature of the president's budget, because it would cement a permanent voting majority with no stake in controlling the cost of general government. [139]

Michael Reagan would comment, with a little more of the plain-talking vitriol for which he is famous:

Obama is deliberately attempting to create an economic system where more people live off the government than by their own efforts, thus creating a permanent underclass utterly dependent upon the largesse of the government and therefore ever-beholden to it. . . . This gigantic voting bloc can be depended upon to march obediently to the polls and vote to place the full financial burden on the top 2% of American wage earners.[140]

But since only conservatives would tune in to analyses such as these, they would have absolutely no effect on the actions taken unilaterally and without public debate by the Obama administration.

As for the independents, they were generally too busy with their lives to be paying more than passing attention to the goings-on in Washington.

In such a void, the *Revisionists* could push forward their rewrite of the American story. That old fable of *The Ant and the Grasshopper* could be rewritten to the *Revisionists* liking, along these lines . . .

Traditional Version: The ant works hard in the withering heat all summer long, building his house and laying up supplies for the winter. The grasshopper thinks he's a fool and laughs and dances and plays the summer away. Come winter, the ant is warm and well fed. The grasshopper has no food or shelter, so he dies out in the cold. Moral of the story: Be responsible for yourself!

Revisionist Version: The ant works hard in the withering heat all summer long, building his house and laying up supplies for the winter. The grasshopper thinks he's a fool and laughs and dances and plays the summer away. Come winter, the shivering grasshopper calls a press conference and demands to know why the ant should be allowed to be warm and well fed while others are cold and starving.

CBS, NBC, and ABC show up to provide pictures of the shivering grasshopper next to a video of the ant in his comfortable home with a table filled with food. America is stunned by the sharp contrast. How can this be, that in a country of such wealth, this poor grasshopper is allowed to suffer so?

Jesse Jackson stages a demonstration in front of the ant's house, singing "We shall overcome." President Obama rages against the ant for getting rich on the back of the grasshopper, and calls for an immediate tax hike on the ant to make him pay his "fair share." The Equal Employment Opportunity Commission fines the ant for knowingly discriminating against "green bugs." Having nothing left to pay his taxes, the ant's home is confiscated by the Feds. The grasshopper is allowed to move into the home, but it soon crumbles around him because he doesn't maintain it.

As the story ends, the ant has disappeared into the snows. The grasshopper has been found dead in a drug-related incident and the house, now abandoned, is taken over by a gang of spiders who terrorize the once peaceful neighborhood. Moral of the story: Government doesn't know better.

Fortunately, this little parable has not played itself out yet. We still find ourselves in the last act, with options. Not many, but options nonetheless.

President Obama will continue to give stirring speeches about "individual responsibility" and that "gung-ho American spirit." That is his public cover, and he's a pro. Meanwhile, he will continue pushing tax and spending policies that reward irresponsibility and sloth. When folks see their government growing larger and larger, taking away the decisions they once made about the Social Security payments they receive, taking away the decisions they once made about the health care they receive, taking away their need even to file a tax return every year even as new and exciting giveaway programs show up on their doorstep, these people will rationally and naturally feel less responsibility for their own actions. They'll figure they don't have to worry about those things any more, don't have to plan ahead any more. They'll just accept the decreasing amount of personal responsibility in our culture. That'll become the new baseline.

And it will feed on itself.

The less responsibility they're asked to take, the less they'll offer.

Soon they'll experience no guilt whatsoever in accepting the handouts of government. In time they'll consider those handouts their right. How does this end? Ben Franklin warned: "When the people find they can vote themselves money, that will herald the end of the Republic."[141]

We're not fond of quoting the Founders, because it's rather easy to find one to make whatever case you're aiming for. But here we quote not only Mr. Franklin, but Mr. Jefferson as well, for there is an essential point that cannot be emphasized enough, a point about the intrinsic value of human responsibility:

> To take from one, because it is thought that his own industry and that of his fathers has acquired too much, in order to spare to others, who, or whose fathers have not exercised equal industry and skill, is to violate arbitrarily the first principle of association, the guarantee to every one of a free exercise of his industry and the fruits acquired by it.[142]

When our government, however well-intentioned, decides that the people can no longer be entrusted to make our own decisions; and when that same government then takes it upon itself to dictate their idea of our collective best interest, then we have crossed a line that was drawn early in the founding of their republic, contested and decided in a great civil war, then held in the highest esteem by administrations both liberal and conservative through the decades.

We can only hope that we have not crossed too far over that line. We will need to keep a diligent eye on that line in the months and years ahead. Because the financial crisis that rumbled across the globe in 2008 is far from passed, despite any near-term parting of the storm clouds.

We expect the days ahead to be worse than what we've seen.

7

GET READY FOR THE FORTY-CENT DOLLAR

The next Madoff case—the next Ponzi scheme—is the U.S. government.
It will go bust. It is only a question of time."

—MARC FABER

The Great Train Robbery was done on horse. The Baker Street Bank
Robbery was done by tunnel. The Global Currency Robbery was done
with a few keystrokes. Just as U.S. investors sensed recovery and
returned to dollar-based investments, the conspirators moved on every
bourse. They dumped the dollar so fast they collapsed it. Worth about
forty cents now. Shouts of joy circle the globe. Tabloids trumpet 'END
OF YANK $$$ LARCENY.' Global transactions now pegged to a basket
of currencies—yen, euros, yuan *and* dollars in roughly equal portions.
Big losers? Suckers holding U.S. dollars. Big winners? Cads known as
Killionaires, including Soros who got his wish—he's first ever to make
a hundred billion euros in one day.

—FROM SOME FUTURE BLOGPOST

FALL OF 2009. Beaten-down, financially-strapped Americans con-
tinued to cling to the fond illusion of hope. "Try to ride it out until
the recovery kicks in," they told the mirror every morning, "then all
will be well again." They needed that hope, depended on it. Last thing
they wanted was some know-it-all prattling on about future portents.
Denial was easier.

When in July the government announced that the federal deficit
would top $2 trillion before year end, the news shows mentioned it
only in passing. Nobody wanted to hear.

Economic activity had ground to a standstill, so the government's slopping away at the debt trough had no discernable impact on interest rates. There was no other demand for money, so no pressure on rates. Consumers weren't borrowing. Businesses weren't borrowing.

Pretty much everywhere, pretty much everyone was doing the same thing—watching TV at full denial-enhancing volume.

Mr. Obama could have dissolved the union and gotten away with it. He was free to do as he pleased. The GOP was incapable of mounting a potent defense. They'd become the Genocidal Old Party—eating through the stomach lining of a glorious past. Yes, Mr. Obama was a free man in a money arcade. Just one more quarter into the slot and let the pinball fly.

It was borrowing and spending that had gotten American into the mess, so Mr. Obama's solution was to borrow and spend even more—in hopes it would miraculously restart the American engine. Miraculous, because how else could it occur? When economic growth is generated by the hard work and investment of people, you can draw a clear line between cause and effect. But how can economic growth be generated by creating artificial money? Isn't that artificial growth? Or perhaps it's something else. Perhaps it's magic . . .

Sim sala bim . . . growth!

Only one thing is certain: the hocus pocus cannot go on forever. So in opening this chapter with a fictional blog post from a few years into the future, we betrayed a suspicion that the United States is about to pay dearly for the hocus pocus that began on Mr. Bush's watch and escalated on Mr. Obama's. This is the thumbnail forecast:

In throwing trillions at the economy, there has to be at least a few billion in financial gains. And there will be. From the Fed we'll hear cautious talk of "recovery." A few months will pass, and then some trigger event—something very positive, such as a boost in new homes sales—will reignite the national greed glands. Americans will fast and furiously shovel what remains of their wealth back into U.S. equities. Right about then, a merry band of international bankers who have been lying in wait will step out of the shadows and effectively crash the dollar on global markets. Net net: the dollars in your pocket will, practically overnight, be worth about forty cents each. And Mr.

Obama's economic recovery will go into the record books as a goose egg, a "Big O."

Here's the details on how we expect it to unfold.

THE FINAL BURSTING OF TWENTY-FIVE YEARS OF CREDIT BUBBLES

For at least twenty-five years, depending on which economist you talk to, we've been inflating asset bubbles in this country and then popping them. In our view, it began when we made the decision to leave manufacturing behind and become a "fire" economy—so called for a financial, insurance, and real estate focus. No longer would we manufacture things, now we would pass pieces of paper back and forth.

How has that worked for us?

America's manufacturing base is 60 percent smaller than at its peak. The number one sector for new jobs in America is the service sector. Nine out of ten new jobs were created in services in 2008. And what was the number one new job creator?

You guessed it, McDonald's.

The decision to create this new economy was a deliberate one, made as we've seen by *Revisionist* Killionaires through legalized crime syndicates abetted, often knowingly, by both political parties. Killionaires understood that a "fire" economy could be fueled and fanned in ways that most people would never understand, allowing all kinds of mischief. And so in those twenty-five years, they built up one bubble after another.

Tech stocks, residential housing, credit derivatives, commercial real estate—pop, pop, pop, pop. Each new bubble was larger than the previous and faster to arrive—such is the complicated calculus required to sustain an inflationary bubble cycle—and each time the bubble expanded higher, we fell back harder.

And there are at least two more bubbles being inflated right now.

The first will be in government debt. It will be the biggest bubble of all time—that is not hyperbole, those numbers are already baked in. Some, like the forecasting genius Marc Faber, call it a Ponzi scheme. Some, like our partisan friends on the right, call it socialism. We call it a bubble in government debt, and when it pops, Mr. Obama's rich friends will make a fortune, Mr. Obama's poor voters will get government assistance, and entrepreneurs will get screwed if they haven't gotten busy.

The essential question for entrepreneur investors is which assets will perform best as the government debt bubble inflates, and which will perform best when it explodes.

THE IMPORTANCE OF FANNING UNCERTAINTY

Mr. Obama is, by choice and design, attempting a most dangerous balancing act. He's up on the high wire with a balancing pole. Hanging on to one end of the pole are his benefactors—the people who put him in office, and who can ruin him if he displeases them. On the other end of the pole are millions of moochers and freeloaders waiting for the goodies they've been promised. The wire he stands on—that's the entrepreneur investor who is, in fact, the only group capable of creating a prosperous American tomorrow. Mr. Obama knows all this. He knows his political survival is entirely dependent on triangulating a balance between these three groups with their at-odds agendas. His task is a difficult one. So he would be shrewd to keep everyone a little off balance. If the three groups are all uncertain about what's coming next, they'll be less likely to make any sharp movements.

In our little mind-meld with Mr. Obama here, we imagine him sporting a big knowing grin for the public below as he inches out onto the high wire. But in his mind, he has to be fighting butterflies, desperately trying to calm his nerves. He's a Harvard-trained lawyer and no slouch in the mental department. He has to know that there is no regulating our way out of the economic mess; no taxing our way out; no spending our way out. But those are the only options the folks attached to his balance pole will accept. What to do?

Try all three options at once, so everyone's scratching their heads.

So it was on the regulatory front that Mr. Obama announced a whole new layer of bureaucracy to ensure that Americans would "never again" be so vulnerable to those SOBs on Wall Street. Like with all his speeches, Mr. Obama chose the right words and sounded awesome. But it was all mere window dressing. There was no real reform of the twin problems of Wall Street: how the banking system operates and the grand hubris that led to the crisis.

If anything, Mr. Obama fortified the financial sector lobby; it grew in size when he took office.

Fact is, Mr. Obama never had any intention of reforming his Killionaire benefactors. His goal was merely to convince supporters that big actions were being taken, change was afoot, hope bubbling anew. The Leftstream media reported all this faithfully.

Mission accomplished.

On the tax front, Mr. Obama announced that he would not tax anyone making under $250,000, igniting a kind of class warfare not seen since medieval times.

Again, Mr. Obama was just keeping everyone off balance.

He knows the truth. He knows that we cannot technically tax our way out of current deficits and achieve a balanced budget without tearing down government brick by brick—and that's not going to happen on his watch.

For just the commitments that Mr. Obama made in his first six months, the taxpayers are on the hook for an additional $55,000 per household. That raises the total each household *should* be paying in taxes to meet our spending obligations to . . . $546,668.[143] Call us crazy, but we don't think the average family of four will be able to scrape up an extra half million a year for Uncle Sam.

But it gets better. Mr. Obama has also insisted, straight-faced, that he's exempting all but the top 5 percent of income earners from tax increases. And, he says, the bottom 50 percent of the country will pay no taxes at all—in fact, they'll "earn" tax credits that mean they get money back that they never paid. A clever bit of wizardry, that.

So if half the nation is exempted from taxes, what does that do to the tax bill of the successful breadwinner earning $200,000 a year? By our estimates, that breadwinner's tax bill would increase from half a million to three million a year.

For some reason, this seems unworkable.

But wait, like a bad infomercial that won't go away, there's more! We've only discussed current expenditures. What then of the fast-increasing costs of Social Security and Medicare?

Analysts at the Social Security Administration tell us that their programs alone will require a 50 percent increase in payroll taxes in the next decade, and a 200 percent increase in the decade after that. Then there are all the "unfunded liabilities" in retirement and health care—that is, money the government has promised to pay out in benefits down the road, but has no idea how it will ever pay. That figure, according to the analysts at the Dallas Federal Reserve, will sometime in 2010 cross the $100 trillion mark.[144] In case you're tracking, our breadwinner would see his tax bill bump to about $7 million a year to pay off the nation's bills.

Right.

The one option Mr. Obama should have embraced up there on the high wire was a little Schumpeterian creative destruction. He should have allowed every dinosaur industry to fail and begun the long painful process of building a new twenty-first-century America. But to do that, he would have had to toss the balance pole, sending the Killionaires and freeloaders to their demise, and somehow still hold on while the entrepreneurs and investors bounced the wire in violent fits and starts of creative renewal.

Not likely, huh?

CO-OPTING THE FED—STEP ONE TOWARD THE DOLLAR'S DEMISE

When U.S. markets were thrown into a tailspin in 2008, all the world's markets went stumbling as well. Only a few isolated island republics escaped unscathed. The world had grown as interconnected as the pundits had been saying. All the investment gurus with their fancy asset diversification strategies and the hedge fund jockeys with their "market-neutral" computer trading programs were shown for what they were: someone trying to sell you something.

The world was flat—and financially flattened.

But those with serious money in play kept their eyes on the ball and on the guy standing behind the plate, Ben Bernanke???

Central bankers around the globe were following the Federal Reserve Chairman's moves with special interest. They could see that Mr. Bernanke was being painted into a corner by the new politicians in town. He was facing two messy options: Either step all over the whitewash Mr. Obama was slathering across the economic catastrophe he'd inherited or allow the Fed to be co-opted by the new administration and risk blowing up the entire economy.

These central bankers had listened to Mr. Obama's speeches ad infinitum. They had nodded sagely as the new president spoke of the sacrifices that had to be made if America was to dig back out. They had watched his actions—the elimination of taxes for half the nation, the attempt to create 5 million new federally funded jobs, the bailouts to every large company with connections in Washington, and a massive stimulus program that was showy but unlikely to have any effect. They saw the disconnect between Mr. Obama's call for sacrifice and his eagerness to throw money at the problem.

They knew what all this really meant.

They knew that quietly, behind the scenes, Mr. Obama would be leaning heavily on the Fed to pay for all his spending. In official parlance, this leaning on the Fed is known as "monetizing the debt." In realspeak, it means the dollar was being ripped in half. Literally.

The Fed was originally set up as a private company operating with government blessing, and for good reason. You don't want the politicians raiding the treasury every time it suits them. You want arm's-length transactions. Oh sure, there are plenty of conspiracy theorists on both the left and the right who ascribe sinister motives to the Fed, and regularly accuse it of undermining our republican form of government. But watch what happens when the Fed drops all pretense of independence and becomes a foot soldier for the politicians at the White House and on Capitol Hill.

It gets messy fast.

All those financiers around the world know as much. They know what happens next.

Mr. Bernanke is, by all accounts, a genuinely likeable person with a deep knowledge of how the financial world really works. His misfortune was in taking over the reins of the Fed at a perilous time. His predecessor Alan Greenspan created the era of cheap credit that enabled one bubble after another. Within months of taking over, Mr. Bernanke was beset by well-wishers who came with hat in hand, knowing full well he had a book of blank checks in his hand. That the checkbook is the work of a conjurer mattered not to the well-wishers seeking bailout funds. As our friend Terry Easton reminds us: "The result of all this newly-created money is that the Fed's own balance sheet—which took 90 years to reach the first $800 billion—is now well on the way to $3 trillion, and that's all money created out of thin air."[145]

With all of the new credit facilities available to Mr. Bernanke, he was in the bittersweet position of deciding who lived and who died in the new economy. Who would get credit and who wouldn't? The Fed had formulas for deciding these things, formulas that bore the handprints of the folks in the White House and Capitol Hill. Some businesses would qualify for Fed funding, others wouldn't. This created a scramble to become the kind of company the Fed was thought to be funding. This also filled the market with uncertainty about the rules of the game going forward. A lot of important questions were being asked, practically into a vacuum:

- Should a company restructure itself to get better access to cheap capital?
- What's the real cost of that capital, given that intense inflation may be triggered?
- What about taxes—will the president and Congress exploit the hidden tax that would result if the Fed bought and paid for government deficits?
- Having guaranteed the deficit spending of a government bent on spending their way out of a spending problem, when will they shut off the spigot, or will they ever be able to?
- Having offered companies cheap credit, how will they wean the companies off so they can stand on their own?
- What happens when Congress steps in and starts dictating which industries shall continue receiving cheap capital?

With questions like these being asked, and no acceptable answers coming from anyone in power, there was confusion aplenty. Folks were kept off balance, as per design.

The Obama administration should have forcefully demonstrated to bankers and investors around the world that the Fed would remain an independent entity, no matter what. No such assurances were offered. Few understood the consequences of this better than Richard W. Fisher, president and CEO of the Federal Reserve Bank of Dallas. In an interview he acknowledged that the financial crisis required extraordinary Fed action, but he worried that the trillion-dollar bailout would be "one more straw on the back of the frightfully encumbered camel that is the federal government ledger."[146]

HOW THE DOLLAR-DUMPING PARTY COULD UNFOLD

On an abstract level, every American knows we've been spending a lot more than we've been making and that the good people of the world have been lending us money to keep our spending binge alive. That's the big picture. The specifics are straightforward:

The Treasury Department estimates that in June of 2008 foreigners held some $10 trillion in U.S. dollars. China held $1.2 trillion, so did Japan. England held $800 billion, Luxembourg $600 billion, Ireland $400 billion, Russia $200 billion.[147] So the good people of China, Japan, Russia, Saudi Arabia, Brazil, and other productivity-oriented countries own trillions of dollars of U.S. government debt, Treasury bills for the most part, but they have a problem.

They can't do a thing with their investments.

They can go on earning a measly 2 or 3 percent on their money, but that's all. They might greatly prefer to use their capital to acquire more profitable assets or to fund projects for their own people in their own countries. But when their Treasury bills mature, they can do nothing but purchase new Treasury bills. If they tried selling all those Treasuries on the open market, all hell would break loose—in theory, anyway.

As that theory goes, dumping gobs of dollars on the market would create a situation where too many dollars are suddenly chasing too few products. Cue up the dark days of the Carter administration. Panic would spread faster than you could get to a money-changer. Other nations would leap into the dumping, out of fear of losing their reserves to a devaluation. The final step is hyperinflation.

For instance, say Luxembourg suddenly announced that they were converting their $600 billion in dollar holdings to euros at the prevailing exchange rate. The currency market might melt down, but it might handle the trade just fine if executed professionally, as it would be. Other nations might follow suit. All those dollars would be shipped back to the United States and we'd be forced to accept them because, well, they are legal tender. With so many dollars floating around, prices would soar and most likely lead to hyperinflation, possibly collapsing the entire monetary system.

The net effect for Americans, in barber shop terms, would be a forty-cent dollar. That car that used to cost $20,000 would now cost $50,000. Few would escape the pain.

Decades ago, the great economist Milton Friedman warned that "the fate of a country is inseparable from the fate of its currency" and that "inflation is a disease, a dangerous and sometimes fatal disease that, if not checked in time, can destroy a society."[148] More recently the investing genius Warren Buffett began a very public series of public warnings that the only way the United States could ever hope to solve its spending addiction was to inflate away the value of the currency.

This fear of hyperinflation in the United States and a tanking of the world's largest creditor kept a lot of people fairly honest for a long time. It created a kind of codependency through all of America's wild spending years. We spent, they lent. We both benefited, or thought we did, in a kind of fiscal tango not unlike the "mutually assured destruction" of the Cold War years. Then, the nukes that the United States and Soviets had pointed at one another on a hair trigger supposedly guaranteed that neither would fire first. Now, if overseas nations stopped financing U.S. deficits, it would drive up the value of their currencies, raise the price of their exports, and thrash their hopes for economic growth. All bad.

This was the game we played for two decades, a delicate *pas de deux* with the world, enforced by a big American stick. America enjoyed the benefit of seignorage — that is, the dollar was the world's currency reserve and so we could arbitrarily increase or decrease the value of the dollar as it suited our economic needs, and the world had to go along. As Nixon's Treasury Secretary John Connolly famously told

European financial ministers in 1971, "The dollar is our currency, but your problem."[149]

But even the most lopsided games in which both sides feel compelled to keep playing do stop, often abruptly.

It happens when the stakes are raised.

Those stakes were clearly raised when the Obama administration made it clear in mid-2009 that it would run $2 trillion deficits for as far into the future as the eye could see. That moved the game into what you might call the "impact" stage.

Central bankers watching from overseas got the message: They would never get their money back. The United States would either default—not likely—or choose to inflate away the debt in the classic Argentine fashion—more likely. Either way, they were screwed. They had to take action.

The only question was "when?"

Glimpses into that "when" came fast and furious in 2009. The Russians, as usual, were most boisterous in venting their anger. Russian President Dmitry Medvedev had been warning for several years of the need to create a new supranational currency:

> We need some kind of universal means of payment, which could create the basis of a future international financial system . . . Naturally, because of the crisis in the American economy, attitude to the dollar has also changed.[150]

As we write, Mr. Medvedev is holding meetings with the financial leadership of Brazil, India, and China. They are discussing a new world currency, as they have many times before. There will be no leaks of their discussions. Publicly we'll hear only the usual prattle—most of it coming from China, holder of the largest amount of U.S. dollars and ground zero for any global currency switch. People like the former head of China's foreign-exchange, Guo Shuqing, will insist that no replacement currency is in the offing. People at high posts in the European Central Banks will chime in, volunteering that they remain positive on the U.S. dollar.[151] People will keep mumbling these dismal nothings until the knife drops and everyone is stuck trying to grab it.

Now that the United States has raised the stakes, the global markets have a new impetus to unload the dollar. It's a lose-lose proposition now. They aren't likely to catch the knife, but they have to try or else take it in the chest. So why not get it over with at the best possible time?

In our estimation, the "best possible time" will be when it's least expected—that is, when the global stock markets begin to recover and investors are showing a renewed appetite for risk, a renewed interest in commodities, a renewed willingness to chase the higher yields of emerging markets. If overseas investment yields are tempting enough, and they can surely be made to look that way by crafty market makers, then investors won't think twice about converting their dollars into whatever currency those investments happen to be denominated in.

That brings the "implosion" phase of the shriveling U.S. dollar.

The first early warning sign that the world is deserting the dollar will come from the central banks of smaller, less-prosperous countries. They'll have to move fast for fear of being swamped by the movements of the major powers. Most of them will fail, sadly, and will be facing wipeout scenarios of their own. But they are the most reliable barometer we've got for assessing the dollar's fate and giving the go-signal to our entrepreneur investors to take the swift action that will be required.

We know that through indecision, opportunity is often lost. In the case of an imploding dollar, the loss could be immense. So in follow-up briefings to this book we'll provide regular updates on a "dollar defense strategy." We most highly recommended this strategy to anyone holding U.S. dollars or doing business in U.S. dollars who isn't eager to see those dollars suddenly worth only forty cents each.

We'll also be taking action ourselves. We don't intend to sit our butts on the sidewalk as smug Chinese and Arabs parade up the Main Streets of America, scooping up our national treasures at the equivalent of forty cents on the dollar, because America is too broke to resist.

There may come a time soon when we will have to fight for a decent standard of living for ourselves and our families. We may have to fight the way Yanks used to fight—the way we fought at Fort McHenry when the entire British Navy spent an entire night blasting away at our new American flag, trying to fell it. As morning cleared, the flag still flew, shredded but unbroken, and America refused to retreat.

Again, we'll refuse.

We pray that every American who cares deeply about this country is up to the challenge. We believe it is up to us, now. Our future and our children's whole way of life are tied to the decisions we make in coming months.

8

POWER TO TAX,
POWER TO DESTROY

I can make a firm pledge. Under my plan, no family making
less than $250,000 a year will see any form of tax increase.
Not your income tax, not your payroll tax, not your capital gains taxes,
not any of your taxes.
—BARACK OBAMA in Dover, N.H., September 12, 2008

AMERICA IS PAYING dearly for the George Bush presidency—for he did more than discredit the great conservative traditions of this country, he also gave Barack Obama license to discredit the great liberal traditions. Such is the current state of American politics—loathing the lessons and wisdom of the past, blindly striking out in audacious new directions regardless of the consequences.

Conservatives are in retreat, so utterly lost they appear condemned to wander the wilderness for many years. They deserve only a full canteen and some jerky.

Liberals are still so intent on exacting revenge for the perceived slights of the 2000 election, they are building bunkers against reason, tradition, and compromise. They understand quite well, as Supreme Court Justice John Marshall reminded us, that "the power to tax is the power to destroy." And they are vengeful. Merely shoving conservatives into the forest is not satisfying enough for them. They mean to destroy every last remaining vestige of conservatism using the sugar/sugar/shaft strategy.

They are likely to succeed.

Their first tool has been spending. Their second is taxation. They will shout from the rafters that they are "taxing the rich" even as, privately, they take good care of their rich benefactors. Taking care of these Killionaires is a Faustian bargain that surely makes Mr. Obama feel dirty. But to a man of unbounded ambition, what's an extra shower or two a day? Mr. Obama will also take care of all the subclasses of people needed to eke out electoral victories for decades to come. Whatever these subclasses want—free health care, fully funded retirements, shorter work weeks, freedom from paying any taxes at all—Mr. Obama will deliver. As strategies go, it is more caustic and mean-spirited than anything this country has yet seen—and is thus in keeping with the *Revisionist* script. It would be summarily discredited by people of honor in normal times. But these are not normal times.

George Bush killed normal. Through his words more than his actions, Mr. Bush lowered the bar so low that "doing the opposite of Bush" was taken seriously as a strategy by otherwise reasonable and intelligent people.

Now Mr. Obama is free to do as he pleases. Even when he gets pushback from his own partisans, it is more of a lover's quarrel—shoes may fly one day, but all is forgotten the next. The real activity of undoing twenty-five years of conservative rule and replacing it with a European-style social democracy is proceeding apace. And somebody has to pay for it all. Somebody has to be beaten down for a new political order to live strong.

That somebody is the entrepreneur investor. "This move to go and tax the so-called rich," Congressman Eric Cantor reminds us, "that's small business."[152] There is a target on the backs of the productive class—a red dot guided by a laser following us wherever we go. Or trying to follow. We will have to take evasive measures if we wish to remain free. The alternative is unacceptable. We will not succumb to the intellectual concentration camp of the freeloaders, muddling along, taking the handouts, lost to the reality TV gods they worship.

That is *so* not us.

Of course Mr. Obama will never get caught saying "we're targeting the entrepreneur." But he will say, through his surrogates, that taxes should be "progressive" and levied based on the "ability to pay." Team

Obama knows these phrases work because they play right into the class envy that he's such a pro at stoking.

This "ability to pay" concept caught on big with liberals when the great political sage Paul Newman started saying it everywhere he went. Mr. Newman insisted that it wasn't fair that people like him who could afford to pay more in taxes didn't pay more. We understand. When a nation is so morally lost that it pays actors such obscene sums that they lose track of how many homes they own in how many cities, and then whine in public about how much better the world would be if only actors didn't have so many homes, and others such as teachers, firemen, and coffee house workers could have more of life's sweet benefits—please!

The idea behind "progressive taxation" is that the larger your disposable income, the larger percentage of that income you should pay in taxes. Proponents claim it is the fairest approach to the messy business of taxation. But even John Stuart Mill, the most influential liberal thinker of the nineteenth century and a supporter of progressive taxation, called it "a mild form of robbery."[153]

Mr. Mill knew what Mr. Obama knows: call it ability to pay, call it progressive, call it cricket, it's all about redistributing wealth from the makers to the takers. It masquerades as class warfare against the rich. But the rich don't pay taxes—or not much, anyway—and liberals know this. The bulk of the taxes collected in this country come from the hard labor of working stiffs. Liberals know this. So they rail against the rich in the public surreality of their public speeches, but tax entrepreneurs in the private reality of the tax code they write.

The more the Obamacrats have revealed of their policies, the more obvious their real agenda. They prize income redistribution over job creation and economic growth. That turns entrepreneur investors into targets. In this chapter we'll look at how they intend to tax you into submission, and how to fight back.

MADOFF'S PONZI: CHILD'S PLAY, SAYS TEAM OBAMA

Commentators such as Marc Faber have found a striking similarity between Bernard Madoff's Ponzi scheme and Barack Obama's Ponzi scheme, with three rather important distinctions.

One, Mr. Madoff sweet-talked folks into parting with their money, while Mr. Obama will use the laws of the land and the guns of federal agents.

Two, Mr. Madoff made off with $60 billion, while Mr. Obama, with the help of Mr. Bush before him, has enabled what will ultimately tally up to a $25 trillion heist by our calculations. (If a jury was to agree with this assessment, and they took into account Mr. Madoff's sentencing of 150 years for his crimes, Bush-Obama would get 150,000 years at Club Fed, assuming the sentence was befitting the crimes.)

Three, the Madoff Ponzi was rather traditional in its structure, whereas the Government Ponzi is inverted. As explained by Ari Fleischer, press secretary to President Bush, the tax plans coming our way crucially invert the pyramid so that it stands on its vertex, upside down, perilously unstable:

> The only way the pyramid can stand is by spinning fast enough or by having a wide enough tip so it won't fall down. The federal version of this spinning top is the tax code; the government collects its money almost entirely from the people at the narrow tip and then gives it to the people at the wider side. So long as the pyramid spins, the system can work. If it slows down enough, it falls. [154]

How long can such a pyramid spin on its vertex?

When Mr. Obama took office, about 10 percent of Americans paid about 75 percent of the income taxes.[155] Yes, just one in ten of us provides more than seven in ten of the dollars the government spends (excluding deficits). Then Mr. Obama came along with his "Make Work Pay" tax cut. That meant that suddenly about half the taxpayers in this country would be taxpayers no more. They'd go on permanent tax holiday. So what happens next? Mr. Fleisher goes on to explain:

> The economic and moral problem is that when 50% of the country gets benefits without paying for them and an increasingly smaller number of taxpayers foot the bill, the spinning triangle will no longer be able to support itself. Eventually, it will spin so slowly that it falls down, especially when the economy is contracting and the number of wealthy taxpayers is in sharp decline. [156]

We expect the inverted pyramid to come crashing down in President Obama's second term, as we'll explain shortly. In the interim, the entrepreneur investor will be almost defenseless against the attacks that'll come. Once, the Republican Party could be relied upon to protect business and nation from the wealth-taxers. Once, the nation's chambers of commerce would lobby forcefully on behalf of small business and large business alike. But in recent years, many chambers of commerce have abandoned these goals and sided wholly with big business Killionaires—using their tremendous financial clout to expand the taxing, spending, and regulating power of government.

There are no protectors left standing. So Mr. Obama was free to begin breaking his "no tax increases" pledge within forty days of the oath. He first slapped a 62-cent tax increase on each pack of cigarettes in hopes of generating $5 billion in tax receipts from (mostly lower-class) Americans. We suspect he wanted to get these tax increases over with early, so that when mid-term elections come up he can deny it ever happened, and rely on the Leftstream media fact checkers to "confirm" as much.

THE HIGH COST OF "HOPE"

As a candidate seeking the presidency, Mr. Obama insisted that he had a plan to pay for all the programs he wanted—"I've laid out how I'll pay for every dime—by closing corporate loopholes and tax havens." As a president seeking to explain himself, Mr. Obama finally admitted the obvious: he couldn't possibly pay for all his big plans, and the nation would be strapped with outrageous deficits for decades to come.

Surely Mr. Obama now longs for those hopeful days of campaign glory when inspired phrasing around words such as "hope" and "change" could compel millions to their knees in adoration and worship. We commented at the time that Mr. Obama was running on a platform of "hope" because it was the best he could offer; he had little in the way of a resume or credentials. It turns out that "hope" was his entire game plan. He wanted to remake government tip to stern and he . . .

- *hoped* he could collect enough in taxes to pay for it all,
- *hoped* he wouldn't have to keep dreaming up ever more inventive taxes to pay for it all,
- *hoped* that tax revenue would just . . . appear.

So what happens when hope dies? That will be the tell on Mr. Obama's presidency.

More urgently, what happens when his plans to shake down entrepreneur investors still leaves his coffers bare? Alan Reynolds of the Cato Institute ran the numbers on Mr. Obama's tax plan. Jacking up rates on the salaries, dividends, and capital gains of people making $250,000 or more would, even in a stronger economy, raise only about $35 billion a year.[157] That's the equivalent of about two days' spending for Team Obama. Much more will be needed.

Since there are no plans to cut spending in any area except national security, and there only lightly, where will the tax revenues come from? Remember that red dot lasered on your forehead? It will increase in size as heavier weaponry is trained on you. (Some callously suggest that Mr. Obama is not cutting Defense spending much because he may need to train those guns domestically.)

So what does Mr. Obama's tax plan have in store?

When the tax sausage finally shoots out of Congress, it will contain a number of smelly things not advertised on the label. But one thing is clear: We're going back to 1977 when Rita Coolidge's "Higher and Higher" was a hit single about ecstatic love, though it could well have been about the economic misery Jimmy Carter's policies gave us.

Under Mr. Carter the maximum tax on entrepreneurs was 50 percent, and we expect the maximum rate to top 53 percent in 2010. The top personal income rate will go from the current 35 percent and shoot past the 41 percent of the Clinton era to 46 percent when certain deductions and exemptions are phased out. This hits entrepreneur investors hardest, because six in ten of us fall into this tax bracket. Owners of more than 500,000 sole proprietorships and subchapter S corporations pay taxes at these individual rates.

But the 46 percent top rate is only the official *pretend*—allowing Team Obama to duck for cover while the red laser dot enlarges. For those stuck in the *reality* of actually paying taxes, there will be a less-publicized "surtax" slapped on us starting in 2011. On adjusted gross income above $350,000, the surtax is one point and rising to two points in 2013. Above $500,000, the surtax is 1.5 points, rising to three points in 2013. Above $1 million, the surtax is 5.4 points in 2011 and beyond.

The Obamacrats said they want a European-style social democracy—they're overstepping even that. The top tax rate combining both federal and state taxes in the United States could hit 53 percent in the tax-happiest states. This rate is higher than France, higher than Germany, higher than all but three countries in Europe—Denmark, Sweden, and Belgium.

For businesses trying to compete globally, the outlook grows bleaker. The corporate tax rate averages about 25 percent in the countries we trade and compete against—the OECD countries. So entrepreneur investors are basically facing the most punitive taxes in the world.

There's also a payroll tax surcharge in store, earmarked to help fund Mr. Obama's health care plan. If you have twenty-five or more employees and you don't offer health insurance, then your current 15 percent payroll levy will increase to 23 percent for starters. This translates into a 25 percent increase in labor costs. Big business will have less trouble swallowing these labor cost hikes—or using taxpayer money to bail them out. But small business won't have it so easy. Margins are already tight. A 25 percent increase in labor costs means that some businesses will simply not hire, leading to a higher structural jobless rate, exactly what Europe saw as its welfare state expanded.

Taxes on investment profits will be increased a whopping 60 percent or even higher. This will represent Mr. Obama's biggest flip-flop from his campaign promises. Back in the campaign he promised to *cut* capital gains taxes. His campaign website touted a "Small Business Emergency Rescue Plan." His advisors told the *Wall Street Journal* to expect additional tax cuts that included "the elimination of capital gains taxes for small businesses and start-ups."[158] But of all the campaign pledges, this is the one he was expected to renege on fastest.

Even if Mr. Obama had wanted to cut capital gains taxes, or even leave them at the current 15 percent level, he stood no chance. House

Democrats object to cutting any kind of tax because that might be construed as legitimizing the Republican argument for tax-cutting—and everything Republican is wrong, as anybody in a leadership role in Congress will tell you. So Mr. Obama was stuck. He could pick a fight with Mrs. Pelosi and company and risk losing. Or he could cave. It was, for him, an easy decision. He followed in the footsteps of his predecessor, refusing to fight Congress on principle. As a result, capital gains taxes are expected to increase to 24 percent, and the economy can be expected to stall as small business owners and investors think twice about taking a 24 percent haircut on the capital they put at risk.

STATE TAXES MAY ULTIMATELY SLAM ENTREPRENEURS HARDER

States faced combined budget deficits of nearly $100 billion in 2009, drawing more and more governors to embrace the Obama solution: gouge entrepreneurs, investors, and small business owners.

California, Connecticut, Delaware, Illinois, Minnesota, New Jersey, New York, and Oregon all moved to raise income tax rates on the top earners in their states. As a result, at least half of all states will have combined state-federal tax rates topping 50 percent, according to the Tax Foundation. Residents of California and New York City will see their top rate hit 58 percent or even higher.

Then there are states not even pretending to care about business. Illinois Governor Patrick Quinn has proposed a 50 percent increase in the income tax rate on higher earners. He says this is the "fair" way to pay for all the money Illinois spends.

California politicians have long operated on the principle that government exists to feed the insatiable appetites of public employee unions, and if any money is left over then it should be spent as wastefully as possible on public services. The Golden State has a wildly antigrowth tax code, second only to the Big Apple, and ranks worst or second to worst on most ratings of state business climate. This drives away entrepreneurs and high-income taxpayers, which in turn translates into fewer tax revenues. It's a death spiral. Yet it continues.

As more and more states decide to slap the most productive to win the votes of the least productive, entrepreneurs are stuck wondering if they should pull up stakes. Entrepreneurs prize freedom most, and many of us can leave tax-unfriendly states and move freely to tax-friendly states. We can take our businesses, our capital, and some of our employees, and go mobile. Increasingly we will have to.

A mini-migration is already underway. Thousands of people are relocating from high-tax states such as California and Ohio to low-tax states such as Texas and Tennessee. The move can translate into 10 to 15 cents more profit per dollar earned. For a business operating with tight margins, those 10 to 15 cents may represent the entire profit. Moving then becomes an easier decision; a hassle, sure, but a solid move.

Arthur Laffer, Stephen Moore, and Jonathan Williams authored *Rich States, Poor States*, and they shed important light on the mobility of entrepreneurs:

> Updating some research from Richard Vedder of Ohio University, we found that from 1998 to 2007, more than 1,100 people every day including Sundays and holidays moved from the nine highest income-tax states such as California, New Jersey, New York and Ohio and relocated mostly to the nine tax-haven states with no income tax, including Florida, Nevada, New Hampshire and Texas. We also found that over these same years the no-income tax states created 89% more jobs and had 32% faster personal income growth than their high-tax counterparts. [159]

In their analysis, the authors looked at what happened when a state raised taxes on its higher earners. One group of people left the state; another stayed but reported less taxable income; another cancelled plans they'd had to move to the state. These are the three actions we can expect entrepreneurs to take in the years ahead.

Business location decisions will be made based on a number of factors, of course. Not every business can move—retailers with storefronts come to mind. Not every business owner wants to move—as infuriatingly unwelcoming as California is to business, it's hard to beat the weather. Nonetheless, many businesses are mobile. Their owners will make the go decision when the full bulk of state tax decisions begin to weigh on the company's bottom line.

Several states are in the process of creating bigger and broader welcome mats for business. They are breaking away from the national rush to be more European than the Europeans. They are in fact behaving in a wonderfully entrepreneurial fashion—figuring out how to transform their states into competitive launching pads for entrepreneurs, investors, and small businesses. These states are delivering eager customers to support businesses, paths to capital through partnerships with local banks, motivated workforces, and more.

As these states turn plans into action, we will be tracking them and offering in our follow-up briefing a full assessment of the opportunities and risks of relocation. We call these the "breakaway states" because they are leaving the failed models of old behind and creating opportunities for growth and prosperity in a new, old-fashioned American way.

Not everybody appreciates this "migration." Many politicians, especially those in high-tax states, bemoan what they call a "race to the bottom." They accuse breakaway states of cutting taxes so low that vital services must also be cut. The poor suffer, school quality declines, and police protection plummets—that's the claim. There is some truth to that, but just as much sour grapes.

New Hampshire is a good example: no income or sales tax, yet great schools and public services. Students in public schools boast the fourth-highest test scores in the nation, though state spending on schools is far below the national average. Then there's California. Teachers there are the best paid in the nation, yet student scores have been for years the second-lowest in the nation.

Some states are too badly broken to be fixed. Others are limping along too dysfunctional to do more than appeal to Washington for bailout funds. All of these states will be eclipsed by "the breakaways" in coming years. Your two authors have already moved away from dying California to two of these growth-minded states. Maybe we'll run into you in one of these up-and-comers and swap ideas for "freeing wealth."

COULD MASSIVE TAX INCREASES HELP THE ECONOMY?

Chief White House economist Christina Romer drew the assignment of selling ObamaTax to business. She met with a number of business groups in the early going, and argued that tax increases would be good for the economy, and thus good for business. It had to be a weird assignment for Ms. Romer. An academic of some renown, she had previously authored a study of tax policy changes going back a century, in which she concluded quite the opposite:

> Tax increases appear to have a very large, sustained, and highly significant negative impact on output. Since most of our exogenous tax changes are in fact reductions, the more intuitive way to express this result is that tax cuts have very large and persistent positive output effects.[160]

We can only guess what goes through Mrs. Romer's most capable mind when she finds herself opining that tax increases will deliver us unto the economic Promised Land . . . when in fact she knows that's hokum.

Remember that inverted pyramid—the government's reverse Ponzi scheme to take from the few and give to the many? With all the tax increases Mr. Obama has proposed, the pyramid gets even shakier. Increasing the top combined tax rate on earnings to 52 percent in some states, and taxes on capital gains and dividends to 24 percent, will reduce incentives for our most productive citizens to create, produce, save, and invest.

Another way to view the distortions caused to the economy by capricious tax policy is to consider how people respond to incentives. Horrific tax rates crippled the economy in the 1970s; huge tax cuts ignited a decade of growth in the 1980s. But how did these macroeconomic trends play out at the shop table level?

Turns out that people, like rats in a maze, respond predictably to incentives. If you increase a high earner's tax rates 10 percent at the margin, he will lower his taxable income by 4 percent. So he has reduced his earnings 40 percent at the margin. That's significant, with implications for the amount of tax revenues the government will collect.

Let's play this out in a real-world small business. An entrepreneur friend of ours creates video games in Silicon Valley. He voted early and often for Obama. He's not politically savvy, though that may change when his CPA lays out his new tax liability. Our game maker had a taxable profit in 2008 of just under $500,000. Under the tax policies of what he called the "evil villain reign of Bush-Cheney," he paid about $143,000 in personal income taxes, plus $27,000 in Social Security and Medicare taxes, plus $46,500 in California state taxes, for a total of $216,500. If he again shows taxable profits of a half million under the tax plan of "messiah Barack Obama," he'll be whacked with $154,500 in personal taxes, a $58,000 increase in Social Security taxes, and the $46,500 in California taxes. That's a combined tax hike of 25 percent, and it means that after making a half million dollars in profit he has only $232,000 to show for it. We'll see how it feels for our friend to send more than half of his income to the government and barely afford the cost of living in Silicon Valley.

An added wrinkle: If our friend responds to the tax increases the way the economic models predict, the figures above must be adjusted. The models tell us that his taxable profit will drop to $444,000. When all the dust settles, our friend will see his income decline by $70,000 to produce a net revenue gain to the government of $14,000.[161]

Put differently, Mr. Obama is taking away almost five dollars from the private sector for every dollar he adds to the public sector.

A lot of productivity loss for little tax gain.

That productivity loss, if in service of a greater national good, could be accepted or even applauded. But the barrage of tax increases in the works could choke off the economic recovery that we all hope will come. This choking action, in the form of stalled economic activity, zero productivity growth, and stubbornly high unemployment rates, could be capturing the headlines as you read this.

No credible economist will disagree that the tax increases slapped on workers in the middle of the Depression in fact derailed the recovery and halted jobs creation. The 1935 tax on corporate earnings and the 1937 payroll tax acted like a one-two punch to the unguarded belly of economic recovery, doubling the nation over in painful misery for another half decade. The same mistake was made by Japan in 1997 when leaders there increased the value-added tax and hurtled the nation into a second lost decade.

As we enter 2010, two years after the financial panic erupted, the economic story is still bleak and worrisome. Consumers are still reeling with not a dime in savings, home construction is at a standstill, banks are only lending to people who don't need the money, exports are weak as other nations suffer their own financial pain, and global protectionism is on the dangerous rise. Each of these are symptoms of a deeply crippled economy, down on its knees, sucking air. It can't take any more blows—and however justified, and that's what tax increases translate into.

Seriously crippling blows.

If Mr. Obama was truly interesting in reforming government, he would trash the entire tax system and replace it with something fair. Former IRS Commissioner Charles O. Rossotti has talked often of how a dysfunctional IRS is at the root of many of our tax woes:

> [The federal tax system is] so shot through with deductions, credits, exclusions, loopholes and outright noncompliance that it fails in its essential job of raising revenues efficiently. . . .

> The complexity and instability of the tax system also leads people to believe that the average person always gets stuck, while the big hitters find ways to avoid paying, regardless of the advertised tax rates.[162]

Mr. Rossotti speaks of the "big-hitters"—we call them Killionaires because of all the wealth they're killing. They love how the tax code now contains more than 70,320 pages of fine print that only their lawyers can understand. They love that 60 percent of individual tax returns are now signed by professional preparers and that folks spend an estimated $90 billion a year on tax compliance. That is the public face of a system spinning out of control, incapable of catching them in their tax-avoidance schemes.

THE RICH PAY ONLY PENNIES IN TAXES UNDER OBAMA

A few years back, David Cay Johnston wrote *Perfectly Legal* in hopes of exposing how the superwealthy escaped paying taxes altogether. The antiheroes in Mr. Johnston's eye-opening book were the New York lawyers who had charted secret routes through the maze of the tax code. At the top of the heap was Jonathan Blattmachr of Milbank, Tweed, Hadley & McCloy and Carlyn S. McCaffrey of Weil, Gotshal and Manges. These two keep well out of the public eye, for they trade in discretion and count among their clients the Forbes 400 richest Americans.

For his client Bill Gates, Mr. Blattmachr devised a way to reap $200 million in profits on the sale of Microsoft stock without paying the $56 million of capital gains taxes that was owed. In fact, the software mogul would be entitled to a tax deduction of $6 million! This was not a one-time deal. It could be worked at every stock sale in the future, so that Mr. Gates was free to present himself as a selfless international philanthropist while dodging the whole taxpaying thing.

The secretive devices of the rich that Mr. Johnston reported in his book continue today; there is no intention to crack down on them. Mr. Obama needs the rich, and they need him. The rest of us are just bit players in their board game. Fair taxation of all, regardless of wealth, is something every honest American can support. That's the kind of genuine "change" political aspirants should bring to Washington. Instead we're stuck with the situation well summed-up by Mr. Johnston:

> The tax system is becoming a tool to turn the American dream of prosperity and reward for hard work into an impossible goal for tens of millions of Americans and into a nightmare for many others. Our tax system is being used to create a nation with fewer stable jobs and less secure retirement income. The tax system is being used by the rich, through their allies in Congress, to shift risks off themselves and onto everyone else. And perhaps worst of all, our tax system now forces most Americans to subsidize the lifestyles of the very rich, who enjoy the benefits of our democracy without paying their fair share of its price. [163]

ONE CIVIL RIGHT LIBERALS OPPOSE—TAXPAYER PRIVACY

Liberals have taken so much pride in the advancement of civil rights, they've lost sight of genuine civility. The least perceived sleight against one becomes the pressing liability of many. And in the process, we *all* lose something valuable that we once had.

The stain of slavery means blacks are rushed by well-intentioned liberals to the front of the line regardless of talent, dumbing us all down. The improper behaviors of a few in the workplace means workers are afraid to touch one another, having the effect of rubbing raw our basic tactile nature. The loss of a lizard to a strawberry field or a seagull to an oil spill has resulted in the formation of environmental defense funds that view humans as some kind of alien predators. But there is an area where liberals have no concern for civil rights—the area of taxpayer compliance.

Since they need to strip as much cash from taxpayers as possible to fund their spending schemes, their concern for civil rights gets lost in all the grubbing for cash. Like kids diving for the goodies from the busted piñata, liberals expose their true civility.

One of the Obamacrats' first requests of Congress was to double and ultimately quadruple the IRS budget for taxpayer harassment.[164] They didn't call it "harassment" exactly, but they want to spend more than $2 billion a year to squeeze more cash out of taxpayers. So call it what you will, but $2.1 billion buys a lot of "action."

It is true that the IRS enforcement division has been lax in recent years. Taxes need to be collected for our many shared needs best provided by government. But when the IRS Enforcement Division is given marching orders by a new president, they hop to. Quotas are set—and met. Field agents have to deliver results so that, in turn, the IRS Commissioner can have lunch with the President and report a net increase in per capita tax collections.

But the Obamacrats' best-laid collections plans are not likely to yield the net revenue increases they seek, if history is any guide.

Back in 1995 one of the authors wrote *How to Disappear from the IRS*, a fun little book about how the IRS really works and how honest Americans could protect themselves from the stepped-up IRS enforcement that President Clinton had ordered. In researching that book something was learned that remains true today. That is the ugly hidden truth about collecting taxes. Simply put, you can't squeeze blood out of a turnip, but you can attract quite a crowd trying to.

What this means is, the IRS will be sending out a lot more dunning notices in the mail. They'll be asking a lot of little questions, requesting tidbits of information. There will be more knocks on the door from agents. All this activity is likely to be short of harassment, but just.

Remember, they have $2.1 billion to spend on enforcement, thanks to Mr. Obama's immediate doubling of the budget, and quadrupling over five years. That buys a lot of "enforcement." If you figure the average auditor costs about $200,000 a year for pay, support, and travel expenses, the IRS could be deploying 10,000 auditors across the taxpaying nation in coming years. Yes, that buys a lot of enforcement.

The super rich have nothing to fear—they've long been protected by their political benefactors from the petty inconveniences of audits and tax compliance. The targets for the Obama auditors will be individuals with income above $100,000 and sole-proprietorships above $250,000. They will try to squeeze out a few more cents out of us. But it will be all for show.

The hard fact, revealed by IRS agents gone rogue, is that most of the audits the IRS conducts yield nothing. In nine out of ten audits, the agent finds that the taxpayer had in fact paid what was owed, or close enough for government work. Indeed, the net proceeds scooped up by the government from these audits don't even cover the cost of conducting them in most years. It's a losing proposition. It is done to harass, intimidate, and frighten good people into paying their full share.

While we agree that people often need prodding to part with their hard-earned money, the net result of the new IRS audit schedule is many more taxpayers being forced into the freakish frightening hell that is an IRS audit, neglecting their families and jobs as they struggle to piece together all the forms and find all the receipts, spending huge amounts of money on their CPAs and tax counselors to line everything up just right, all despite the fact that they probably complied fully with the law and don't owe a dime.

What of these Americans' civil rights?

Aren't taxpayers the most important special interest group? Don't they deserve the very best treatment? Not from the Obamacrats, they don't.

If the Obama IRS is serious about jacking up tax receipts, they should take their enforcement activity offshore. Many thousands of citizens have stashed cash in island tax havens. U.S.-based companies have parked big bundles of cash in overseas accounts. As much as $700 billion in taxable earnings are estimated to be in hiding.

It does appear that the Obama IRS is targeting offshore cheats. New rules are being written to require more open reporting of overseas accounts, increase penalties for tax evasion, strengthen the government's hand in cases that are brought to court, and crack down on the tax havens themselves to the extent possible.

They may be successful. Offshore tax cheating is something the Obamacrats know a lot about. Early on, Mr. Obama was finding it hard to fill senior administration posts because every other individual he nominated, it seemed, was in violation of the U.S. tax code.

Treasury Secretary Timothy Geithner, House Ways and Means Committee Chairman Charles Rangel, former Senate Majority Leader Tom Daschle—all of them didn't report their overseas earnings correctly. That's the nice way of putting it. When ordinary citizens behave as these powerful Democrats behaved, they're called frauds, and they become felons.

If the Administration decides that catching offshore tax cheats is too much work, and their fallback position becomes cracking down on overseas tax shelters, there will be serious repercussions on U.S. businesses. In the view of Cisco, which sells computer networking hardware worldwide, any change in tax rules would put U.S. companies at a distinct disadvantage. Cisco spokesman John Earnhardt explains:

> If rules are changed on tax deferral and we are taxed in the U.S. on non-U.S. profit, this significant additional U.S. tax cost would adversely impact our ability to invest and grow our business in the U.S. . . . and to compete against our foreign competitors who are not subject to this U.S. tax.[165]

Cisco is a successful multinational with issues very different from the entrepreneur investors we know and talk to. Yet some of the problems Cisco faces will also be faced by entrepreneurs with overseas contracts and earnings.

The whole reason Washington has long tolerated the abuses of offshore tax havens—and there are abuses aplenty—is that U.S. companies needed the help. They needed to be on equal footing with their foreign counterparts who are not taxed.

If for example you have a Nevada company and you want to sell computer equipment in Germany, you would hope to be taxed at the same rates your German competitors are being taxed at. That makes you competitive at the margin in Germany. But under tax proposals floating around liberal water coolers in Washington, U.S. companies may soon be paying higher taxes on overseas earnings, making it tough to compete.

We understand that Mr. Obama is not just looking to increase tax receipts. He also wants to create more jobs in the states. His tool for accomplishing his "jobs" goal is reverse psychology. If you're less able to earn profits by producing abroad, maybe you'll bring your company back home again. Tax specialist John McKinnon sought to explain recently why Mr. Obama will be disappointed in both goals:

> Bringing production back to be taxed at the higher U.S. tax rate would raise the cost of capital and make the products less competitive in global markets. American corporations would therefore have an incentive to sell their overseas subsidiaries to foreign firms. That would leave future profits overseas, denying the Treasury Department any claim on the resulting tax revenue. And new foreign owners would be more likely to use overseas suppliers than to rely on inputs from the U.S. The net result would be less revenue to the Treasury and fewer jobs in America. [166]

We believe Mr. McKinnon will be proven correct, and the IRS crackdown will become one of the embarrassments of Mr. Obama's first term, only to fade away as an agenda item in a second term. But along the way, U.S. businesses of all sizes will face sharper anticompetitive restrictions, thicker mind-numbing rule books, and tighter profit margins that combine to make life all-around more difficult.

There are tax-wise money policies that America could follow—policies that make business more competitive at home and overseas, rewarding savings and productive investment. We know from our own nation's experiences, and from the experiences of other nations, that we can reduce tax rates and simplify the tax code, and in so doing actually win the hearts of taxpayers and strengthen the nation's economy at once. We will talk further about these policies in the next section of this book.

9

THE MONSTROUS GUILT OF LABOR UNIONS PAST

So tell me, what's wrong with unions? Nothing. They are great on fajitas and pizza and fried in rings.[167]
—Blogger at FreeRepublic.com

FOR NEARLY A half century America has been trying to gently coax labor unions into a nice enough retirement home. Like a crazy old uncle who won't wear his hearing aid and blurts off-color remarks at the party, everyone would love to shove him into a closet. But once he was young, once he was vital. And everyone has dutifully read Upton Sinclair and so they treat him as agreeably as they can, too respectful to kick his sorry ass like he so richly deserves.

Not that the "coaxing" hasn't yielded some accomplishments. Ronald Reagan famously broke the air traffic controllers union (while abetting the victories of Solidarnosc and Lech Walesa in Poland). George H.W. Bush allowed workers to withhold any "political" dues demanded by their unions. Bill Clinton slapped the unions hard with NAFTA. George W. Bush gave them eight years of deserved corruption probes and forced more openness in their financial dealings.

During this time the U.S. workforce evolved beyond the need for unions and came to view them with something approaching contempt. Today only 7.4 percent of private sector workers are members of a union.[168] And a poll conducted by the nonpartisan Opinion Research Corporation found that 82 percent of nonunionized workers had no interest in seeing their jobs unionized.[169] With such clear feelings held by everyone at the party, you'd think that crazy old Uncle Labor could be shut up for good. But apparently the hardest thing to kill is a good idea gone bad.

And oh how labor went bad.

If there is any institution in American history that should be raised onto the highest pedestal, it is the American Labor Movement. The great middle-class prosperity that our nation enjoyed—at least until the Killionaires destroyed it, possibly forever—was directly attributable to the sweat and blood of valiant boycotters at the Pullman railroad yards, the strikers taking blow after blow from armed thugs at Henry Ford's Dearborn plant, the terrible loss of life in the Triangle Shirtwaist Fire sweatshops. Organized labor played a vastly important role in our nation's history—fighting for fair pay in a safe workplace. It's easy to forget that the eight-hour work day did not become the standard until the 1950s; the five-day work week until the 1960s; paid vacation days, maternity leave, health insurance—not until the 1970s. Nobody of conscience or principal can refute the great accomplishments of labor unions, just as nobody can honestly argue they should continue.

Perhaps the worse offense of labor unions is how they drive up the cost of living for everyone else, a problem summed up nicely by Matthew Continetti, editor of the *Weekly Standard*:

> Nor is it an accident that as union membership has declined, global markets have become increasingly integrated and the price of consumer goods has fallen. Unions seek to close markets in order to bid up wages. This is good for the union members but lousy for the rest of us, because it means we pay higher prices for the stuff we buy at the mall.[170]

Organized labor has so thoroughly outlived its usefulness that they now resemble the thugs they once stared down. Their organizing tactics have become deceptive and mean-spirited. Workers tell of getting visits night after night at their homes by union reps—often finding it easier to agree to join the union than resist. Companies tell of being forced into arcane, outdated, and inefficient work rules while foreign competitors get smarter, faster, better. Society has come to expect endemic corruption from unions and a self-serving willingness to destroy industry rather than sacrifice a single dime. Every honest observer sees the union bosses for what they are: trapped in a time warp and unable to shake their 1930s glory days, or dirty rotten scoundrels, or both.

Where ever you find a heavily unionized workforce, you find problems. A study was done of the comparative economic performance of the fifty states by Arthur Laffer, Stephen Moore, and Jonathan Williams in their book *Rich States, Poor States*. Over the last decade seven out of the ten best performing states have been "right-to-work" states—where workers can decide whether or not they want to join a union. Eight of the ten worst performing states have been heavily unionized—where workers are forced into unions, like it or not.[171]

It's important to make clear that our beef is with union organizers, not necessarily union workers. We know many union workers of high caliber, especially in the teaching profession, but the system is rigged against them. They are under constant pressure by their unions to deliver an inferior work product as a bargaining chip for the negotiation table. They tend to be insulated as well from the pressures of the real world, since it is much harder to fire a worker in a unionized shop.

True story—happened at a municipal zoo. The crew there was unionized under AFSCME—the Federal, State, County, and Municipal Employees union. One of the guys on the crew kept showing up to work drunk. After multiple warnings, his supervisor finally fired him. The union stepped in, filed a grievance, and harassed the zoo supervisor until the drunk got his job back, with damages. A short while later, the drunk ran over another employee with a floor buffer and injured him. Now the zoo had to pay workman's comp for the injured employee and risk a negligence lawsuit. In the end, the zoo gave the drunk an office, and a title, with no duties. They had to hire someone new to do the drunk's old job. Union's orders.

Stories like these tan the hide of any entrepreneur, and we consider ourselves blessed to be able to steer mostly clear of the public sector with all this foolishness. But the "zoo story" isn't confined to municipalities or larger companies. Smaller businesses face very similar risks the moment they allow union organizers into the shop, as we will see.

But first, we want to again emphasize that there was a time when unions mattered. They fought for the right of collective bargaining against unfair employers, poor management practices, and unsafe working conditions. There was a need for organization in the ranks of labor. Without it, we wouldn't have the National Labor Relations Act of 1935, the Labor Management Relations Act of 1947, the Fair Labor Standards Act of 1938, the Labor-Management Reporting and Disclosure Act of 1959, the Civil Rights Act of 1964, and the Occupational Safety and Health Act of 1970—all of which put a mirror to business for examining its blemishes, cleaning them up, and getting on with business with workers as capable partners in the enterprise.

In this sense, the unions outlived their usefulness. They completed their good work. When the harsh reality of their obsolescence dawned on the union bosses, they had a decision to make. They could move on to some other productive pursuit. Or they could become greedy parasites making endless and unreasonable demands on business. They chose the latter course, obviously, and our nation is about to pay a staggering price for their selfish refusal to go gently into that good night.

This is the point in the story where Barack Obama enters.

Union bosses have felt the jilt of universal rejection for three decades now. They are past the crying, past the denial. They've become almost pathological in their attempts to keep themselves in a job. But their successes have been few and far between. And they've been linked rather convincingly to the destruction of America's proudest industries, to persistent high unemployment, and to a flood of job losses to overseas competitors. This has created something of a desperate situation for union bosses, requiring desperate measures.

What could be more desperate than identifying a lowly state lawmaker with no track record whatsoever and then allying with that lawmaker in a grand scheme to ultimately spend more than $1 billion to get him elected president of the United States?

OBAMA IS MORE DEEPLY IN DEBT
THAN IS COMMONLY KNOWN

Back in 2000, a young Illinois state legislator was trying to figure out his future. He fancied the job of mayor, but the Daley machine had a lock on that. So he fished around and found that a fellow named Bobby Rush represented the Chicago welfare projects in Congress. Mr. Rush could be vulnerable to a primary challenge, the legislator figured, because Mr. Rush had done nothing while in office and his only credential was his Black Panther lifetime membership card. So the legislator jumped into the race. But soon he found himself the object of unexpected scorn. "Just what's he done?" Mr. Rush asked. "What's he done?" The message hit home with voters. The legislator lost by thirty points. But, no fool, he learned some valuable lessons. He took some meetings with new handlers and went back to the Illinois statehouse to begin refashioning a new mask for himself with regular speeches telling of "new politics" from a "change agent" working with a "higher ethical bar."

In between giving speeches, one of the legislator's best talents, he ramped up the number of new bills he shepherded through the legislative process. There was HB3396 that made it much easier for unions to organize workers by sidestepping the "secret ballots" that had long balanced the desires of workers and employers. There was SB230, which granted union teachers a six-year leave of absence if they wanted to take a job strengthening the teachers' union. There was SB1070, which allowed college teaching assistants to join a union. This legislator was making quite a name for himself in the labor community. So many liberal politicians paid lip service to the "importance of organized labor," but this politician delivered.

Soon the union bosses began urging him in private to run for the U.S. Senate so he could continue his lonely crusade for union legitimacy. He had to be pleased with himself—he'd come a long way from that mayoral bid! And fortune was again smiling—he won the Senate seat. Right away he began pushing the legislative agenda of his benefactors. He was so intent on delivering that he tried to force employees of the

Homeland Security Department to unionize. He failed, but we can only imagine what might have been:

> Sorry, Los Angeles, we cannot move forces into the vicinity of the bomb detonation, it constitutes an unsafe workplace!

This was just one of many outlandish plans to which the young senator attached his name. Another involved a bill designed to protect businesses that preferred English to be the language used in their workplaces. You may be wondering why such a bill would even be needed? Well, it turns out that a bunch of dunderheads had tried to sue companies to force them to speak some other language while at work. Our young senator voted with the dunderheads—trying to strong-arm business in a way that no sane observer of business could ever hope to understand.

Our senator voted time and again to slap tighter rules on employers to weaken their hands against union organizers. He voted to increase the minimum wage. He sponsored a bill for a new Air Traffic Controller's union—because when thousands of planes are in the sky, it's a good time for a walk-out.

Union bosses were so impressed with his attentiveness that they decided to go all in. They supported his run for the presidency in 2008 in hopes that he would do well on the national stage, and then run seriously once he wasn't so green and had earned some chops. He was such a talented speech giver, they reckoned, he might actually win some day. They decided to commit every resource they had to getting him elected. This might be their last chance ever to save the union movement.

We know the identity of young legislator, of course, and how his story took an unfathomable twist in the 2008 election. With the Republican Party disgraced and the Democratic frontrunner a hard-swallow even to perennially forgiving liberals, a good speech giver could come out of nowhere and win, or rather, buy the presidency.

"We spent a fortune to elect Barack Obama," admitted Andy Stern, president of the Service Employees International Union (SEIU). Some

have said the unions spent a billion dollars on the 2008 campaign—
we don't know for sure, but they may well have. It was an audacious
gamble on the part of organized labor. If they had failed in their
mission, the SEIU, Teamsters, AFL-CIO, and UAW may well have
sunk under the burden of their debts. But the bet paid in spades.

Now it's payback time.

Labor has a long list of wants, and with the help of Mr. Obama they'll
get a lot of what they paid for. Not all of it, but a lot. As Mr. Obama told
the AFL-CIO Executive Council in March 2009:

> I do not view the labor movement as part of the problem. To me, and to
> my administration, labor unions are a big part of the solution. We need
> to level the playing field for workers and the unions that represent
> their interests—because we cannot have a strong middle class without
> a strong labor movement.[172]

How does Mr. Obama intend to level the supposedly unlevel
playing field?

WHAT UNION BOSSES WANT, WHAT THEY'LL GET

Within hours of Mr. Obama striding across the threshold into the
most important office in the world, we witnessed the cold calculus
of political payback. He immediately issued three executive orders
reversing Bush-era labor policies. His $787 billion stimulus bill
included "buy American" provisions. He shut down a NAFTA program
that would allow Mexican trucks to come into the States—you could
just hear Jimmy Hoffa chortling over that one. And for the coup de
grâce, the United Auto Workers (UAW) were handed 55 percent
ownership of Chrysler and 17.5 percent of GM, plus billions of dollars
in special favors. It was the biggest political boondoggle to come out
of Washington in decades—and that's saying something. As Newt
Gingrich commented:

> In a rigged proceeding in which the federal government disregarded
> bankruptcy law in favor of the political outcome it desired, the

Chrysler bankruptcy laid the predicate for the much larger General Motors bankruptcy to come. Against law and precedent, the unions were moved to the front of the line when it came to who would benefit from the bankruptcy. [173]

Chrysler's investors and GM's bondholders got clocked, paid only pennies on their investment. Meanwhile, the unions, which were more responsible for the automakers' demise than anyone else, got a sweetheart deal. Indiana State Treasurer Richard Mourdock looked beyond the obvious political payback to an essential issue of law: "The issue of secured creditors' rights is bigger than Chrysler. It's an essential foundation of our capital markets. And fundamentally, this is about the law."[174]

Those laws were trampled in a brute move to pay back unions. Not only did the UAW secure ownership stakes in two giant companies, but they were granted ongoing protection and subsidization by the U.S. taxpayers. While the rest of America struggles to find jobs, autoworkers get lavished job security of the highest order—taxpayer funded.

What's more, Mr. Obama agreed to the UAW's demands that GM not be allowed to import the fuel-efficient cars it makes in its overseas Opel operations. That makes no sense, of course. Out of one side of his mouth, Mr. Obama is urging green innovations, fuel efficiency initiatives, and "cash for clunkers" programs to get gas guzzlers off the road. But out of the other side, he's not letting GM compete—further crippling them and no doubt lengthening the time they'll be stuck on taxpayer-financed life support. That's the game Mr. Obama plays. Because, as UAW President Ron Gettelfinger boasted on PBS: "We, quite frankly, put pressure on the White House, the [auto] task force, the corporation" to bar small-car imports from overseas.[175]

In the GM and Chrysler bankruptcies, the Obama administration trampled on the rule of law. It used taxpayer money to pay back the unions. As Mr. Gingrich observed: "Nobody's calling this a scandal. It's time we start."

We've learned that the union bosses are expecting payback from their investment on eight major fronts. The bosses won't get everything they want, but they'll get a lot. Mr. Obama will do everything in his power to ensure key legislative victories. He will work tirelessly because he needs their support come re-election time. He cannot hope to win a second term without another big infusion of cash from labor and tens of thousands of paid labor organizers hard at work getting out the vote.

So Mr. Obama will deliver a lot.

Unions want Mr. Obama to pass the Employee Free Choice Act, making it easier for unions to organize and shelving longstanding rules that require unions to work with management when organizing employees. This is known as the "card check" fight and it's taking center stage in Washington (much more on this shortly).

Unions want Mr. Obama to rewrite U.S. trade agreements with other nations to give union workers "favored" status. This will be called a "leveling" of the field when it's a clear "tilting" toward U.S. workers, inviting retaliation and trade battles with other nations. We expect Mr. Obama to succeed on this front because the rules of international trade are too murky for the rank-and-file to follow, and Mr. Obama can score some easy first-term points while hoping that any significant retaliation from our trading partners will not occur until his second term. On that score, he will be sorely disappointed, in our estimation. Already, America's trading partners are crying foul and launching retaliatory campaigns that will soon spiral into global trade conflicts.

Unions want Mr. Obama to repeal parts of the 1947 Taft-Hartley Act that allowed twenty-two states to enact "right to work" laws that made businesses in their states more competitive nationally and globally. We expect Mr. Obama to wax eloquent about Taft-Hartley whenever he finds himself in a room of labor organizers and kindred socialists, but that will be the extent of it. He needs comity in the statehouses, and prodding them to undercut small business owners in their own states is almost certainly a losing battle.

Unions want Mr. Obama to set aside government projects for only unionized shops to bid on. Unions will get an embarrassment of riches in this regard. All presidents get to reward their supporters. But as the biggest spender since the pharaohs, Mr. Obama will see to it that spending bills are reported out of Congress with certain provisos that lock out nonunion shops, or at least unfairly favor union shops.

Unions want Mr. Obama to boost unemployment insurance benefits. He delivered the boost within hours of taking the oath. And he'll keep those benefits coming uninterrupted until the day he is re-elected. At that point we expect him to push back, in a gallant eleventh-hour conversion to fiscal conservatism. His closest advisors will have a good laugh at that one.

Unions want Mr. Obama to slap punitive tariffs on imports so that uncompetitive union shops can stay in business. Unions don't care if these actions spark global trade conflicts in which everyone loses. And apparently neither does Mr. Obama. In September 2009 the president slapped a 35 percent tariff on Chinese tire imports, precisely what the United Steelworkers union had asked for.

Unions want Mr. Obama to penalize companies that hire overseas. This will be a difficult demand to meet, and little will come of it.

Unions want Mr. Obama to require small companies with fewer than twenty employees to allow union organizers in the doors. This is such an absurd request on face value that when legislation bubbled to the surface in 2009, a number of Democrats jumped ship to shoot it down. Small businesses cannot function under all the rules and requirements of unionization. That is plainly obvious. But this is a key priority of labor. They know that small businesses are the most easily penetrated, for they lack the legal sophistication and resources to resist an organizer's onslaught. Labor will insist that Mr. Obama breathe new life into the legislation, offering it up in a different guise, trying again to slip it into law. They will succeed. There will be precise strategies entrepreneur investors can use to protect themselves; we will return to those shortly.

Unions want Mr. Obama to unionize the entire public sector in hopes of lending some legitimacy to the continued existence of unions when the private sector has moved beyond them. Unionizing more of the public employees who are already guaranteed high job security and low performance standards seems wasteful to us. But expect it to happen, nonetheless.

Unions want the Department of Labor to turn a blind eye to union shenanigans while beefing up regulatory oversight of business in general. They'll get their wish and more. In selecting former

Congresswoman Hilda Solis for his Labor Secretary, Mr. Obama has labor unions' biggest advocate right where labor wants her—on point, very public, for all to see. When she was in Congress, Ms. Solis co-sponsored the Employee Free Choice Act (EFCA) that will wreak such devastation on small business in coming years. So labor may get two blind eyes from Madam Secretary.

HOW UNION ORGANIZERS MEAN TO INFECT SMALL BUSINESS

When fighting a parasite such as ivy, a few good whacks with the machete to the early vines and you are good to go. But wait too long and the vines will thicken and wrap themselves around the vital fiber of the host, and any attempt to cut it back will cause serious damage. That is the situation small business owners are in today.

Faced with declining membership, setbacks at larger companies, and general public disfavor, unions are resorting to trickery and deceit. They're pushing EFCA and lining up the Leftstream media to make the legislation appear so appealing, everyone will be out planting ivy—or at least that's the hope.

Fortunately for business, there are still members of Congress who read bills before they vote. And the finer points of EFCA are so appalling that the Obama administration's mid-2009 efforts floundered when they attempted to ram it into law without debate. Now the unions and their congressional allies are regrouping, trying to figure out how to slap a less offensive face on EFCA so that it's not so obviously an Employer Fastened in Chains Act.

The most offensive piece of EFCA is the highly questionable organizing practice known as "card check." If this practice becomes federal law, the unions will have a much easier time organizing workplaces, from the largest to the smallest. As an August 2006 *Hartford Courant* editorial explained: "The card-check procedure almost always results in a union victory because the union controls the entire process."[176]

The way it now works, employees in a workplace can vote in a secret ballot whether or not they wish to unionize. No pressure can be applied—not from the employer, not from the union. Balloting is secret. Union organizers want to replace this with "card check." That system would allow union organizers to approach employees and coax, coerce, bribe, or otherwise corner them into signing a card saying they want the workplace unionized. When the organizers get a majority convinced, the shop goes union. It's an obviously lopsided system, which is why the unions are pushing it so hard.

Just because card check failed in the first legislative attempt in Congress doesn't mean it won't come to pass. SEIU's Andy Stern has made it clear that he's still expecting payback: "The Employee Free Choice Act is going through the usual legislative process, and we expect a vote on a majority signup provision in the final bill or by amendment in both houses of Congress."[177]

Labor leaders like Mr. Stern meet daily with members of Congress and the senior White House staff to figure out tweaks to the legislation so it will squeak through and become law. They will succeed. They have Mr. Obama attending one labor event after another saying he is "standing behind" the Employee Free Choice Act.[178] This is payback in action. And both the union bosses and Mr. Obama believe they have the perfect cover. The irresponsible behavior of the U.S. financial services sector has convinced enough people in this country that big business is the bigger problem. With all the attention focused on executive bonuses and bailouts, unions mean to slip in the back door.

We must keep an eye on that door, machete in hand.

HOW TO KILL THE PARASITE AT ITS ROOTS

If you own a small business with twenty or more employees, you should be making preparations now. Union organizers have your name on a list.

At the very least, teach your trusted managers how to respond to union organizing efforts without running afoul of the fast-growing list of laws. Taking a few simple steps now could save months of aggravation down the road. Here's good advice from Harrison Darby and Margaret Bryant, authors of "When Unions Knock, How Should Employers Answer?":

As union leaders commit serious money, time, and attention to organizing new members, employers should heed any warning signs and take steps to prepare for a union campaign. The best preparation is to anticipate issues that a union would be likely to raise and minimize the potential for union support. By identifying and correcting vulnerabilities, employers can blunt the edge of a union's strategy.[179]

New rules will be raining down on your business, making it all the more difficult to keep abreast of the latest. But the top rule to keep in mind is this: You must have posted a written company policy on unionization *before* the start of any union organizing or else you risk the charge of unlawful retaliation. Your policies should be clear on three fronts:

1. Distribution of union literature is banned.
2. Signing of union authorization cards by employees on company premises is banned.
3. Solicitations by noncompany organizers on company premises in banned.

Making sure that all employees are clear on these matters will offer protection down the road, come what may.

Recognize that the unions are not the only beneficiaries of an Obama presidency. The lazy and slothful are winners, too. Any company that grows in size to fifty or more employees is likely to have a few employees trying to skate by, emotionally detached from the company's mission. They will feel increasingly empowered by the Obama-Oprah-Unions victimization train when it arrives to say, "You've been exploited, honey, but we're here to make it right!" The indolent and the lost glom onto this stuff. They will begin to talk with others in the workplace. A little talk here, a little talk there, soon it adds up to serious shouting.

If one day one of your marginal employees walks into your office bearing a petition demanding a vote on unionization, all is *not* lost. Your legal bills are about to skyrocket; your business will be tossed in turmoil; your attention will be sorely diverted from profitable enterprise; but if you respond in just the right way you may avoid the wrath of Mr. Obama's rather far-reaching Labor Department, and you may just pull through.

In the *Legal Handbook for Small Business*, Marc J. Lane pointed out the importance of following the letter of the law or risk losing a unionization election automatically:

> Be careful to avoid any unfair tactics. . . . Improper conduct can induce the NLRB to set aside a management victory; and your repeated violations of the National Labor Relations Act can force union recognition even without an election.[180]

Mr. Lane also offered guidelines for defending your business interests in the weeks leading up to the NLRB-supervised election. There is a thicket of legal strictures imposed on you, detailing what *you may not do* in a number of areas:

- Polling employees about their attitudes toward the proposed union.
- Threatening or otherwise implying that a union victory will spell a loss of employment or benefits.
- Withholding employee names and addresses from union organizers once an election agreement has been made.
- Visiting employees at their homes to lobby against the union.
- Unequal application of rules about solicitation on company grounds and company time (regarding pro- and anti-union forces).
- Favoritism toward antiunion employees.
- Discrimination against pro-union workers.

As the owner, you will have the opportunity to make your case and tout the many advantage of keeping the company nonunion. You'll want to lay out the benefits you currently provide to employees, such as how:

- Employees benefit by having direct "one-to-one" interactions with management instead of dealing with an external layer that has no vested interest in the success of the company.
- Employee wages, benefits, and working conditions are already above the norm.
- Seniority rules will change under unionization—those who have been employed longer will have seniority rights that trump younger employees who may be more accomplished.
- Employees will find it difficult to decertify the union if they become unhappy with it.

In any companywide meeting with employees, it is most important to maintain a high level of integrity and forthrightness. For example, do not call the union organizers what they are . . . parasites. (Use the word "ivy").

Once the election is over, it is not over. Even if victorious, your company will remain in turmoil for months. Stress levels will remain high, resentments will linger. The union may try to nullify the results or simply regroup and try to take over your company again down the road.

Alternatively, if you lose the election you have recourse. You can charge the union with unfair labor practices and, if you have the stomach for a long sit in court, have the election results overturned. You could acquiesce and enter into collective bargaining arrangements in good faith—hoping for the best. Or you could try to sell your business—but it won't be easy because the buyer would have the pending liability of a union shop. Or you could just shutter the business.

It's a grim scenario all around.

And it promises to grow grimmer in coming months as a snarl of red tape coming out of Washington wraps itself tighter and tighter around your ankles. Fortunately, some of the right-to-work states are studying the ways they can resist Washington and lay out welcome mats for small business.

We're tracking the early efforts in these states. As concrete measures are put in place, we'll share them with readers in our complimentary follow-up briefing.

10

THE BIGGEST FINANCIAL BUBBLE IN HISTORY

Humanity is sitting on a ticking time bomb. If the vast majority of the world's scientists are right, we have just ten years to avert a major catastrophe that could send our entire planet into a tail-spin of epic destruction involving extreme weather, floods, droughts, epidemics and killer heat waves beyond anything we have ever experienced.
—AL GORE in 2006

I believe it is appropriate to have an "over-representation" of the facts on how dangerous it is, as a predicate for opening up the audience.
—AL GORE in 2009

W**E HAVE UNCOVERED** a disturbing and potentially criminal connection between Silicon Valley venture capitalists and the Democratic Party leadership. The revealing of even the broadest outlines of this connection could prompt investigations into several high-level Administration officials. We take this very seriously. So we have taken extra caution to present our findings faithfully, and with integrity. Everything we've uncovered is truthfully presented and accurately sourced, and in places where we have been left to conjecture, we say so. We know that doesn't matter to the partisans, but it matters to us.

And so we begin.

. . .

DISTRACTING A NATION WITH "CAP-AND-TRADE"

In June 2009, Congress passed H.R. 2454, calling it an urgent and necessary solution to America's energy problems. With this bill, its proud sponsors announced, the looming threat of global warming would be reversed; the widely sought goal of energy independence would be met; and it wouldn't cost Americans any more than a "postage stamp" a day.[181] This bill came to be known as "Cap-and-Trade" because it would slap business with some strict rules on emissions (the "cap") and penalties for not complying (the "trade"). By 2010, the legislation is expected to clear the Senate and be signed into law by President Obama.

Businesses will be required to cut harmful emissions 17 percent from 2005 levels by the year 2020, and then cut them a full 80 percent by 2050.

This is certainly a worthwhile goal, since nobody in their right mind advocates increasing pollution. The legislative trick is to design a system that's workable. Under the cap-and-trade legislation, companies would be allowed to release only so many tons of pollutants into the air before being slapped with huge penalties. There is a lot of fine print involving the buying and selling of these allowances, and feel free to wade into all of it if you like. But if you want the summary view, cap-and-trade will come down on business like a mallet coming down on a grape. Big business will hustle out to build protective enclosures for themselves; small businesses will be staring up helpless as the mallet comes down.

As potentially disruptive as cap-and-trade will be, it's important to keep in mind that it's only a distraction. It is not the main agenda, in our view. We believe cap-and-trade was crafted for the purpose of appeasing the tree-huggers and helping environmental organizations with their fundraising efforts. All mere payback to liberal donors.

And a great cover for the real agenda.

But first let's be clear. We applaud President Obama for any ambition he musters in tackling our energy problems. Energy is a $5 to $6 trillion market worldwide. It affects everything we do. Yet our nation's energy policies are outmoded and in desperate need of redirection. Whether you believe that our planet is warming to the danger point, or that the whole green movement is a joke, it matters not. Informed people can agree that we should lower our dependence on fossil-fuels and work toward a cleaner, energy-independent future.

So from the beginning we hoped that Mr. Obama would work with both parties in Congress, with energy producers and environmentalists, with inventors and consumers, in crafting a forward-looking energy policy. That was our hope.

What did we get?

As early as 2007, then-Senator Obama had called for price controls on energy. He lectured audiences about driving SUVs and absently leaving the house lights on. "It is undisputable that the climate is getting warmer," he insisted, so habits had to be changed. Reporters asked, "How do you convince people to change their lifestyles?" Mr. Obama's answer: "It is important for us to send some price signals to change behavior."[182]

Interestingly, the controls proposed in the candidate's platform were similar in form to those forced on Americans by President Nixon in 1973. The effect then was to trigger the worst recession in decades. Mr. Nixon wanted to force wages to keep pace with prices; Mr. Obama wants to force Americans into more environmentally friendly choices. He will learn, as Mr. Nixon learned belatedly, that people, like horses, can be led but not easily forced into anything.

Once in office, Mr. Obama stayed on message. Responsibility for selling his energy plan went to Secretary of Transportation Ray LaHood. He said that the administration would, "coerce people out of their cars."[183] Yes, his words. Mr. LaHood's office even planned to open up an "Office of Livability" to monitor the way we live and ensure that our lifestyles are in compliance with new federal statutes.

If we could stop laughing, we might be afraid.

In a June 2009 radio address, delivered a day after the House passed the cap-and-trade legislation, Mr. Obama was feeling the heat of the kitchen and launched a spirited defense of the bill:

> We must not be prisoners of the past . . . don't believe the misinformation out there that suggests there is somehow a contradiction between investing in clean energy and economic growth. It's just not true.[184]

Is this a fair and honest thing for Mr. Obama to have said? Can America invest in clean energy as we should, and not pay a financial price for abandoning fossil fuels? After studying the legislation and its $150 billion price tag, Dan Kish at the Institute of Energy Research concluded: "Greenhouse gas taxes that are going to be implemented by the Obama administration—with or without help from Congress—will raise the cost of everything."[185]

David Kreutzer, Senior Policy Analyst in Energy Economics and Climate Change at the Heritage Foundation, concluded:

> The economic impacts of this cap-and-trade program in just the first two decades are extraordinary. The estimated aggregate losses to gross domestic product, adjusted for inflation, are $4.8 trillion. By 2029 the job losses in the manufacturing sector will be nearly three million.[186]

Since the Heritage Foundation tends conservative, one might view Mr. Kreutzer as merely partisan. Well, here is the information he used to base his conclusions. More than 85 percent of our energy use comes from CO_2-emitting fossil fuels—that's a fact that none deny. Our ability to switch to "clean" energy over the next twenty years will be limited and expensive—another fact that none deny. To meet Mr. Obama's goals, then, we must dramatically reduce our use of fossil fuels, and dramatically increase the cost we pay for those fuels, and somehow at the same time accelerate the development of alternative energy sources. Cutting usage and raising prices can be expected to hurt economic activity and destroy millions of white- and blue-collar jobs—yet another fact that cannot be denied in any honest assessment of the situation.

Conservative columnist Doug Patton has also crunched the numbers on the legislation and concluded that cap-and-trade would kill at least two real jobs for every "green" job it created; home utility bills would increase by 50 percent or more; gasoline prices would increase by 50 percent or more. Even if these estimates are incorrect by double, they still translate into skyrocketing energy prices which are a far cry from the "postage stamp" a day costs promised by Mr. Obama.

So apparently Mr. Obama is not being honest.

Douglas Elmendorf heads up the Congressional Budget Office. His is a nonpartisan job, but he's also careful not to upset the guys writing the checks. That would be Democrats at this juncture. He told Senators in May 2009 that the cap-and-trade scheme resulting from a mandated 15 percent cut in CO_2 emissions would cost the average household about $1,600 a year.[187]

Even Mr. Obama's own advisor, billionaire investor Warren Buffett, conceded that the energy programs would cost more than advertised: "Regulated utilities would pass the costs on to customers, effectively resulting in a carbon tax. . . . It's a tax like anything else. . . . Probably going to be pretty regressive."[188]

Seeing an uncompetitive trucking industry after fuel price hikes is likely the reason that Warren Buffet made his single biggest investment in recent years when he bought the BNSF railroad in November 2009.

It's the harsh regressive nature of cap-and-trade that is its most surprising feature. Many of Mr. Obama's working-class supporters will be slammed hard by the price increases it will bring. If the cap-and-trade scheme implodes politically, it will be because ordinary people realize it's one income redistribution program that doesn't benefit them at all. Instead, cap-and-trade takes cash right out of their pockets and gives it to rich Killionaires. It takes from Miami, Ohio, and gives to Miami, Florida. It takes from the struggling smokestack regions and gives to Silicon Valley investors. A lot of people took a liking to candidate Obama when he promised to cut taxes for the working man and rip into the rich man and special interests. Will they reconsider when President Obama slaps hefty new costs of living on the working class for the express benefit of the rich folk?

Our friend Brian Sussman, San Francisco's KSFO talk show host and author of Climategate, makes the case that cap-and-trade is "simply an excuse for another massive government attempt at control and giveaways." Mr. Sussman is one of the few who actually read the thousand-plus-page legislation and identified one item after another intended to expand government based on junk science. But he also recognized that in the eyes of the radical left, the expansion of government into all aspects of energy was just gravy; the real coup was all the money they would be making for themselves even as they publicly blasted "the whole rotten system of capitalism. . . . "

A MAN SCORNED PLOTS HIS REVENGE

The 2000 election cost us more than we realize.

It launched George Bush into a presidency that began quite well, and ended quite badly.

It launched the Democratic Party off the deep end, with loyalists convincing themselves that the election was stolen, pathologically oblivious to the fact that *both* candidates tried to win by the rules established by the electoral college and *both* candidates tried to settle the election in their respective favor using the courts.

And lastly, it launched Al Gore into a loser's exile, unlike anything this son of privilege had ever known, and, trapped, by demons and torments he was no match for, he spawned a revenge scenario that will in coming years wreak global economic destruction even as it makes Mr. Gore wealthy beyond imagination.

We cannot imagine the personal hell Mr. Gore must have endured in the weeks following his 2000 loss. But we do know he believed himself the winner—and from such delusions terrible outcomes come.

In the eyes of his adoring public, Mr. Gore journeyed to the mountaintop and, as his beard came in full, consulted with the swami and sought a more enlightened path for himself. That path, fans say, was to go out and save the planet.

We have a different view.

We suspect that Al Gore, having both time to think and a good grasp of history, reflected on his generation's glory days. There had to be the fond memories of offing the pigs, burning bras, spelling it Amerika. But beyond that, there was the effort to convince people of global . . . cooling. Yes, that crusade got some purchase back in the 1970s.

First there was an article in *Science News* predicting "a full-blown 10,000-year ice age" by the end of the decade. Then came Lowell Ponte's 1976 bestseller *The Cooling: Has the New Ice Age Already Begun? Can We Survive?* That was all it took to convince a nation of the need to act.[189] And fast. Liberal believers grasped hands to sing "Kumbaya" and save the planet from the advancing glaciers. Millions bought into global cooling.

It had been so easy to shape these starry-eyed liberal minds, Mr. Gore had to be thinking. If people could again be "convinced" of the urgent need to save the planet from yet another apocalypse, there were fortunes to be made! And if he could get rich enough, that would be revenge indeed for a "stolen" election.

If Mr. Gore ever shared his grand plans with anyone, they might well have asked a few pertinent questions. Such as, "If scientists in the 1970s had predicted an impending ice age—and yet been so wrong— why would anyone believe any forecasts of greenhouse warming today?" In this imagined scenario, we see Al simply smiling that awkward smile of his. For he had a long family history of trading on the gullibility of party regulars.

Plus, as a deeply wronged former vice president, he had sympathetic connections across the land. The right people would return his calls— at least for awhile. So early in the going he placed a call to David Blood, an eighteen-year veteran of Goldman Sachs. Together they began talking about the potential for the largest swindle in history. Gore chose other words to explain himself to rapt audiences, but in the very words he used you can begin to see the method to his madness: "What we are going to have to put in place is a combination of the Manhattan Project, the Apollo project, and the Marshall Plan, and scale it globally. . . . "[190]

By 2003, Mr. Gore and Mr. Blood had established Generation Investment Management and created a $1 billion fund to invest in the "green technologies" that would save the planet. They issued all kinds of press releases portending the end of Gray Nation, and fashioning themselves as the new leaders of Green Nation, details be damned.

Those details?

Anyone who bothered to look into Mr. Gore's bona fides on the planet-saving front may have been underwhelmed. While George Bush had built a 100 percent environmentally friendly home for himself in Crawford, Mr. Gore's 10,000 square foot Nashville home was grabbing headlines for consuming more electricity in a month than the average American household does in one year.

Less known at the time, because the Leftstream media enforced an official blackout on the news, was the awfulness that was delivered on those living downstream from the Gore family homestead. Turns out there was a zinc mine on Mr. Gore's property, a mine that paid him $577,000 in royalties over the years, possibly to buy his silence. As reported in *The Tennessean*: "[Mr. Gore's mine] emitted thousands of pounds of toxic substances . . . nearby rivers had levels of toxins above what was legal."[191]

So we see that in 2003, at the same time Mr. Gore was repackaging himself as Mr. GoodPlanet, he was responsible for extremely toxic chemicals leeching into the groundwater, finding their way into the stream, and carrying dangerous toxins into the drinking water of nearby residents.

Some would call that criminal.

Mr. Gore called it an excellent time to go green. He pushed ahead on two important fronts: First with a remarkably bright bunch of venture capitalists, and second with an eagerly co-opted bunch of environmental Pollyannas.

The first foray took Mr. Gore deep into the heart of Silicon Valley, to its most successful venture capitalist firm, Kleiner, Perkins, Caufield & Byers. This firm had backed the biggest names in the tech boom, and one of their brightest stars was John Doerr. His was the financial acumen behind the success of most every major technology start-up, from Amazon.com through Google. Mr. Gore was Mr. Doerr's dinner guest at his home in June 2005.[192] Over coffee and dessert, Mr. Gore whipped out his laptop to give the financier a preview of a feature-length documentary he was working on, a film that might make a little change at the box office, but that wasn't the point—the film could change the face of the investment world in ways previously unimagined.

Mr. Gore had Mr. Doerr's attention. And in the ensuing weeks, the men grew close as friends and associates in a new understanding: "global warming" involved neither the earth nor heat.

Before long, Kleiner Perkins had moved an initial ante of $100 million into "green" investments.[193] The firm announced publicly that they would "advocate for policies that reduce the climate crisis and increase energy innovation." Doerr booked himself into a series of lectures and strategic public appearances preaching the gospel of green. At least eight of the nineteen partners at Kleiner Perkins began actively pushing for government subsidies for alternative energies at the state and federal levels. They enlisted the Environmental Defense Fund to design and promote a carbon emissions–trading scheme (which would evolve into cap-and-trade). Lobbyists in Washington began converting politicians to the cause. They were so thorough, a firm partner, Floyd Kvamme, landed a spot as an adviser to President Bush and was successfully selling the green-tech message to senior administration officials.[194]

Meanwhile, Mr. Gore was moving ahead on the retail front as well. Out came the biggest gun in his arsenal—his documentary film, crafted to invent global warming as a full-blown crisis requiring an immediate crusade with every American joining in to save the planet.

The release of *An Inconvenient Truth* was a huge success, earning $49 million at the box office. The Green Nation plan was on track and chugging—er, biomassing ahead. The previously suspect proposition of "global warming" had become real for millions.

There was one problem, though . . .

THE BUBBLE-MAKING MACHINERY
WHIRLS INTO HIGH GEAR

As long as President Bush was in office, Green Nation could never attain widespread acceptance—there's just too many people with half a brain in this country. Mr. Bush did buy into the concept, but within the bounds of reason. His 2006 speech on the subject made it clear that he was on board, but not foolish:

> Keeping America competitive requires affordable energy. And here we have a serious problem: America is addicted to oil, which is often imported from unstable parts of the world. The best way to break this addiction is through technology. Since 2001, we have spent nearly $10 billion to develop cleaner, cheaper, and more reliable alternative energy sources. And we are on the threshold of incredible advances. . . .

So tonight I announce the Advanced Energy Initiative—a 22 percent increase in clean-energy research—at the Department of Energy, to push for breakthroughs in two vital areas. To change how we power our homes and offices, we will invest more in zero-emission coal-fired plants, revolutionary solar and wind technologies, and clean, safe nuclear energy.[195]

Many readers will be surprised to know this was Mr. Bush speaking. How could that be? Wasn't he the crazy-talking, river-fouling, temperature-rising, environment-hating stooge of Polluting Dick Cheney, as portrayed in the Leftstream and even the Rightstream media? This speaker sounded like quite the tree-hugger!

Well, in fact, Mr. Bush was an incremental environmentalist, on board with the concept, but not about to try anything rash.

That was unacceptable to the crusaders.

They wanted a full run of the house. So they campaigned more strenuously for Mr. Obama than for the last several liberal presidential candidates combined. And they took tremendous pleasure from his victory.

Here was a man they could work with.

Within hours of Mr. Obama's victory, Kleiner Perkins had upped their investment in forty-eight clean-energy-technology companies to the tune of nearly $2 billion. They also invested hundreds of millions in start-ups serving dirty old fossil-fuel-belching oil and gas industries, but those weren't trumpeted so loudly in the company's press releases. For all intents and purposes, the venture capital firm was totally "green"

If you followed the venture capital industry newsletters, you saw the maestros at work—building the market opportunity. In an interview in Portfolio.com, Mr. Doerr called alternative-energy "the mother of all markets" and "probably the largest economic opportunity of the twenty-first century." If he could bring disruptive change to even a narrow slice of worldwide energy market, he said, it would "set off an IPO frenzy that would make the Internet boom look like chump change."[196]

The problem Doerr & Company had faced was that green investments were very different from what Silicon Valley was used to. None of the alternative energy technologies being developed—solar, wind, geothermal, or biomass—were financially sustainable. That meant the supersized investment returns that Mr. Gore and Mr. Doerr were banking on would require massive government subsidies, regulations, and mandates. And that would require a Democratic president—and a very liberal starry-eyed one at that.

Mr. Obama was perfect.

Now with Democratic control of Washington, the green campaign had all the pieces in place. Now the bubble could begin to be properly inflated through massive government subsidies, a labyrinth of funding partnerships, and favored-status laws that were crucial to the eventual success of those companies.

Also important was keeping the public on board. There was a bit of a snag in 2009 as Mother Earth appeared to have fallen into a most contrary, decade-long cooling trend—but fortunately for the plotters, "green" was hot and nobody wanted to hear otherwise. None of the crusaders, anyway.

"Green" had become so popular that every media outlet covered it as a regular beat. Entire commercial campaigns were organized around it. The Internet was thick with it. Everywhere you looked there were signs that everyone had bought into the green exaggerations and hypocrisy, just as they had bought into technology hype before the bubble collapsed in 2001, and just as they bought into the housing mania before the bubble popped in 2008.

The Green Bubble was inflating as planned; everyone wanted in—reason be damned.

As expected, the first to profit from the Big Green Bubble was Mr. Gore and his pals at Kleiner Perkins. One of their investments, Silver Spring Networks, was first in line to receive a chunk of the $3.4 billion the Energy Department allocated to smart grid development. As a result Mr. Gore is expected to become the world's first "carbon billionaire," profiting from the laws he helped Congress write.[197]

Did Mr. Gore break any laws, or merely step on toes?

If we learn that the green companies Mr. Gore invested in were given preferential treatment in securing the "green milk" of government grants, then yes—laws were broken. But there will be no

Congressional hearings or oversight committee investigations as long as the Democrats control Congress.

During that time, only one thing will happen: The Green Bubble will continue to grow larger and larger. We expect this dangerous phase of expansion to continue through 2012 or 2013, at which point Mr. Gore, Mr. Doerr, and fellow Killionaires will cash out, billions into the black, as speculation in green technologies overexpands and the bubble bursts.

Those who are capable of riding the expansive phase of the bubble, and getting out before it pops, will make fortunes along with the Killionaires. But it will be a tough hoe.

Most will fail.

If you wish to try, be sure to get our follow-up briefing for all the investment details that matter, as well as timing considerations.

In our follow-up briefing, we'll also look further into the potentially criminal connection between Silicon Valley and the Democratic Party. It is too early to report with greater certainty on the methods Mr. Gore, Mr. Doerr, and the Killionaires are using to funnel federal dollars into investments they own, the methods they're using to circumvent the competitive bidding requirements of government contracts, or the vehicles they're using to funnel profits back into the campaign coffers of Mr. Obama and Democratic candidates. But just as the bursting of last two bubbles carried with them several high-profile arrests on charges of fraud and racketeering, we expect the same this go-round.

If you choose to sit this bubble out—which may well be the wisest course—be sure to keep in mind who's responsible for the bubble. When it pops, they'll be telling you those nasty greedy Republicans are to blame. And Republicans will have joined in the money making with sufficient gusto to appear sullied, their ability to fight back compromised. In that sense, it will look a lot like the housing bubble.

Keep that in mind as you approach what promises to be the biggest financial bubble, and bursting, in history.

11

GIVING LAWYERS LICENSE TO STRIP SMALL BUSINESS

Some men inherit money,

some men earn it,

and some are lawyers.

ENTREPRENEUR INVESTORS KNOW the caustic effects of litigating lawyers—we live it daily and end up, all to often, on the receiving end of frivolous lawsuits. Less known is how indebted Mr. Obama feels to the lawyers' lobby for helping him move from 5046 South Greenwood Ave. to 1600 Pennsylvania Ave. But early in the going, just nine days after being sworn in, we gained insight to that indebtedness.

Get ready for Hurricane Tort!

Two bills came whirling out of the 111th Congress and each appeared safe enough from a distance, but as they grow nearer they will be revealed for the lawyer-full-employment measures they were furtively intended to be—with entrepreneurs squarely in the path of destruction.

The first bill President Obama signed into law was the Lilly Ledbetter Fair Pay Act. This bill amended Title VII of the Civil Rights Act of 1964 to make it easier for female employees to sue employers for alleged gender discrimination. This is the "equal pay for equal work" controversy coming to a head. Before the law passed, a woman had a maximum of 180 days to sue her employer. Now those 180 days are "rolling days" pegged to the last paycheck the employee feels she was discriminated on. It doesn't sound like such a big change in policy.

Is it, though?

The Lilly Ledbetter case had been a sleeper for years, but in the 2008 election liberals seized on it as a tool for whipping up audiences. Left unmentioned in the rousing "Yes We Can!" rallies, however, were the actual facts of *Ledbetter v. Goodyear Tire & Rubber Co.*

Ms. Ledbetter had been a manager at Goodyear from 1979 until accepting early-retirement in 1998. During that time, her performance reviews had been consistently poor, and she received commensurately small salary increases. Over time a large pay gap grew between Ms. Ledbetter and more competent coworkers. In 1998 she filed a charge with the Equal Employment Opportunity Commission (EEOC) claiming that she had been unlawfully discriminated against because she was a woman. Her case went to trial, and a jury agreed with her, awarding $3.5 million for lost pay, mental anguish, and punitive damages.

Our purpose is not to second-guess the jury—though there was ample reason to do so. On one level, it doesn't matter whether she was discriminated against because she was incompetent, because she was a woman, or both. In the view of the lawyer lobby, "Who cares?" This case broadened the precedent for lawyers to bring all kind of new and exciting lawsuits against unsuspecting employers.

"Yee-Haw!" is their official position on the matter.

The American Bar Association actively supported the Lilly Ledbetter Fair Pay Act, of course. But a few forthright lawyers vented their concerns publicly. They argued that the bill would strain an employer's chances of mounting an adequate defense. Under the new law, a disgruntled employee could wait for many years before suing for discrimination. Records could be lost. Memories fade in the haze. And poor, poor juries are often eager to side with poor, poor plaintiffs. Just the kind of situation lawyers love and employers rightly loathe.

The second bill reported out of Congress early in Mr. Obama's term was the Paycheck Fairness Act. Sponsored by then-Senator Hillary

Clinton, the bill hiked up the damages that employees can seek in court if they feel wronged. What's more, the bill set up a government mechanism through the EEOC to help employers make hiring decisions. Whereas once you hired folks based on the skillset and talents of the candidate pool, now you will have to hire based on the dictates of a distant government bureaucrat. They call it the "pursuit of equality," and they believe they are doing good things. With little experience in the private sector, they *would* think that.

What these bills are actually creating, as the *Wall Street Journal*'s Daniel Henninger described so aptly, is a "world being drained of oxygen for the kind of people who build the nation's economy."[198] In public statements, Mr. Obama professes great admiration for the private sector and what it needs to function. But in signing these two bills within weeks of taking office, he was, by his actions, siding with the destructive class—lawyers—over the productive class—entrepreneurs.

This should not be surprising. The Democratic Party long ago decoupled from the marketplace, viewing business as some primitive tribe requiring a whip and chains. Al Gore and John Kerry ran on anti-business platforms. Barack Obama proved himself a quick study in the Democrat Two Step: privately sidle up to big business to secure deep wells of campaign cash and union contracts, then with a wink denounce greedy businessmen in any forum attended by the liberal faithful, all the while hoping that neither side catches on to the cynical insincerity of it all.

Entrepreneurs will suffer greatest from Mr. Obama's handing the city key over to the lawyers—since entrepreneurs can least afford to retain the high-priced legal eagles that help big business soar above the litigation train coming out of Washington. In the story ahead, we see what happens when that train runs right over a small business owner.

TRUE STORY OF A SMALL BUSINESS
BESIEGED BY LAWYERS

Not long ago, on the central coast in California, there was an advertising agency of some prominence. The agency was small, with only sixteen employees and $8 million in annual billings, but the owner, Will, liked it that way. He loved the uncertainty of the business, and often quoted the Ray Bradbury line, "Living at risk is jumping off the cliff and building your wings on the way down."

Will tried to hire carefully, and treated every employee like family, partly because a happy workplace led to happy clients, and partly because he spent more time at the office than at home. He liked having an office where everyone was valuable, everyone made at least $50,000 and felt like an equal, and everyone knew that profits were being distributed fairly.

One especially happy day was the announcement by one of the graphic designers, Ruth, that she was pregnant. Everyone was atwitter, excited for the new addition. Ruth worked harder and more impressively than ever, determined not to miss a beat. And she didn't, until the seventh month. That's when her work turned to crap. Nobody said a thing, of course—the woman was about to burst! Everyone just picked up the slack, and soldiered on. Will finally insisted that she take some paid leave, to ease the tension. Ruth refused. Soon enough the baby arrived, and within days Ruth was back on the job, baby in tow, creating a distraction—but worse, her work product was unusable. Again, everyone tried to cover for her, but as the weeks wore on, patience wore thin.

Exasperated, Will finally told Ruth that she could stay on if she worked from home at 50 percent time for 50 percent pay, allowing her to balance baby and work and hopefully regain a sense of self. This arrangement went on for four months, according to court records. Because yes, Ruth sued Will.

She charged him with discriminating against her because she was a woman, paying her less than men were being paid. Will couldn't believe she'd parade such an obvious lie into their small-town environment. He became visibly distraught, and soon his own work began suffering as he attended to the details of the pending trial. The firm lost two clients in two months as Will's day was taken over by depositions, mandatory written documents, and long expensive meetings with lawyers. When a rumor began circulating that Ruth had been talked into suing by an attorney she had met at childbirth classes, that was the final straw. Will became a basket case, volleying between rage and sullen withdrawal. Everyone dreaded coming to work. Month after month of hefty court costs ate into the company's few remaining profits—two people had to be let go, with those remaining taking a pay cut. Three more left to find new jobs.

Fifteen months later, a jury found Ruth's charges baseless. But Will felt no relief, no reprieve. He felt violated, bitter, and vindictive. He had always been fairly liberal in his views, a believer in the courts as the righter of wrongs, the doer of good. But no longer. His business had been effectively ruined by a woman who should have had no right.

But she did.

And many more like Ruth will have the "right" to sue and ruin broadened in coming years, thanks to the Obamacrats' control of the White House, Congress, and Supreme Court appointments.

GOVERNMENT SHOULD FEED CREATORS, STARVE DESTROYERS

The bottom line in any analysis of public policy is that our government should feed those who create, not those who destroy. Everyone can readily agree to that. Small business creates, lawyers destroy. Lawyers as a lobby have a right to support the Democrats almost exclusively, with the tribute lawyers pay ensuring favorable legislation. But the nation must understand where this will lead.

Lawyers will keep pushing for new and more entangling laws, because that's what lawyers are trained to do. Each new regulation will tighten the noose around free enterprise and kick the stool out from beneath it. Each new law will leave Lady Liberty angrier, shaking her fist at her destroyers.

With all the attacks that will be leveled against entrepreneurs, it could be worse. Imagine if John Edwards had not withdrawn from the Democratic primaries early! If ever there was a poster boy for all that is contemptible about lawyers—bankrupting good and decent doctors by the hundreds; living large on contingency fees from trumped-up jury settlements; spending hours in front of mirrors working toward the perfect do; cheating on a wife undergoing chemotherapy treatments for deadly cancer—John Edwards was the worst of the worst. Had he won, it would have been Katy bar the door and Molly tap the keg for the plaintiff's bar. As lawyers go, Mr. Obama is about the best we could have hoped for. He practiced law for such a brief time—what, two years time if you stretch it?—he couldn't have much practice.

A TELLING EXCERPT FROM THE NOVEL *OUT OF ORDER*

The last time lawyers enjoyed such clout in Washington was during the tenure of Bill Clinton. As a lawyer himself, Mr. Clinton felt a certain kinship with those who take from the productive and give to the unproductive, keeping a big slice for themselves. So it was back during Mr. Clinton's term that one of the authors wrote a fictional piece about a scientist who had been so royally screwed by his attorney, he decided to seek revenge in a most disturbing yet satisfying way. A decade has passed since the writing, and still the book rings true—so we chose a brief excerpt to adapt to our purposes here.[199]

We pick up the story in the final scene with a surprise admission of guilt from the scientist Janek Twisselman to his attorney Canada Glenn. There is in this a fair warning of the hell we'll be facing from lawyers under a Democratic regime. And there are hints at a solution, though it's not a solution we're likely to see jumping off the fiction pages . . .

"I knew what I was doing," Janek began. "Every step was premeditated. My defense will not be insanity."

Several of us fidgeted, and started to interrupt him, stop him. None of us wanted to hear this, but what choice did we have? We had come too far together.

"I had an opportunity few have ever had," Janek continued, "an opportunity to balance the scales of justice. Lawyers were draining us, so I drained them. I sound glib? I assure you, I'm not. It was a frighteningly hard decision. I agonized over it for months after finding that my lawyers sold me out. There are no words for what I went through. I knew good people would be hurt—lawyers who'd kept their honor intact in a dishonorable system—and I have felt their misery as if it were my own."

Abruptly, Janek slammed fist into palm. "But the whole system had to be smashed! It was rotten. What reform would have worked? Capping victim awards? Insisting on binding arbitration? Hiring more judges? Streamlining the appeals process? That's just chipping at stone with Popsicle sticks. Gets you nowhere. Lawyers can block any real reform because our elected officials are all . . . what? Lawyers! Spending their days regulating every waking moment of our lives, handing down vague admonitions in favor of all things good, creating so much confusion that lawsuits naturally follow. Our elected leaders are part of the problem, not part—"

"All these laws are just the byproducts of progress," Canada interrupted, though feebly. Her heart wasn't in it.

"Sure, technology has given us some knotty legal issues," Janek said, "but we can't continue the direction we're going."

"How about stronger judges?" Canada asked

"Judges! Once, they revered judicial restraint. Now they hand down landmark decisions every chance they get, and for what? To become celebrities? To go on talk shows? To write best-selling books? Have I forgotten anything?"

"You sure have," Canada replied. "You've forgotten all the people who benefit from these landmark decisions."

"Have I?" Janek asked and then opened an arm wide to the picture window. "Look out across America. Look at doctors. They used to pay ten thousand a year for insurance; now it's a hundred thousand. Half the country's OB-GYNs have stopped delivering babies; they can't afford insurance. More malpractice suits were filed in the last decade than in the entire history of American tort law. Are today's doctors that bad, or has something gone terribly wrong? Look at the police. Most of their day is spent doing paperwork for court. Are our streets any safer for it? Look at the courts. They're so backlogged from lawyers' never-ending motions and pleadings and stalling techniques that folks just expect miscarriage of justice. Look at the Boy Scouts—the Boy Scouts, for crying out loud! They can't even have a baseball game in a city park because they can't afford the insurance. Look at the prices of products.

A third of the price of a jet and almost the entire price of children's vaccines go to keep lawyers at bay. Something's terribly wrong. Last year we had 750 verdicts of a million dollars or more. Lawyers say these large settlements are important because they send a message loud and clear. If that were so, there'd be less wrongdoing. But is there? Hah! There's only higher and higher awards from easily manipulated juries. One defendant got ninety-two million dollars for exposure to asbestos. Ninety-two million could've built factories, engineered new products, employed thousands of people. Instead we got two more millionaires: the plaintiff and his lawyer. Bottom line, the scales of justice are out of whack. There are so many lawyers, there's no law anymore. Something has definitely gone wrong and someone had to right it!"

Janek fell back into the couch, spent.

Canada started to speak, caught herself, then shook it off. "It's no secret lawyers deserve a heap of abuse. But how can you deny all the good we do? Lawyers have fought racism and inequality; we've prosecuted society's worst criminals; we've acquitted the wrongly accused. Lawyers aren't perfect, but I'd hate to live in a world without them."

"In a world without lawyers," Janek asked her, "or in a world without law?"

"There's no practical difference!"

"No? There was a time when people had precise ideas about lawful and unlawful, moral and immoral. Ideas based on the Bible and Greek concepts of, of . . . virtue. Ideas which made it right into the twentieth century, when all of a sudden we saw some kind of metamorphosis and all that had been virtuous suddenly was naïve and narrow-minded, when all that was immoral became tolerable and something to be protected. What brought on this metamorphosis? Where did we go wrong?"

None of us in the room had an answer.

Janek did, though. "People blame drugs, TV, modernity, technology, liberals, Freud, but I think there's a better explanation, something nobody talks about. Why hasn't anyone pinned the blame on the Warren Court's 1964 decision to implement a system of public defenders?"

Canada's jaw dropped. Finally, she asked, "Why not just blame Thomas Morton, the first lawyer in the colonies?"

"Wasn't he jailed and shipped back to Europe?"

But Canada was still talking, "Gideon versus Wainwright? Guaranteed counsel to all, regardless of ability to pay? You're joking!"

"Hear me out," Janek said.

"No, you hear me out!" Canada shrieked at Janek as she too shot to her feet. "Public defenders have long existed at the state level, where they're needed. Adding them at the federal level didn't make any big whoop."

"Your opinion of my opinion doesn't change my opinion," Janek said oddly. "I believe the public defender system created a sudden, unprecedented need for thousands of new lawyers. To meet the demand, law schools popped up across the land and good people attended the schools and went on to become PDs. Then something happened. They found out how much more money they could make in private practice, and they jumped ship. Word got out that the law was a gravy train. More law schools opened. People who had once become engineers and scientists opted for the law. More lawyers bred the need for even more lawyers. Soon they were generating twenty million lawsuits a year. Twenty million lawsuits do not come from handling people's base instincts. They come from giving people a license to be base. Lawyers themselves created the litigious society, the sue-reflex. They taught us to salivate over big money settlements. Lawsuits have become everyman's lottery ticket. People now take for granted that if they suffer an injury of any sort, someone else should pay. Phrases such as 'tough luck' and 'bad break' have fallen out of use, along with 'thank you' and 'sorry' and other niceties of old. Lawyers have created a society in which moral people can no longer act morally, a society in which the immoral rule and crime pays. And the only way I could see of ever returning to a semblance of the Golden Rule was to genetically reprogram the entire legal profession, or enough of them anyway . . . "

"Who in hell are you to play God?"

"That's an unanswerable abstraction! The fact is, I chose to play God. I was ruthless because I had to be!"

"Exactly what Hitler claimed," Canada hissed.

"More like Einstein. Confirmed pacifist, but when his former countrymen handed their allegiance over to a madman, Einstein knew the world had to intervene with force, so he argued for the Manhattan Project, he even consulted on it. America today is in a similar situation. The legal chains around us are no less appalling than the gas chambers; they just appear so because death comes more slowly."

Canada was aghast. "Surely you don't believe that?"

"I do believe! By terrorizing the whole profession, I could hope to make a change. I knew all along I was doomed, of course, but I had to make my stand. If I spend the rest of my days in a four-by-six, at least I made a stand."

12

THE PERILS OF ONE-PARTY GOVERNMENT

Never let a serious crisis go to waste. What I mean by that is, it's an opportunity to do things you couldn't do before.
—RAHM EMANUEL, White House Chief of Staff, shortly before doubling the size of government.

IN POLITICS, AS in business, crisis means opportunity. Rahm Emanuel can be excused for getting caught up in the Obama victory frenzy and blurting out in public that which is often contemplated in private. Liberal ideas had been in disrepute for most of his adult life—maybe, just maybe, he had to be thinking, it was finally his time in the sun.

In fact, all new presidencies begin this way, with a cocky belief among captains and yeoman alike that anything is possible. This is good, and as it should be.

And as history goes, the election of Barack Obama was certainly one to be celebrated. We're personally proud of America for shattering the race barrier and electing a half-black man to our highest office.

Sure, he was not our first choice, and we even wrote a book detailing in some length how he would rule—as has been borne out— differently from how he ran. But he won.

And sure, the Boise dogcatcher could have beaten whomever the Republicans nominated—given their sorry state. But Mr. Obama did win, and he did it through a brilliant exploitation of media imagery in the fashion of our time. He told a wonderfully "post-racial" American story that offered hopefulness to every young child: *Yes, any man can still become the main man.*

It will, nonetheless, be difficult for Mr. Obama to write the post-racial chapter for America that he seeks. He's up against unyielding opponents—not from Republicans, who are weak, but from the race-baiters, shakedown artists, and victimologists of his own party who feel emboldened and entitled. The people who played key roles in his victory—the Reverend Wright's, Jesse Jackson's, Henry Louis Gates's, Oprah Winfrey's, Louis Farrakhan's—they have a vested financial interest in scraping raw the scab that good people have long since grown over the terribles of old. Mr. Obama bested the conservatives in 2008, but not his own.

We've also learned to our great dismay that in his more candid moments, when the true heart of a man is revealed, Mr. Obama himself is not nearly as post-racial as other great black leaders. Colin Powell, Condoleezza Rice, and Bill Cosby come to mind.

The most telling example was the offhand comment he made upon learning that Harvard professor Henry Louis Gates had been stopped from breaking into his home by Sergeant James Crawley. It was one of those black-and-white moments that Mr. Obama thought he knew. Without a pause and knowing none of the details of the case, Mr. Obama called the police officer "stupid." That was his gut reaction. Surely he regretted his words at once, though he never apologized in public. And surely he will mature into the office and learn to hold his tongue when uncertain—qualities to be admired in anyone, and required of a president. But however much he may desire to be a post-racial leader, he entered the presidency a bit shy of that goal.

CONTROL THE MEDIA, CONTROL THE AGENDA

The first real insight into the methods the Obama administration hoped to pursue vis-à-vis the media came in May 2009 in an innocuous package. It was a visit with the University of Connecticut Huskies— the NCAA women's basketball champions. It was a standard photo-op, an honor for the young ladies, some fun for the president. And off they went to shoot some hoops on the White House court. Only without the photo-op part. The press corps was barred.

No explanation was offered, and the media were left to speculate. ABC's Jake Tapper filed this story, not altogether tongue-in-cheek:

> Do Obama White House officials think their media coverage isn't flattering enough? Is the goal to ultimately replace the pesky photographers who film what they want to and not what they're told to (not to mention the annoying reporters who ask uncomfortable questions about, say, detainee policy and bank bailouts)? Do you want your OTV? (I'll bet there are a few takers out there.)[200]

Later that day the White House put out its own version of the event. They created an entire video release, complete with interviews, captions, and a cute little White House logo. Was this a test of the White House's ability to both make the news and report it, eliminating the middleman?

We know a little about this. One of the authors worked in the Reagan Press Office and had responsibility for producing the radio "actualities." These were packaged audio clips on the "news of the day" and were made available to radio stations around the world via phone lines. They were supposed to be fair and objective. One day the clip was (correctly, if memory serves) tagged as "too partisan," and CBS News sent Bill Plante to do a hatchet job on the offender for the nightly news. Wrists were slapped, lessons learned. Now fast-forward two decades. You could infer that Team Obama was simply updating an old tradition into video.

Okay, but there is a difference in the *impact* of audio and video communications. And the Reagan White House never barred reporters from an event. It merely put out a supplemental news report for media outlets that didn't have a Washington correspondent. With Mr. Obama, the goal appeared to be complete control over the message.

Given what Bernard Goldberg has correctly called the media's "slobbering love affair" with Obama,[201] it first struck us as odd that the administration would risk angering their allies in the media by cutting them out of the deal. But that appeared to be the gambit.

The photo-op with the Huskies was but one example of the almost authoritarian management style that Team Obama aimed to bring to media relations. Such is the partisan control-freak nature of the Obama White House that they tried to starve any formidable opponent of oxygen.

One victim: Glenn Beck. The crime: reporting the truth about ACORN, truth that even the Leftstream media had to finally acknowledge. The strategy: Accuse Mr. Beck of "racism" loudly and publicly and threaten a nationwide boycott against FoxNews.[202] This should have been much ado about nothing, since partyline liberals are too busy fluttering like moths around the CNN flame to ever watch Fox in earnest. But big advertisers were threatened, and at least five yanked their advertising dollars. They had no choice. No advertiser in their right mind could risk offending the president over an ad buy.

The boycott was the handiwork of a former Communist, avowed anarchist, and special assistant to the president, Van Jones. Such flagrant abuse of presidential power is akin to what drove Richard Nixon from office. But across the land, with the shoe on the left foot, liberals cheered.

That kind of hypocrisy makes a joke of Mr. Obama's smiling-face insistence that he is the change we have sought.

At the first whiff of opposition to their policies, Team Obama became good students of the Clinton years. They went straight for the kneecaps. Just ask Eric Cantor. As the Republican Whip, he had reached out to the White House from the very beginning in a genuine display of bipartisanship. He had suggested that there may be a better approach to fixing the economic crisis than doubling the size of the federal government. He presented his position reasonably, tactfully, intelligently. So how did Team Obama respond?

They launched a character assassination campaign. While Mr. Obama gave his stirring speeches about working with Congress, lesser liberal assets were deployed to smear Mr. Cantor's good name. Blogs, pundits, 527s, even the White House press secretary joined in the attack. It was an old-fashioned hatchet job, reported as such in the Rightstream media, ignored by the Leftstream media, and so it goes. But it certainly gave the lie to the Obamacrats claim to post-partisan politics.

More hardball hypocrisy came amidst the health care battle of 2009. At one point it must have became apparent to the president that he had blown a historic opportunity. He was the first president since Roosevelt to have bipartisan agreement that America's health care system needed fixing. Everyone was on board. The obstacles that Hillary Clinton faced in the 1990s were no more. But rather than manage the writing of a health care plan from the White House, Mr. Obama outsourced it to partisan crazies in Congress. The "ObamaCare" plan they came up with in a staggering 1,900-page document offended everyone. A deep gloom fell upon the White House. Then the oddest string of events unfolded.

First, there appeared on the official White House website a message urging partisans to become "brown shirts" for the cause: "If you get an email or see something on the web about health insurance reform that seems fishy, send it to flag@whitehouse.gov."[203]

Odd choice of words, "fishy." On its own you could dismiss this request as an overreaching but harmless gaffe by a junior aide. But this stuff was sitting on an official, taxpayer-supported website. And soon after its posting the president appeared at a political fundraiser in Virginia with some choice words for his opponents, as reported in the *Roanoke Times*:

> I don't want the folks who created the mess to do a lot of talking. I want them to get out of the way so we can clean up the mess. I don't mind cleaning up after them, but don't do a lot of talking.[204]

When a president tells his political opponents in thuggish terms to shut up and get out of the way, he's in need of a time-out. Ours is a democratic republic, and people are entitled to talk and get in the way. Liberals know that better than anybody. Was Mr. Obama suggesting otherwise? His authoritarian threat sent a chill rippling across official Washington. Worry escalated to fear when in this string of events White House Deputy Chief of Staff Jim Messina next told an assembled group of ObamaCare true-believers: "If you get hit, we will punch back twice as hard."[205]

Politics is a contact sport, yes. But this was incendiary in a borderline criminal way . . . especially since later that day the White House was publicly portraying citizens who oppose ObamaCare as a *"violent mob."* Those words flirted with something that is outlawed in all fifty states—inciting to riot.

In fact, supporters in St. Louis took the message to heart. At a health care town hall meeting there, Ken Gladney sat handing out American flags when he was attacked by members of the infamous SEIU (Service Employees International Union).[206] Bystanders disagree on how it all started. Those attending a "tea party" insisted that Mr. Gladney was attacked, unprovoked. Union members said Mr. Gladney started it. Whatever. There's still no call for any president or his senior staff to incite supporters to hit back at those they disagree with. That kind of behavior, like, say, slavery, is supposed to be behind us. If it is not, then Mr. Obama's senior advisors will come to be known as ObamaThugs and their time in Washington will be limited.

For now, with the White House moving toward unobstructed management of news content, the Leftstream media more interested in praising Obama than analyzing him, and Democrats in control of two, possibly three, branches of government, the Obama administration is free to transform the nation as they see fit. The only remaining obstacle could be a legitimate counteroffensive from the Republican Party, but they remain stuck like a dog in a cone of shame.

REPUBLICANS DON THE CONE OF SHAME

Since the global wealth killing went down on the Republicans' watch, they will be long stuck. To folks outside the Beltway, it's laughable to hear people like Representative Paul Ryan offer a "GOP Alternative Budget." They want to know where Mr. Ryan and his kind were during the eight years Republicans tossed financial responsibility out with the bath water. As one blogger put it, "I put no more faith in his claims than in a late night infomercial." And this from a conservative.

Mr. Ryan is in fact a talented politician with a big future, in our view. But it's cone-time for Republicans for as long as the economic downturn lasts. We may well see a temporary economic recovery in 2010 because the Obama administration will have spent trillions to inch the nation's GDP into positive territory. But when the stimulus spending is reeled in, as eventually it must be, most Americans will still be in the same financial mess, nervous, anxious, and uncertain. So even those who prefer limited government in theory will be open-minded to government activism.

Not surprisingly, then, a May 2009 *Wall Street Journal*/NBC News poll found the number of Americans self-describing as "Republican" dropped from 37 percent at the start of George Bush's term to just 31 percent at the end. This decline was registered across the nation in every state and age group. Commentators began portraying Republicans as the "very picture of a minority party."[207]

Republicans looked as desperate as Democrats had been in the years they wallowed in the Slough of Despond. Blinded by fear, the GOP fell into the same petty squabbling and small-minded tactics that had so entertained them when it was liberal doing. One faction of the party insisted in most strident tones that the key to a GOP comeback was to refurbish the contract of 1994 or the victory of 1980. Like so many generals fighting the last war, they hadn't a clue to the conflict of 2008.

Another faction looked to the future with an eye to forming a new governing coalition. But only certain people would be allowed into that coalition, and to hell with the rest. So they could only form a losing coalition in the real game that is electoral politics.

With the Republicans in such obvious disarray, the few conservative ideas that made sense found little in the way of purchase. And the vacuum gave Mr. Obama an open field to compete for the allegiances of voters who otherwise would be suspect of his agenda, and to define a new political center well to the left of the old one.

OF ANGRY MOBS SIPPING MINT JULEPS

"Repeal the Pork or Our Bacon Is Cooked"
"Obama Lied, Liberty Died!"
"You Can't Blame Bush Anymore"
"Obama—He's Robbin U.S. Not Robin Hood."
"The Problem With Socialism Is That You Eventually Run Out of
Other People's Money"

All those conservative protestors at the tea parties of 2009 must have appeared quite the spectacle to observers on the left who actually have some experience at the ramparts. Conservative protestors—isn't that kind of like government efficiency or airport security? We can imagine the conservative rabble marching in the streets, mint juleps in one hand, fancy pre-printed signboards in the other, chanting with feigned fervor:

"We Want Normal, Much More Normal"
"Status Quo, Cannot Go!"

Such a hoot, conservative protestors. But after getting over the incongruity of it all, a question is begged: Is there more to these tea parties than meets the eye?

There was no "official" Republican Party involvement in these tea parties. This protest movement was a self-organizing, mass movement of Americans who instinctively raised hackles at the sudden penetration of government into the economy. While a few existing organizations, like Dick Armey's FreedomWorks and Newt Gingrich's American Solutions, got involved, they played only limited and belated roles. At most of the many protests across the nation, the professional politicians were kept at a distance.

That was the point.

Conservatives knew their leaders had failed. Folks across America understood at the gut level that a grassroots effort was needed— for some to vent, for others to begin anew the building process. Importantly, this protest movement was less about saving capitalism and more about saving a nation. Indeed, the very name "tea party" chosen initially by options trader Rick Santelli in a now famous rant from the floor of the Chicago Board of Trade, suggested that these protests would become a new chapter in a great vein of American movements dedicated to bettering our nation.

That was healthy.

It meant that the protests might have an impact on the 2010 and 2012 elections, might lead the Republicans out of the wilderness, might even lead to the formation of new third party to supplant the

Republicans. We'll return to this in the third section of the book. Our concern here is whether the current Democratic Party dominance of politics will lead to a "realignment" that alters the political landscape, possibly for decades.

Results from the elections of 2009 could be an indicator. Conservative Bob McDonnell won the governor's race in Virginia by eighteen points. Considering that Mr. Obama won that state in 2008, it suggests the possibility of a near 25 percent swing in public opinion in that state. In extremely Democrat New Jersey, incumbent Democrat John Corzine was defeated by Republican Chris Christie. Early harbingers?

Perhaps.

IS A SERIOUS POLITICAL REALIGNMENT IN STORE?

While in the thrall of the 2008 Democratic sweep of Washington, liberal wags such as Lanny Davis crowed that Democratic victories were "likely to create a new governing majority coalition that could dominate American politics for a generation or more."[208] But is that likely?

We know that Mr. Obama is very keen on presenting himself as the change agent that people seek, an amalgam of favorable images that satisfy without being too filling, a hybrid vehicle that can deliver liberal social reform and traditional economic policy that pleases the majority of people who call themselves independent thinkers, while picking up some of the old Reagan Democrats who felt betrayed by George Bush. Such a presentation would be a tall order for any politician to fill, but Mr. Obama succeeded at it in the early going of his presidency.

Then he took a meeting with the Speaker of the House.

If Mr. Obama is capable of moderation and compromise—and all good leaders are—Mrs. Nancy Pelosi is not. As the putative leader of the Democrats in Congress, she proved early on that she meant to be the steamroller and Republicans the smoking asphalt on the road toward the Democrats' agenda. While publicly declaring a new era of bipartisanship, the Democrats on Capitol Hill excluded every single

Republican from the drafting of the then-legendary $787 billion bailout bill. Instead of it being a bailout bill, it was a payback bill. Something for every Democratic subclass. As Ms. Pelosi herself said, "We won the election, we wrote the bill."[209]

So began another term of strident partisan fighting in Washington, a lot like the past terms. Both sides fell into the easy rhythm of demonizing their opponents, rather than debating them. And so crumbled any hope Mr. Obama might have had of building bipartisan coalitions behind important legislation to advance the social and economic interests of our nation.

"Felled by his own party" may become Mr. Obama's obit.

Had he tried to rein in the wild partisans in Congress, and publicly work with reasonable Republicans to write solid compromise bills— the way Reagan did, the way Clinton did—Mr. Obama could have succeeded in redefining the political center of politics in this country in his own image. He could have realigned the country behind his vision. But he didn't. He let the crazies on Capitol Hill off leash; he even outsourced the writing of key legislation to these crazies. This demonstrated either an appalling lack of judgment, or a revealing insight into his true ambition.

We had initially reserved judgment, offering Mr. Obama the courtesy deserving the office. But six months into his presidency it became clear—or at least clear to that point—that Mr. Obama's vision of America was very different from the majority of people in this country.

His was not a centrist or moderate vision.

His was the same leftwing vision that he had pursued as an Illinois legislator, and as a U.S. Senator. He had not shifted to the center, or even center-left. He wanted to create an America most closely modeled after the European socialist democracies.

Even as those European countries were actively seeking a way out of their socialist-rooted malaise, Mr. Obama was seeking a way in.

This is not to say that Mr. Obama himself is a socialist. That's a loaded word that triggers stereotyped reactions. He's too pragmatic for such an idealistic label. He recognized that to get elected, particularly without any resume of note, he had to offer himself as a shill to the rich Killionaires to get the cash he needed, and offer himself to the poor Freeloaders to get the votes he needed. As political strategies go, it was one for the ages. It will be studied for years to come. Students will ask, "But why did millions of middle-of-the-road folks vote for Obama in light of what he did?" Those few students who have honest professors will be told, "People needed to reset the leadership; they didn't care who came next."

But clever and well-timed election strategies do not political realignments make. Realignments come when men and women of vision offer compelling word pictures of a new morning in America, and then work with the leaders of the both parties to paint that picture with fidelity and with patience for the endless series of refinements that will surely follow. That hasn't yet happened under Mr. Obama

Instead, Mr. Obama has offered a radical blueprint for extending government deeper into our lives—deeper than we as a people are willing to accept. So we are expecting a lot of pushback at the polls in 2010 to signal our dissatisfaction for the government intrusions that we did not sign up for. And as result of this pushback, Mr. Obama will end his term viewed as yet another divisive leader who could have done big things.

But didn't.

As for the Republicans, they are limp and disorganized and will likely end the term much the same. They won't be able to muster any kind of serious competition to Mr. Obama, setting us up for single-party control over our lives for the short term.

There is peril in that . . .

13

HOW WILL AMERICA BE CHANGED?

Inflation or deflation / Tell me if you can / Will we become Zimbabwe /
Or will we be Japan?
—MERLE HAZARD

Trying to predict the future is like trying to drive down a country road
at night with no lights while looking out the back window.
—PETER DRUCKER

THIS CHAPTER IS something of a summary, pulling up the strings on our reporting thus far, and tying it off with specific forecasts of value to entrepreneurs and investors. These forecasts come with the usual caveats, since the future rarely unfolds the way anyone expects. It's as easy to get it right as wrong—because good forecasts are part watchful wisdom, part witchcraft. And then, just because a forecast is correct doesn't mean you can make good use of it in your situation.

That said, we had to be pleased with the accuracy of the forecasts made in *Obama Unmasked*. Having called the U.S. stock market crash to within one month and 50 points on the Dow, many readers were able to take defensive action. And we were urged to include similar forecasts here.

Keep in mind that these are unprecedented times. Our world has never seen every major nation's economy crash simultaneously. It simply wasn't possible previously. Only through recent advances in information technology have we had supply chains, credit systems, and capital flows all synchronized across global markets. So, just as the global economic engine sputtered to a standstill in ways unprecedented, it could just as easily spark back to life in ways unexpected and with speed unanticipated.

Staying on top of the unfolding events that impact your personal life, business ambitions, and investment choices requires reading books such as this. It also requires follow-up to get a handle on how current projections will evolve into tomorrow's opportunities. We'll help in that challenge through a complimentary follow-up briefing that continues the threads begun in this book.

WHAT THE PROS ARE PREDICTING—
BEST CASE & WORST CASE

Predictive models and econometrics, while only marginally useful in forecasting the future with any degree of accuracy, are nonetheless a good place to begin.

Perhaps the most comprehensive of all the studies on economic collapses is being conducted by Carmen Reinhart of the University of Maryland and Kenneth Rogoff of Harvard.[210] In their various studies spanning eight centuries of financial crises across sixty-six countries, they have analyzed dozens of variables. Here's a summary of their findings that are relevant to us (Figure 13.1):

An 800-Year History of Economic Meltdowns			
	PREVIOUS CRISES (average)	2008 U.S. MELTDOWN (as of Feb. 2009)	YEARS TO RECOVER (if average)
Home Price Decline	-35.5%	-25.0%	6.0
Stock Price Decline	-55.9%	-51.1%	3.4
Unemployment Increase	7.0%	3.2%	4.8
Per Capita GDP Decrease	-9.3%	-1.5%	1.9
Public Debt Increase (cum.)	86.0%	30.0%	3.0
Source: Aftermath of Financial Crises, Reinhart & Rogoff			

Figure 13.1 An 800-Year History of Economic Meltdowns

If the history in these chart numbers is any guide, the U.S. financial crisis shot to the top of its bell curve relatively early in the going as compared to past crises. Within its first six months, housing prices and stock prices had already approached the average loss for past crises. The increase in unemployment had reached half the expectation in this time, but was clearly on an upward trajectory. But there was an obvious divergence from past crises.

Our nation's GDP and public debt were only still in the early stages of pain, suggesting that we were a long way from knowing the effects that collapsing businesses and government bailouts would have on the overall economic outlook.

With so many uncertainties swirling around the 2010 economy, most of the economists looking at these historical comparisons are coming to the conclusion that our nation's current economic downturn will be "just another average downturn." They are buttressed in their thinking by the sucker's rally that came, as predicted, in late 2009 when a trillion dollars of government bailout money managed to temporarily lift the fortunes of those groups lucky enough to get that free cash—compliments of American taxpayers for generations to come. But what happens when the artificial pumping up of the economy stops, and the underlying problems still remain?

That question is not being adequately addressed—not by the politicians, of course, and not by the investment managers either. Neither group has any interest in facing up to the harsh realities of our situation. Instead, all of the financial advisors who didn't see the economic misery coming are now quick to forecast a "cautiously optimistic recovery," and so, clearly, their credibility is entirely suspect.

Fact is, there is a thundering herd mentality in the financial advice-giving business. Most advisors are charging ahead with the "things will return to 2007" talking points because they're eager to get back to making big trading commissions again. Representative of this pack-think is John Waggoner, financial writer for USA Today and author of Bailout. "The economy will recover, earnings and personal income will rise and life will be good again," he predicts.[211] Okay, but when?

Trying to figure out when the economic hell will end turns a lot of people into baseball fans. "Are we in the fifth inning or the fourth?"

"Will we hit our way out, or tighten up the field?" "Will we turn it around in 2010, 2011, 2012 . . . ?" There's a shocking naïveté to these questions. They're all based on the assumption that the powers that be can just decide to bail us out and get the good times rolling again. They've been bailing us out for most of our adult lives, the thinking goes, so why can't they do it again?

Maybe they can.

But an honest assessment of the "state of the union" strongly suggests otherwise. In previous economic disasters, we Americans and our government were never so deeply in debt. Official estimates put public debt at about $10 trillion, or roughly equal to the gross domestic product of the nation. If our nation's creditors were to call our debt, then, every dollar of output for an entire year would be transferred to those creditors, and we would starve. It won't happen that way, of course. So what will happen?

We could face an even worse scenario.

This is because estimates of public debt do not include the so-called off-budget obligations. These are debts the government has run up, but officially ignores. The practice began in earnest under President Clinton and was largely why he could boast—that is, lie—that he had balanced the federal budget. When you factor in off-budget obligations, says former U.S. Comptroller General David Walker, the public debt shoots up above $59 trillion.[212] That's the same as every citizen owing $192,000 on top of our existing debt obligations.

Who among us can afford that?

The story gets worse. Americans as individuals have been just as reckless in our own borrowing. Back in 1972, individuals borrowed about $100 billion a year for various expenses. By 2004, we were borrowing ten times as much—over $1 trillion according to the Federal Reserve. So when the economy collapsed in 2008, many millions of people were overleveraged, with not a dime in savings and no defenses against the nationwide wave of layoffs that are still only in their early stages. Americans are, consequently, in a dangerous mental state.

It is not clear how we can make our way to a happy ending soon.

A two-decade-long financial scam promoted as "cheap money" and "easy credit" should be dead and done—exposed for the fraud it is, shamed out of existence. Everyone knows this. Yet the leaders of both political parties are still in on the scam, still promoting it. And why?

Because the values of Yankee thrift that they were raised on are now so murky and distant in their minds?

Because they profit so handsomely from the campaign contributions of the Killionaires running the scams?

Because they're reluctant to tell voters the unpleasant truths until they are comfortably elected or re-elected?

All these.

Few among us have seen an economic reality as destructive as what we face now. The harsh fact is: we are in the early stages of something that will in our estimation come to be known as a "rolling stall" and could easily endure for the rest of our adult lives. As bad as things are as we write, the pain is still in its early stages, and the healing still far off.

We do not, however, believe in the worst-case scenarios floating around. We are not end-of-timers. Tales of the fiery inferno, like the wretched poor, have always been with us. We are realists. We play the short odds, knowing we can stack one little victory on top of another and make a reasonable living in the doing.

We follow the doom-mongers closely, not just because they are endlessly entertaining, but also because woven amidst all the clever turns of phrase are usually a few nuggets of wisdom, worth a closer look. So we read Doug Casey,[213] and especially his "Street Fighting Man," and we marvel at the eloquence of James Howard Kunstler, as he looks to the future:

> We're not going to rescue the banks. The collateral for their loans is no good and it will only lose more value. All those tract houses on the cul-de-sacs of America and scattered on the out-parcels of our tragically subdivided farming landscape will only lose value, one way or another, in the years ahead. Right now they're simply losing inflated cash value—and that has been bad enough to sink the banks. In the months and years ahead, they'll lose their sheer usefulness as the distances once mitigated by cheap gasoline loom larger again, and the jobs vanish and incomes with them, and the supermarket shelves cease to groan with

eighty-seven different varieties of flavored coffee creamers, and one-by-one the national chain stores shutter, and the theme parks, and the NASCAR ovals, and the malls, and the colossal superfluous cretin-cargo of consumer nonsense that we've been daydreaming in gets blown away in a hurricane of change that we were not ready to believe in.[214]

THE HIGHS AND LOWS OF A "ROLLING STALL"

We are expecting both mildly pleasant economic highs and painful lows for the next ten years, possibly quite a bit longer. This period ahead can be characterized as a "rolling stall," in which the U.S. economy continues to roll ahead while experiencing zero forward growth.

We do believe Mr. Obama will be able, with his pals in Silicon Valley, to engineer one more bubble in "green" energy. As outlined in Chapter 10, we'll see tremendous run-ups in green technology stocks as the bubble is being inflated, followed by a sickening bursting of the fortunes of millions of Americans. That green bubble should be the final product of the Great American Bubble-Producing Machine. It should be preceded by, and then followed by, periods of anemic growth, with isolated pockets of opportunity for the nimble and the informed.

Positioning yourself to act on these opportunities will require a clear understanding of the nine biggest trends driving the years ahead:

1. Credit-Crunched Consumers Remain Flattened

We will at last see the end to the American Junk Empire. No more buying Slurpees on credit cards. The wild and crazy era of free money from madcap lenders is over. Universal easy credit will be the thing we look back on with only a tinge of nostalgia—because it papered the excesses of an era that we will be paying for for the rest of our lives. From 2008 until 2018 at least, consumers will have to save for the things they want, and businesses will have to run largely on accounts receivable. As a nation we will find our way back to concepts such as value and principle—though it will be a struggle and it will take us an entire generation to get it right.

2. When the Banking Holiday Comes, Business Goes

The next "big slam" is looming even now. Advance word of this came to us from Terry Easton. We listen closely to him because he's not only a street-smart economist, but also a successful entrepreneur. Indeed, it was his warnings about a national banking crisis that initially prompted the writing of this book. We feared that millions of entrepreneurs like ourselves would be the primary victims of a "bank holiday" that could easily come within two years. Mr. Easton has explained the details of the briefing that bankers have received on executing an actual bank holiday. There will be limits on how much money you can take out of a bank. And probably limits on what you can do with it.

The trigger for this banking holiday—in which all your assets will be frozen, your access to those funds cut off, and the future value of those funds left in limbo pending the most watched presidential press conference of all time—will be the downgrading of Moody's rating for the United States. The threat to the nation's triple-A rating has been looming for years. Trillion-dollar spending surges have opened up debate anew on whether the U.S. is creditworthy. Yet Moody's has never budged in its official outlook for U.S. debt. In May 2009, the rating agency publicly declared: "While government financial strength is weakening as a result of interventions to support the financial system and the economy, other factors supporting the AAA rating remain intact."[215]

When asked about those "other factors," Steven Hess of Moody's warned of "longer-term pressures on the rating," suggesting that developments now unfolding in international markets could cause the United States to lose its coveted AAA rating. Indeed, Bill Gross, who manages the giant PIMCO bond fund, has publicly stated that the United States will soon lose the rating because it is running massive deficits for as far as the eye can see.[216]

When the rating is in fact downgraded, expect an old-fashioned run on the banks and the equity markets.

. . .

3. Asset Deflation + Price Inflation = Pain For All

In light of all the borrowing and money printing we've seen in Washington, the conventional wisdom is that we'll see hyperinflation, and soon. "Inflation could return sooner than you think," *MoneyWeek* reported. "By the end of this year [2009] we could have the beginnings of really rapid inflation which could get out of control," said hedge fund manager Jim Mellon.[217] These prescriptions could come true. They certainly should come true. But it may take several years for inflation to unfold.

Given the trillions Mr. Obama wheelbarrowed into the economy at the beginning of the crisis, it's hard to argue against the "too many dollars chasing too few goods" case. Especially since the last several presidents have demonstrated a clear intent to spend whatever it takes to nip any deflationary force in the bud. Through the government's steady doses of inflation, we have already seen how a dollar today will buy only 77 percent of what it bought a decade ago, and 56 percent of what it bought a decade before that.

But we suspect that the "Japan or Zimbabwe?" question will resolve in ways surprising to all. Inflation will surely come roaring back in a vicious business-killing way, but that pain may well be years into the distance. And it will just as likely take on a different form than in the past.

We expect to see key assets that don't produce steady cash flow such as homes flatlining and even declining in value, while the cost of everyday goods increases. In short, asset deflation combined with price inflation. So a home that appraised at $1 million in 2005 may actually sell at $600,000 today and then $400,000 in a decade, while a dollar will only buy 40 cents worth of groceries in a decade. It'll be a double whammy that will require people to do something painful and entirely radical to them.

They will have to live within shrunken means.

Old assumptions about market cycles will no longer apply. Homeowners should forget about houses going up in value. That's history. Houses have to be viewed as shelters from the weather, not appreciating assets. Before the housing slaughter is completed, more than 5 million homeowners will be converted into shamed, credit "dings" in search of affordable rentals. Their new landlords will be the Killionaires who stepped in to buy up so many real estate assets on the cheap. Many of these new landlords will be U.S.-based, but many more will be from overseas. And they will have renters over a barrel. Rental prices will approach mortgages in monthly outgo, with no equity building.

On the wage front, the age-old expectation of regular pay raises will be no more. Wholesale pay cuts will become more common as foreign creditors take over companies and lean them down in line with international pay standards. This will translate into 40 percent to 50 percent pay cuts right out of the gates for employees in companies of all sizes as the adjustments ripple through the economy.

4. Government Rescues Nothing, Including Itself

We have shown the Bush and Obama stimulus plans for what they were: vain attempts to appear to be doing something in the first case, and to pay back some election chits in the second case.

The stimulus plans were based on a simpleton's insight: that if folks can't spend, the government can come to the rescue by printing up new money and handing it out to friends and family; and soon, as this logic goes, the economy will mend. But if fiscal policy were so easy, we would have no downturns *ever*. Politicians would see to that! They'd spend and spend, and the economy would be punch and roses all the time.

The truth of government stimulus spending is quite the opposite. To get that cash to give away, the government goes out and borrows it. That sucks up the available credit, crowding out small business owners from the credit markets, cutting down on our ability to regrow the economy. With business activity in decline, and household income in decline as well, the result is declining tax revenues, which in turn increases the budget deficit. Think of the ever-decreasing concentric vortex of a whirlpool sucking down trillions of dollars' worth of asset values, millions of jobs, and hundreds of thousands of businesses. That's the harsh truth.

Businesses of all sizes will have to adjust to this rolling stall lasting for years. The growth game is over. Too many people still fail to grasp just how dire the situation is, or how difficult life could become.

We are not in a correction, a brief lull before the upward march again resumes. At some point our foreign creditors will discover that U.S. bonds are neither a safe harbor in a turbulent world nor a good investment. They will stop buying. That will feel like a foot stomping down on the bleeding abdomen that is now America. The foot will come down in a manner long predicted by investing legend and budding politician Peter Schiff. He has characterized the U.S. Treasury market as the "mother of all bubbles" and openly wondered how much longer the bubble can last:

> I have often said that the only thing worse than holding U.S. dollars is holding promises to be paid U.S. dollars at some distant point in the future. However, this is precisely what U.S. Treasuries represent. Given all of the inflation that already exists, and all of the additional inflation likely to be created over that time period, why would anyone pay par value for the right to receive $1,000 in thirty years in exchange for a mere 4.5% coupon?
>
> Eventually, the world's lenders will reach similar conclusions with respect to U.S. Treasuries. No matter how low the Fed funds or discount rates get, private savers around the world will simply refuse to lend given the inherent risks and paltry returns. At some point the sheer absurdity of holding long-term, low-yielding receipts for future payments of depreciating U.S. dollars will be apparent to all . . .
>
> The day of reckoning may not be too far off.[218]

There is no way around this reckoning—no matter how dearly Mr. Obama wishes it so. In the affairs of man and state, there is always a balance sheet. It can be out of whack for a period, but it must correct. Whether you are a government or a business, you can only take on so much debt. When you cross the line, you have to stop borrowing and start paying it down—to the detriment of other necessary expenditures. If you cannot pay it down, because your income is insufficient, you either declare bankruptcy or flee the country.

A depression is when the entire nation is dragged into bankruptcy proceedings because it can no longer pay its debts. A "rolling stall" as we've described it is when the nation should declare bankruptcy and get its balance sheet in order, but refuses to be dragged anywhere.

There will come a time when a new economy is born. But at this point in history there is no chance that America will regain the unrivaled financial strength we enjoyed for over a century. The main reason for this is something you won't hear a lot of people admitting publicly. That is: The majority of Americans have decided by their actions that they are less interested in prosperity than in the absence of war. . . .

5. Making Love Not War . . . Results In Neither

A generation that came of age in the 1960s made a decision, not even knowing it. They decided to cast away the long history of America and set out on some new uncharted course.

We've called it the *Revisionist* course.

By actively opposing "war" in nearly all its forms, or by belittling the historic role of war in advancing geopolitical interests, or by simply tuning out all but the gentler pursuits of love and lust, this generation of baby boomers killed off the economic boom for future generations. It was not a conscious decision—quite the opposite. A great many people—most of them good-hearted liberals with fine minds—have no idea the kind of damage they've inflicted through their actions and mindset.

When they spat on the returning soldiers in the 1960s and then pretended to care about those soldiers' sons returning from more recent conflicts . . .

When they burned the flag in the 1960s and then laughed contemptuously at the Fourth of July flag-waving "fanatics" of the post-9/11 years . . .

When they blasted the House Un-American Activities Committee of the 1950s and then declared themselves part of the new millennium's post-national community of nations . . .

When they institutionalized their anti-war, anti-institution, anti-

American concepts at all levels of society, from the classroom to the courtroom . . .

They killed America.

Oh, how we can hear them howling at us! They bring so little perspective and open-mindedness to their views on geopolitics, they can't grasp a word of these last paragraphs. It's an outrage to them. Utter claptrap.

If only.

Want to know what lonely feels like? Stand up in a crowded room and announce that the only reason America was able to create its great middle-class experiment and lift the standard of living of millions of people to a higher level than ever seen in history was because the soldiers of our nation killed all our competitors in World War Two. We won the war and we threw a big party—that's what happened.

Not too many people want to hear this kind of honesty. Certainly not the crowd that thinks the flower mightier than the sword. Certainly not the "flat earth" crowd who genuinely believe that all nations should be on equal footing and that all nations will go along with the notion—a notion that has, by the way, not worked once since, oh, the Bronze Age.

They don't want to hear it, and they will go to their graves convinced they knew better. That is why there is such a partisan rift in our nation. That is why there are two scripts—*Traditional* and *Revisionist*.

Sadly, few of these baby boomers will live to see the unintended consequences of the decisions they made. They will be mostly dead or senile when American hegemonic power, born on distant battlefields and matured in countless boardrooms, yields to the new kid on the international bloc.

And there will be a new kid.

Someone stronger, willing to fight for a better life for his own kids, willing to sacrifice so that someday her daughter can enjoy opportunities she was denied. Those kids are out there—in towns in Brazil, China, India, and elsewhere.

Let us hope that similar kids are also growing up in towns in . . . America. And let us hope, as well, that they are willing to fight for what is right *for them.*

6. Nationalizing The Weakest Makes Us Weakest

In just about every speech he gives during his presidency, Mr. Obama will declare that he wants to run the government—he doesn't want to run GM, Chevron, Delta, or a host of other companies. But then he will return to the Oval Office and do precisely that. He will prop up one company after another because that's the bargain he struck with the union organizers and Killionaires who (1) who got him elected and (2) will be needed to win a second term.

By opening up a dedicated faucet between the Federal Reserve money vaults and major company bank accounts, Mr. Obama creates the illusion that all is well in the world of high finance. But of course it is not, as wonderfully summarized by Bill Bonner: "The feds now pretend to bail out the economy by giving money to companies that pretend to be concerned, run by people who pretend to know what they are doing."[219]

Insurance giant AIG was the first big project of government. AIG has taken nearly $150 billion in bailouts to date, and each time it takes another big loss, it will again look to the master faucet for more sustenance. It's the same for Citibank and dozens of other companies now lapping at the public tap.

Meanwhile, the managers of these companies go about their business secure in the knowledge that market forces no long apply to them, bad business judgments will no longer hurt them, and stronger competitors cannot touch them, because they enjoy the patronage of the king—that is, President Obama and the Democratic Congress.

These wards of the state can continue for quite a spell on the government dole, until some smarter, faster, nimbler foreign competitor comes along and cleans their clock. Then the Obamacrats have a decision to make. Either they double down on a bad bet—dumping even more taxpayer money into these dinosaur U.S. companies to "make them competitive"—or finally let them fail.

By now, we all know the approach the Obamacrats will take.

Meanwhile, in very different office buildings across the country, entrepreneur investors are groaning under the collective weight of the Big Government Big Business Big Wealth Transfer Complex. It's the little guy who is being increasingly leaned on to cough up the added tax revenue needed for the government tap. It's the little guy who will also struggle with lack of credit—since the government has crowded out smaller borrowers; struggle with waves of new regulations—since the big business wards will need them to pretend at competitiveness; struggle with an unfair playing field—since the union bosses will need them to keep their cozy extortion rackets churning out mediocrity and ruin.

7. Idiotic Fall From Energy Leader To Laggard

The most dysfunctional scenes in the "two script" narrative involve energy and the environment. Republicans invented environmentalism and stood as proud stewards of our natural resources for decades. Democrats stole the issue, fair and square, and today both sides have dug stubbornly into positions that are together killing the energy resource lead the United States once enjoyed.

Democrats dig in their heels on the exploration of natural gas in the U.S., despite general agreement among geologists that we have enough natural gas reserves to fuel the bulk of our nation's energy needs for hundreds of years. Republicans pooh-pooh any attempt to develop the alternative energy resources that could, someday, wean us off our dependence on foreign oil and polluted skies.

As a result of clownish idiocy on both ends of the political spectrum, America is stuck. Held hostage by oil producers who hate us, who want to see us brought low, who are happy to play us off against increasing demand from China and other nations. The net effect will be higher and higher energy prices for decades to come.

Cheap energy is over.

Our fondest hopes for widespread use of alternative energy will be wildly inconsistent with reality for decades. We'll have to live differently, having no other choices. Our nation's great love of the open road will be changing dramatically. Not only will U.S. automakers produce fewer cars, but Americans will buy far fewer cars made anywhere. We'll see older cars on the road, retrofitted cars to boost mileage, hybrids and the like, but far fewer cars. Many folk won't be able to afford the luxury of a second car, or even a first car. This will create great resentment for those who can afford good cars. Bitter resentment that will be acted upon.

A once-proud interstate highway system will become a potholed obstacle course as we are unable to afford scheduled maintenance. This *should* prompt efforts to revive the mass transit that once crisscrossed major cities (until the auto barons destroyed it), but that won't happen either. Road rage will disperse beyond the L.A. freeways to the Riviera of Santa Barbara, beyond the Atlanta beltway to the golf cart paths of Peachtree City.

Rage. Potholes. A sense that everything is falling apart. . . .

8. A Nation With No Center Spins Apart

We are told by the U.S. Census Bureau that those groups currently categorized as racial minorities—that is, people of African, Hispanic, or Asian heritage—will be in the majority within thirty years. We'll see the shift earlier though; within a decade, Caucasians under eighteen will be in the minority. The new white minority.

"White" culture is already dead, or at least deeply discredited in most areas. The tell is in the casting notices for TV and film—most roles now call for "ethnically ambiguous" actors. This is the future.

The question is: When the culture of a nation changes, do the values change with it? The answer, to anyone paying attention, is an obvious yes. And when those values change, how? We have already begun to find out. And Mr. Obama will find out, we expect, in ways that boil his blood.

The old white Anglo-Saxon culture had plenty to recommend it, and warts as well. But one thing you could count on with white guys: They played to win. They could be brutish, overly aggressive, cunning, and cutthroat. The result was the strongest, most prosperous, most accepting nation in world history. We didn't get there overnight, and Lord knows we didn't get there being "pretty" about it.

But we got there.

With those ornery old white guys no longer in charge, and their dreams of hegemonic control no longer fashionable, things will change—dramatically. For one, we can expect unemployment to settle in at about 15 percent to 20 percent and not budge for decades. This will happen as a result of:

- Major U.S. businesses being uncompetitive globally—since they're mere wards of Washington and drained of the capitalist spirit.
- U.S. workers being told they must work for less pay under less tolerable working conditions or take a hike—because foreign companies have bought up U.S. companies on the cheap and are submitting workers to international compensation standards.
- Bureaucrats in Washington being impotent in their interventions—for despite all their protests at the UN and their most capable globetrotting negotiators—shock, nobody in the world gives a damn about anyone but themselves.

What happens when those people with jobs see their upward mobility cut off, and those people losing jobs see how unreliable all the bafflegabbers in Washington really are?

We've seen how little it takes for idle, frustrated, angry men to turn to violence on the streets. Even a sore loss at the stadium can throw sports crowds into a frenzy of destruction. So it has not been surprising lately to see runs on ammo at sporting goods shops.[220] People are nervous. When the summer days grow long and hot, and the jobs few and unsatisfying, millions of young men will find themselves standing at street corners with nothing do to. It won't take much to incite violence at that point. Class warfare, so artfully stoked by the Obamacrats, could easily erupt into widespread burning of businesses. Police will be outnumbered and incapable of quelling local uproars. The National Guard will be called in to one city after another.

Maybe we'll survive 2010 without mishap. But soon there will be a situation where National Guardsmen have their rifles leveled at violent rioting youths. And a mixed-race president will have to give the order to fire on mixed-race youths.

Will he?

Will Mr. Obama declare martial law? When unemployment tops 20 percent and the president's policies are to blame, will he quell the mob in the interests of an old, discredited white culture? When some crafty Muslim organizer puts together a "Million Muslim March on Washington" and they arrive with torches and larcenous intent, will Mr. Obama order in the military?

9. Completing a 230-Year Experiment . . . Badly

January 20, 2009 will be memorialized by our futures for the proud historic ascension of a man of mixed race to the highest office in the land, and also for the completion of a 230-year journey, full-circle of sorts, to where we began. This second "event" may well earn more ink, or bytes, in the history books. This is not to take anything away from Mr. Obama, since he figures centrally in both achievements.

It is commonly said that "America" was born out of a fierce love of liberty and disdain for the monarchial regimes of old. And this is true, in the abstract. But "America" was truly born under the rules of law and government—a radically different kind of government from what had previously existed, yes—but *government* still.

Our young nation did not flourish under this experimental government. For quite some time it hobbled along on the bare minimum strength of good intentions and Spanish doubloons—since nobody would take our new currency.

It was *agriculture* that secured the nation. Our ability to feed ourselves, put away stores for the winter, and export surplus crops put the nation on firm footing. Nine out of ten people farmed the land, and those who signed up for military service got tracts of land for free, or for those with $2 and an ox, an acre of land could be purchased and turned into a family business.

As time passed and across the land there were folks with bellies near to full, the more enterprising among the population were freed to pursue *industry*. Francis Lowell could travel to England and brazenly steal the secrets of the remarkable new textile machine, then come home to launch the United States on its way to becoming an industrial powerhouse.

With *manufacturing* might and a capable military, the smartest minds of the nation were freed for less physically taxing pursuits. Soon a nation of engineers and laborers became a nation of lawyers, insurance agents, stockbrokers, and real estate agents. The *service* sector was born, and the idea of actually creating anything, other than paper trails, became practically anathema to the American dream. Factories and mills turned to rust, business turned to foreign suppliers, and the Protestant work ethic became a display in the Smithsonian.

Since little more than paper was being pushed across the country, the U.S. economy became vulnerable to games-playing and elaborate wealth-stripping schemes. These schemes came to a head in 2008, and by design these schemes required the government to step in and "make good," or risk seeing a $12 trillion economy collapse into severe depression.

Thus we came full circle around to *government provider*. In 2008, a nation turned its weary eyes to government, and that government eagerly agreed to become the provider of all things good. The Obama administration sealed the deal with a tax plan that ingeniously (for them, if not the country) allowed half of the nation to pay no taxes. Turning a majority of the country into obeisant wards of the state practically ensures the reelection of Democrats for as long as they can keep the cynical scam going.

So as in the beginning, 230 odd years ago, government will make the big decisions that impact our lives. They'll tell us what to do, when to do it, and if they feel like it, they'll tell us why. Our economic system will have come full circle:

Government > Agriculture > Industry > Services > Government

As in the early years of our nation, we should again expect years of an economy stuck in a rolling stall with a devaluing dollar, persistently high unemployment, declining property prices, increasing cost of goods, with increasing taxes leading to increased violence amidst falling living standards.

We will almost certainly look back on the last decade and think: We didn't realize how good we had it, until it was gone. And yet the American story need not end at this stage. It can cycle on to something better, if we will it to.

14

YOUR PERSONAL CLAWBACK STRATEGY

Americans collectively lost $5.1 trillion of their net worth during the last three months of 2008 and $11.2 trillion for the full year. . . . Anyone who was a millionaire at the beginning of 2008, and had a million dollars invested in stocks, has lost about $300,000 to $400,000.[221]

—JAMES B. STEWART

IT IS SAD and troubling that Mr. Obama and the internationalist left in coordination with the Killionaires have achieved their goal: leveling the wealth of average Americans so that as a people we are no wealthier than the rest of the world.

Rather than pull the world up to our level of prosperity and riches, they've attacked the stores of wealth laid by generations of entrepreneur investors, squandered almost all hope of future inheritances, and condemned our children to living "less than" lives financially.

Like a third-generation heir of a great family fortune, America's leaders have partied, warred, spent, and mismanaged our national family into the poor house. Our children and grandchildren will be called upon to rebuild this great land. But in the meantime, our goal is to help you help them. We are confident that you can claw back much of your lost wealth with the "Personal Clawback Strategy" we've devised.

America may be decaying from top down, but we suspect that your own personal financial goals remain the same today as always:

protecting your family and your accumulated assets while enjoying the challenge of lifting higher your standard of living. You will find in the next few pages a wealth-protection strategy created by enterprising Americans for enterprising Americans—in short, it will work for your family and your business interests. This strategy—*this Personal Clawback Strategy*—is based on the simple fundamental that in good times and bad, there are always those who prosper.

Why should the crooked politicians and Killionaires prosper alone in these times? Why not good people as well, and on our own terms, without resorting to fraud, chicanery, or deceit? Why can't we take advantage of the one asset we have that allows us to stand up to the Killionaires?

If you're thinking that one asset is a slingshot, you're not far off. We are the "David" in this struggle, to be sure. But we can mobilize into what Glenn Reynolds called an army of Davids if it suits us. Joining forces with entrepreneurs and investors like yourself across the country, you can be a part of something raw and powerful.

It can multiply your own good ideas by a thousand, for starters.

It can result in investing tips or business opportunities being shared in a private way with a limited number of people.

It can put you in fellowship with people who all share one passionate goal: to walk away from the unhappy, asset-stripped crowds and choose our own enterprising path to wealth restoration and renewal.

This idea of "fellowship" is such a strong one in our view that we created the *Freeing Wealth Fellowship* expressly for the readers of this book and fellow entrepreneur investors.

When combined together, the *Freeing Wealth Fellowship* and the *Personal Clawback Strategy* become a powerful tool for prospering in the coming years, no matter what comes out of Washington.

We'll talk more about the *Fellowship* at the book's end—for now there are three rules that guide both the *Strategy* and the *Fellowship* that must be followed without exception. (If these rules prove too burdensome to you, then perhaps you should look elsewhere for guidance.) We are firm on this because we know these rules are timeless and powerful, though commonly ignored. We know that if you follow them, you are then in position to achieve prosperity—and everything else is just execution. So let's begin by locking those rules in your personal vault for safekeeping and regular review:

1. While America's fiscal house is out of order, you can still put your personal house in order. Live within your means and save at least 10 percent no matter your circumstances.
2. The greatest engine of wealth creation is your own labor. Control your own labor, and the labor of others, by owning your own business. There is opportunity in the uncertainty and chaos that swirls all around us. As real wages fall for most Americans, those of us who control our own and others' labor will steer clear of the wealth-killing fields and come to know the prosperity of the enterprising path.
3. Invest in those "real assets" that keep pace with inflation. These assets may include stocks, real estate, and natural resources at any given time. Move away from fixed-income assets such as bonds at least until yields are much higher.

PUTTING YOUR HOUSE IN ORDER

The authors of this book have taken major life steps to put our personal fiscal houses in order. During the 1990s and early to mid 2000s, like many Americans, we both ignored warnings that the music would end. America was in the midst of an unprecedented productivity boom. Interest rates were unnaturally low because of Federal Reserve mistakes. Like many, we overindulged in debt—caught up in the society-wide expectation that rising asset prices and increasing wages would keep us ahead of future debt payments.

But the music did stop as America's leadership faltered and her finances collapsed. Faced with crisis, our leaders took the wrong course of action. Rather than pay their bills and let big business suffer from the excess, they doubled down, like the losing gambler in Las Vegas. Then our leaders doubled down again. Rather than allow the credit markets to find equilibrium, our leaders, through arrogance or stupidity, mortgaged our children's future to cover for their mistakes.

However, your authors took a different course than the government.

Rather than double down, we deleveraged. We understand you cannot repeal the laws of economics, so we corrected our personal cash flow until monthly income covered monthly expenses. Debt squeezes are never solved with more debt.

We both left California, a high tax and regulation state that has fallen into the ocean as long predicted—only not physically, just fiscally. We headed to greener pastures—one of us in the Pacific Northwest, the other in the Sawtooth Mountains. We moved to communities with lower costs of living, substantially lower real estate expenses, and the kind of good old-fashioned American values we can abide.

As the economy faltered, we made tough decisions to amend our ways. As citizens we are dismayed our leaders didn't choose a similar course. But just because our leaders faltered doesn't mean you have to follow their example. It's tougher, but inevitably smarter, to tackle the tough decisions sooner rather than later.

If you are in debt over your head, we encourage you to change course now. Yes, it is possible. Cut up your credit cards, sell your cars, your home, your investments, but do not put off the day of reckoning by adding new debt. Repair your finances, so that each month your income is greater than your expenses by at least 10 percent. This may require increasing your income, or decreasing your expenses, or both. But at its core it's a goal that's simply elegant and so easy to execute. Just 10 percent each month—the rest will follow in good order.

START YOUR OWN BUSINESS

The greatest American wealth-creation machine is a personally owned business. Owning your own business doesn't even mean you need to leave your day job, but the national tax regime and system still favors those who own a business.

Today business opportunities abound. In times of crisis, if you analyze the situation around yourself you will find opportunity.

As the current recession worsened, a neighbor of ours lost his job. He had been a highly paid salesman with a firm specializing in construction materials. This recession has been most brutal to the individuals who make a living in construction because it virtually stopped. He found himself unable to find a job in his field; he's in his fifties. He was too young for retirement and too old to start over at the bottom in a new field. He went to work studying the opportunities around him.

His search led him to a brand new business. He went to the courthouse and bought a house in a foreclosure auction. He fixed it up himself with paint, yard restoration, and elbow grease. The next month he sold it, making a profit of $30,000.

At the next auction he bought two houses. Now he is running a crew rehabbing houses and selling them for a profit. He took the pain of others and turned their foreclosures into a business for himself.

We wouldn't be surprised if he started to keep some of these houses in the future and turn them into rental properties. He didn't allow the depression of losing his job to get him down. By assessing the situation, he found he could prosper in the deep recession.

You may not succeed on your first try. You may struggle with bills and hours of back-breaking work, but we guarantee that if you start and run your own business, and keep correcting your personal budget until your income is 10 percent greater than your expenses, then you'll turn the corner to prosperity.

Amid the stark credit climate, raising capital is tougher than ever, so you must be more creative than ever in securing it. Good money for good ideas still exists. Some small businesses are turning to a new breed of incubators providing seed capital, administrative and technical help, and crucial mentoring as well. Notehall.com, an online marketplace for college students to buy and sell class notes, secured a half-million-dollar investment from DreamIt Ventures of Philadelphia. Other startup funders include Y Combinators in Silicon Valley and TechStars in Boulder.[222]

There's a common misconception that new businesses have to have a brilliant idea or breakthrough technology. Not true. Some of the best businesses are the simplest.

One of our family members had washed windows to help put himself through college. When he graduated he continued washing windows. Today he owns a large home services firm that still washes windows, but they will power-wash your home, roof, or deck. They will clean, repair, or replace your gutters. He owns ten trucks and has built an excellent business just providing services that we all could do for ourselves if we weren't so busy running our own businesses. He hasn't washed a window himself in years. He profits through the labor of others.

CAREFULLY INVEST THE 10 PERCENT YOU SAVE IN REAL ASSETS

Because our national government is gorging on debt, it seems likely that in 2010 and beyond, America will experience massive inflation. Record-shattering borrowing by the U.S. Treasury combined with maniacal money-printing by Ben Bernanke and the Federal Reserve leads us to believe a massive inflation and soaring resource prices are looming just around the corner.

We would be enthusiastically bullish on real assets that generate cash flow, such as income-producing real estate, stocks in growing firms with low debt and healthy cash flow, and commodities such as gold, oil, and other natural resources, even if the dollar's buying power wasn't being gutted by our own leaders in Washington.

But there's another reason that has convinced us that energy, metals, food, water, and construction and manufacturing materials are destined to be among the most profitable investments in the world going forward: The emergence of China, India, Brazil, and the Asian bloc as the new economic superpowers of the twenty-first century is truly a defining event.

It's not a new story. It has been unfolding for nearly two decades. But this massive global transformation is now a reality. And even the quickest glance of recent figures on Asian economic growth reaffirms it.

While credit is still difficult to come by in the United States, new loans made by China's banks are exploding higher, more than tripling in 2009. Chinese auto sales surpassed the United States for the first time in history in 2009. While U.S. retailers continue closing stores and downsizing, China's retail sales in July were up over 15 percent in 2009. While the U.S. economy was shrinking at annual 3.9 percent pace, China's GDP was growing 7.9 percent when last we checked in 2009. In 2010, the U.S. economy may see spurts of growth, but overall we anticipate a "rolling stall" in the United States that requires investors to look globally.

These are crucial trends with tremendous consequences for your investments. Nearly one in four human beings alive on the planet today is Chinese. And while most of the world is still struggling through the worst recession since the 1930s, China's economy is continuing to grow. The simple reason is that China as a nation saves more than it spends. Its national fiscal house is in order. Each month China's income is greater than its expenses. This is how America's finances were routinely handled before the 1970's, except during the World War Two years. However, China's not alone.

India's population is 1.1 billion strong, and its economy is booming, too. India's economy was expected to grow 7 percent in 2009, and continue that pace into 2010. Nearly one in every two human beings on Earth lives in one of these two countries, and they are growing their economies the old-fashioned way. They spend less than they make. Much less. That matters.

Less than 5 percent of the earth's population lives in the United States, and for the past 200 years or so, our nation drove nearly all economic growth on the entire planet. Why? Because as a nation we spent less money than we made. We were the largest creditor nation in the world until late in the twentieth century.

In the past it was America's demand for oil and other natural resources that drove prices ever higher. In the future, demand from China and India for natural resources will collide with our planet's dwindling supply of natural resources. The future is on a collision course. Therein lies your profit potential.

Today an investment in natural resource stocks is essential to your future prosperity. Growth in demand for these products is coming even if demand in the United States is stagnant.

Since 2007, the emerging markets of China and India, along with a few other nations that supply them with natural resources, have been responsible for a full 50 percent of global economic growth.

Their citizens' incomes are rising, while ours are stagnant and in many cases shrinking. More than 80 million new middle-class families are being created in Asia per year. These consumers want the goods and lifestyle we have enjoyed for years.

There was a time when investing overseas was fraught with uncertainty and danger. But now because of the Internet, you don't have any reason to invest solely in U.S. companies anymore. Investing in overseas markets with the same level of security and confidence that you have in U.S. markets is now possible. More current information on this trend will be available at FreeingWealth.com.

REAL ASSETS WILL HOLD VALUE IN INFLATION, BONDS WON'T

Much of the pain of the housing collapse of 2008 is now in the rearview mirror. When inflation heats up in 2010 and beyond, certain kinds of cash-producing properties will become very attractive.

Markets are always unpredictable. Market timing doesn't work; that is why we recommend thinking about what is going to happen over the next decade or longer. Think long-term. Think about the purchasing value of the dollar and how you will cope with its demise.

Our financial system is badly crippled. Commercial and residential real estate prices are off as much as 50 percent from the highs. It's very ugly in real estate. That said, as investors, we see great opportunities in a tough environment. The current real estate collapse is an excellent time to opportunistically add to your portfolio. One of the authors recently bought a foreclosure; the bank financed an 80 percent balance at 4.8 percent fixed for thirty years. With just a few years of inflation, the mortgage holder will be in the red on that debt, but the house will likely hold its value—making it a fine rental property throwing off a steady stream of income.

During America's last run of out-of-control inflation in the late 1970s, the Consumer Price Index was climbing as fast as 13 percent. Thirty-year Treasury bonds ended up yielding 15 percent at the peak. We don't recommend owning bonds. We expect a bond rout in the days ahead. After it comes, then consider owning bonds again.

If you have "risk" money for speculation, consider shorting Treasuries. Timing is the question, but with most of our debt sold to foreigners, we will see a day when they will convert from buyers of American debt to sellers. You don't want to be caught in the door when this rush begins. That is why we don't recommend investing in long-dated bonds. They can lose value against inflation, even if you hold them to maturity. Bond market crashes can be as ruinous to your financial well-being as stock market crashes. The 1970s bond crash evaporated billions of dollars of wealth in that decade. (More on these innovative strategies at FreeingWealth.com.)

STOCKS ARE ALWAYS OUR PREFERRED ASSET

Investors will remain shell-shocked by the devastation in the stock market for quite some time to come. Even when a long-term bull market in stocks begins again, most investors will be too afraid to join until they see solid confirmation. It is hard to live by Warren Buffett's words: "A simple rule dictates my buying: Be fearful when others are greedy, and be greedy when others are fearful."[223] Yet in the past, stocks have always provided a defense against inflation. If you position your portfolio with inflation expectations in mind, you can do even better.

We are expecting to weight our Clawback portfolio heavily in oil, natural resources, and high-dividend-paying cyclical stocks in the 2010 period. Cutting back on utilities and consumer-dependent stocks should be a prudent move with unemployment moving well beyond 10 percent and people radically paring back their spending. The real sweet spot is abroad. Stocks that cater to the long-term worldwide demographic and wealth changes are the best protection.

No matter what happens to America's economy, you can expect global demand for oil, natural gas, aluminum, copper, gold, silver, nickel, rice, sugar, cocoa, coffee, coal, cotton, corn, wheat, water, and timber to continue to boom globally. And as demand for these things soars, share prices of the companies that provide them will also. Companies that produce these resources will post ever-increasing earnings. And higher earnings will of course drive the stocks of the best-positioned companies higher. Bottom line: Natural resource stocks are the place to be today.

Obama's runaway deficits and money-printing virtually guarantee sky-high inflation and soaring resource prices. And the demand explosion in emerging markets also means you can expect the stocks of companies that produce oil and other resources to skyrocket.

It's clear that neither of these megatrends is likely to end soon. To the contrary: Every scrap of data we study tells us that these trends are long-term, and despite being subject to the "rolling stall" will be the shiniest opportunities for years to come. Yes, you will hear a lot of chatter about spikes and collapses in these markets—but watch the trend lines. Over the past five years, and into the next five years—blips aside—the natural resources sector will offer the greatest stock returns. Your key, of course, is smart stock selection.

The Keynesian belief that large fiscal stimulus is crucial to ending an economic downturn is nearly a religion amongst policymakers worldwide, yet it goes against common sense. Governments everywhere are fighting against unemployment and the possibility of deflation in this financial crisis. But instead they should let the economy heal naturally. The command-and-control attempt to stimulate demand will only prolong the troubles and lead, inexorably, to a period of rapidly rising prices.

If history is repeated, the Federal Reserve will fail to take the punch bowl away from the party soon enough, keeping monetary stimulus polices going far past the point when unemployment has turned a corner. Despite protests to the contrary and government edicts (remember Nixon's wage and price controls), inflation will hit like a tsunami within three years, maybe sooner.

You must be prepared. Your portfolio must be prepared, and if you position yourself correctly you will profit handsomely, repairing the damage your finances have sustained in the current downturn.

This is the beginning of your Personal Clawback Strategy.

15

FREEING WEALTH

There can be no purpose more enspiriting than to begin
the age of restoration, reweaving the wondrous diversity of life
that still surrounds us.

—EDWARD O. WILSON

FOR THERE TO be strength in numbers, there must first be strength
in one.

For economic revival and political reform to take root and flourish,
each of us must first put our own houses in order. This is not empty
rhetoric. This is simply a core truth we all know to be self-evident, but
our own houses have not been in order. Not for a long time. For us to
find our strength as a nation again we as individuals must rededicate
ourselves to the first principles—virtue, honesty, and humility.

If we consciously live by these principles, they will find their way
back into the national dialogue and into the institutions we depend
on. Just as groundwater finds a way up through the tiniest cracks in
a sidewalk and gives birth to new life, so too can the first principles
of virtue, honesty, and humility give renewed strength to our nation.
With the strength of one, we "force the spring," as the late William
Safire suggested, and find glorious flowers blooming from the tiniest
cracks.

It all begins with the strength of one, and builds from there.

We have already begun the rebuilding. In this book we have talked about the Freeing Wealth Fellowship. In this private network you will find men and women who have joined forces to free our wealth from the sticky-finger attacks of the Killionaires—that is job one. But also important is the work we're doing to free our families from the *Revisionist* attacks on our common decency and character, and free our nation from the grasp of those who don't understand America's unique role in advancing the dignity of man.

Our private Fellowship does not seek to make a big political splash. We are not angling to get onto FoxNews, or form a 527 political influence group. We are simply beginning with the strength of one, and building from there.

We have strong ideas about how to revive our own investment portfolios. We will not be sharing these ideas publicly. We will keep a confidential portfolio, available only to the Fellowship. By acquiring this book, you will be extended an invitation to join us on a provisional basis. There will be no pressure to join, nor will your acceptance be guaranteed. We are looking for people who see the world as we do, people who have something valuable to contribute.

By succeeding financially and freeing our own wealth-building potential, we hope to auger the success of many. It all begins with the first principles of virtue, honesty, and humility as they apply to the challenges facing our great nation. . . .

THE FIRST PRINCIPLES

Freeing our Character as an Exceptional People

In surveying the last decade, Her Eloquence Peggy Noonan called it "the age of the empty suit," with the reigning ethos being "every man for himself." So it did seem, and yet Ms. Noonan thought it appropriate to also remember who we are as a nation:

> We are the largest and most technologically powerful economy in the world, the leading industrial power of the world, and the wealthiest nation in the world. . . .

We are the oldest continuing democracy in the world, operating, since
March 4, 1789. . . .

We don't make refugees, we admit them. When the rich of the world
get sick, they come here to be treated, and when their children come
of age, they send them here to our universities. . . .

We have a supple political system open to reform, and a wildly diverse
culture that has moments of stress but plenty of give. . . . [224]

Yes, we have lived through a difficult period, and the emotional and
financial stresses have cut many of us. Cut us into the marrow. We are
still sore, still beaten down, many of us. But right ahead of us, right within
reach, there is still a "wondrous diversity" of opportunities—if only we are
confident, if only we hew to our essential goodness. Then we will, as Ms.
Noonan concludes, be the one tilling the suit and walking proud again.

We will be walking in the sunny, indomitable footsteps of another
gifted writer, St. Paul: "Finally, brothers, whatever is true, whatever is
noble, whatever is right, whatever is pure, whatever is lovely, whatever
is admirable—if anything is excellent or praiseworthy—think about
such things" (Philippians 4:8).

In seeking the good, however, we cannot ignore the evil. While it
may be true that evil can triumph but never conquer, we know that a
string of evil triumphs in a nation as open and accepting as ours can
lead to some very bad endings.

And evil does exist—let's just be honest and upfront about it.

The hills of Hollywood are filled with soulless scum who
methodically expose our families to the lowest filth in search of profit,
and they must be held to a higher standard.

The high-rises in Manhattan are filled with financiers who
systematically strip the assets of hardworking people, and these
Killionaires, as we've labeled them, must be publicly shamed and
when appropriate, brought to justice.

Radical Revisionists grab headlines with their anti-American tirades,
and we must call them to account as the great patriot and former
Marine, Robert Hall, has admonished:

I'm tired of being told how bad America is by leftwing millionaires like Michael Moore, George Soros and Hollywood entertainers who live in luxury because of the opportunities America offers. In thirty years, if they get their way, the United States will have the religious freedom and women's rights of Saudi Arabia, the economy of Zimbabwe, the freedom of the press of China, the crime and violence of Mexico, the tolerance for gay people of Iran, and the freedom of speech of Venezuela.[225]

America is already well down this road. But we know she has not arrived, nor does she have to. Not if we stand for what is good and right.

Freeing the Country to Be Good and Wise

We proudly fly Old Glory on the fourth of every month, not just July, because there's no other place like America! We mean no disrespect to other countries. Not at all. We are sincerely fond of all the freedom-loving countries of the world. We just know that America still stands tallest among nations in advancing the dignity of man.

Has America ever botched it? Sure, but those are the exceptions and they do not begin to disprove our exceptional character and destiny. We can be tolerant of those who think, as G.K. Chesterton did, that "my country, right or wrong" is as insipid as "my mother, drunk or sober." We just disagree.

We are nationalists, without apology. Accordingly, we hold in no higher respect the young men and women of our awesome military. They deserve our highest praise, and we offer it daily. We cringe when they are exploited by politicians of either party to score cheap points. But we don't worry about them. They're made of stronger stuff than citizen politicians.

The United States is a sovereign nation with borders that must be protected. We take threats to our sovereignty seriously. We believe the Obama administration is naïve to ban the word "terrorism" from the federal lexicon—that just plays into the hands of fanatics who mean our country harm. We hope Mr. Obama captures Osama bin Laden and neutralizes al-Qaeda on his watch. A little less talk and a lot more action is what's called for. That is, after all, what made America exceptional in the first place.

Freeing Our Dollar to Again Soar in Worth Globally

We do not expect the American greenback to regain any of its lost value in our lifetimes. Yet we remain optimistic that despite Mr. Obama, America will return to sound money policies.

We remain optimistic because we must.

Already the bulk of our own personal investments, and the focus of our Clawback Strategy, is with overseas opportunities. We have no choice. But we can hope for a return to fiscal sanity on our native soil. And we will rise in celebration of the political and economic leaders who bring it back—whichever their party.

Freeing Our Laws to Promote Personal Responsibility

"The *first* requirement of a sound body of law," Justice Oliver Wendell Holmes Jr. wrote, "is that it should correspond with the actual feelings and demands of the community."

When Harvard Law gives new graduates such as Mr. Obama their diplomas, the Deans remind them that the *final* requirement of law is that it contains "wise restraints that make men free."

Today's laws fail the first and final requirements of usefulness.

Instead we have a legal morass designed to benefit the Killionaires and their pricey lawyers at the expense of the many. They decide how much they can get away with—then they bring in the lawyers to push the boundaries. As Ken Connor, chairman of the Center for a Just Society, so aptly put it:

> Law today is all proscription and no protection. There are no boundaries, just a moving mudbank comprised of accumulating bureaucracy and whatever claims people unilaterally choose to assert. People wade through law all day long. Any disagreement in the workplace, any accident, any incidental touching of a child, any sick person who gets sicker, any bad grade in school—you name it. Law has poured into daily life.[226]

Mr. Connor's solution is straightforward:

We need to abandon the idea that freedom is a legal maze, where each daily choice is like picking the right answer on a multiple-choice test. We need to set a new goal for law—to define an open area of free choice. This requires judges and legislatures to affirmatively assert social norms of what's reasonable and what's not.

By insisting that laws reflect the needs of communities, we free up people to take personal responsibility for their actions—that's goal one. Then we slap a wall in front of that mudbank so that lawyers and their retainers either rise up and clean up, or get stuck in the mud.

Freeing Our Teachers to Nurture Genuine Excellence

By allying themselves with the Democratic Party exclusively, the teachers' unions have created an unnecessarily subpar educational system, condemning our youth in the doing.

Even more scandalous is the Republican Party's willingness to take a bye on education, caring little for reform, with instead an almost single-minded focus on "vouchers" for fortunate children. Vouchers can be vital and valuable to many parents and their children—but they are a sideshow in the educational crisis we face.

We offered a modest proposal earlier—that lawyers and teachers swap jobs and salaries. We think it would yield most salutary results.

Here's another less modest proposal: We urge Congress to go on posturing about executive pay if they think it will win points back home. Meanwhile, put up legislation that uncaps the pay of teachers who refuse to join the teachers' union. If the self-serving unions can be circumvented, then good smart teachers can focus on real teaching. Let's pay teachers to leave unions behind, so children won't be.

Freeing Our Energy Producers to Deliver Energy Security

As with our schools, our nation's energy supply is a hodgepodge of distortions and missed opportunities. And as with our schools, the mess is a direct result of the political slugfest between the political parties.

Democratic demagogues fight every effort to develop our natural resources—despite the undisputed truth that those resources could give us energy independence and a way out of the Mideast tar pit. Narrow-mindedly these activists insist that clean fuels be pursued exclusively, though those fuels will not (in even the most optimistic scenarios) supply more than 10 to 15 percent of our energy needs for decades to come. The only clean fuel they oppose is the one that could solve many of our problems—nuclear.

Republican Party demagogues fight every effort to clean up the environment—despite libraries of evidence that fossil-fuel pollution causes many of the "new" illnesses our families struggle with. These Republicans act like alternative energies—wind, solar, hydrogen, fuel cells, biomass, whatever—are some kind of San Francisco trick or treat.

Both sides are wrong. Our nation needs to develop fossil fuels and nuclear power, mindful of the environment as we do. We also need to properly incentivize the entrepreneur inventors who will someday give us clean, sustainable, next-gen solutions. We need both solutions. We need to drill hard, and think clean.

What's so difficult about that?

Freeing Our Health Care System to Be the World's Best

Perhaps the greatest tragedy of Mr. Obama's first year in office was his decision to outsource the writing of health care legislation to Pelosi & Company. He blew a golden opportunity, and he must know it.

Despite bitter partisan divides on most fronts, on health care there was general agreement that the system had deteriorated so far, and costs to consumers had spiraled so uncontrollably out of hand, that electroshock was required. Folks on both sides of the aisle were ready to work together in a rare show of bipartisan unity. But the radical leftists got their hooks in and made a botch of things.

Mr. Obama may yet produce a health care plan, but it will be far from workable. It will continue to undermine good doctors, reward incompetence, misallocate resources, and anger everyone involved.

A colossal tragedy, indeed—especially since workable solutions are sitting out in the marketplace in plain sight.

One of those solutions comes from Steve Burd, CEO of Safeway. He took a particular interest in health care when his grocery stores were being strangled by health care cost increases of 10 percent a year. Mr. Burd tossed Safeway's existing health care plan overboard, and replaced it with a market-driven plan that gave employees a financial stake in controlling costs, as well as incentives to take responsibility for their health. It was a more competitive plan that proved affordable.

Safeway's results were astounding: While the rest of the business world has seen a minimum of 10 percent cost increases every year, Safeway's costs are flat. This has not been accomplished by cutting benefits, or increasing costs, for employees. In fact, 80 percent of the 30,000 nonunion Safeway workers who take part in the program rate it good, very good, or excellent.[227]

In Mr. Burd's view, the success came from "removing the obstacles to a free health-care market."

Another similar solution has been figured out by John Mackey, CEO of Whole Foods. His health care plan allows employees to take advantage of health savings accounts for tax savings, move into low-premium high-deductible accounts to save money, and drive down costs by adopting healthy lifestyles.[228] All these free-market, free-consumer initiatives should be part of the Obamacrats' health reform legislation. But they are not.

Both the Whole Foods and the Safeway stories are models of success in the real world. But among the utopian tinkerers now running Washington, the real world is but a distant abstraction.

Freeing Our Taxes from Unfairness and Confusion

When Mr. Obama announced his intention to exempt half the country from paying taxes, he was rekindling an old quarrel. That original "tea party" in the Boston harbor was all about being taxed and having no say in the matter. Today, the more productive members of society are protesting the paying of taxes to benefit nonproductive, nonpaying countrymen, and have no option in the matter once again.

The matter goes straight to the character of society.

Should one set of people hand over half of their income to the government so that another set pays nothing? Is this the kind of country we want to live in?

If Mr. Obama is successful in his tax plans, he will kill upward mobility. Far fewer people will endure the fight to create wealth when they know their gains are going to be confiscated.

When Justice John Marshall said the power to tax is the power to destroy, he never spoke more presciently than for our current age. We are seeing the effects all around us.

People hear Mr. Obama's "yes we can," and they imagine all kinds of bennies coming their way. They look to Mr. Obama as the proprietor of the camp canteen, with a big supply of everything from soup to nuts, womb to tomb.

Yes, there are sloths and fools looking to get fat in ObamaCamp. They either do not understand or choose to ignore the unassailable truth that government is a net destroyer of wealth. While Mr Obama demonstrates a magician's skills in his speeches, he hasn't invented a perpetual money machine. He can only distribute wealth by taking it from someone else. That is, by taxing.

All the lazies in the camp will go along with the ruse until it comes crashing down on them. Then they'll turn on Mr. Obama. Then it will be most ugly. But until then, they'll toss responsibility and freedom to the wind in exchange for a roof over their heads and food in their mouths. They will be no different from slaves, in that sense. Odd that a black man would bind a nation to the fiction that government can be the provider of all that is good.

Government cannot, of course. And it will not, for us.

Freeing Our Entrepreneurs to Create a New Prosperity

Few have been hit harder by the financial collapse than the entrepreneur. Collapsing consumer spending and tightening credit markets have been a double whammy. Four in ten small businesses entered 2010 in dire financial straits.

Big businesses are getting billions in bailouts, the poor are getting billions in tax breaks and giveaways, entrepreneurs are getting scraps. This is wrong, but it has been Obama administration policy to date.

Liberals in Washington believe capitalism failed, and their response has been twofold. First, bail out the big businesses that failed, and keep bailing them out for years to come—for they will need it. Second, fill the capitalist bucket back up with new regulations that keep the failed businesses afloat, but strangle the innovative companies now seeking to invent the future. Through it all, the Obamacrats are either unaware of or indifferent to the irony of their solutions.

In fact, it took a Frenchman to point out the true problem in the financial markets, and to offer his American cousins a solution. Said Nicolas Sarkozy in October 2008: "The financial crisis is not the crisis of capitalism. It is the crisis of a *system* that has distanced itself from the most fundamental values of capitalism, which betrayed the spirit of capitalism."[229]

That "system" he referred to would be the system of Killionaires moving to co-opt a government, distort the free market, and asset-strip a nation. Mr. Sarkozy knows what those in Washington don't: Capitalism didn't fail America, America failed capitalism.

Few have explained this better than Judy Shelton, an economist and author of *Money Meltdown: Restoring Order to the Global Currency System*. In her writings, Ms. Shelton asks about the conductivity that needs to flow between government and entrepreneur if our nation is to prosper again:

> When the owner of a small retail outlet or medium-sized service firm gets into financial trouble, who steps in to help?

> Why are the rules to start a business so onerous, why is the bureaucratic process so lengthy, why are the requirements for hiring employees so burdensome?

> When does the entrepreneur receive the respect and cooperation he deserves for making a genuine contribution to the productive capacity of the economy?

> Equal access to credit is sacrificed to the overwhelming appetite of big business—especially when government skews the terms in favor of its friends.

It is time to pay deference to the real economic heroes of capitalism: the self-made entrepreneurs who have the courage to start a business from scratch, the fidelity to pay their taxes, and the dedication to provide real goods and services to their fellow man.[230]

Yes, it is surely time to pay deference—but it's not likely to come from this government in a form that is valuable or even useful. We alone must choose our path, and with greater tenacity and drive than we've ever had to in the past. That is our roadmap and our destiny. The wealth-killing will continue for the many, but the wealth-freeing can begin for the few.

In that sense, we've come full circle in this book—back to where we began, staring up at that massive boulder at the foot of that imposing hill. It's a situation every entrepreneur knows well—for it is our lot to lean forcefully into the toughest challenges and shoulder our way clear to the top.

It will be harder now, and much is uncertain.

That is why we formed the *Freeing Wealth Fellowship* with a charter that is very different from all the investor clubs, CEO conclaves, and screaming guru groups out there. Those groups serve a purpose. We belong to a few of them ourselves. But they are not sufficient to the task ahead.

More than ever, you need real-time insights into the game-changing moves being made rapid-fire in Washington, and in other political centers around the world. You need to be as politically savvy as business-wise.

So the Fellowship has been designed to put you in contact with political operatives who have a long history of sniffing out the backroom dealings that turn into official policy that affect every business and investment decision you make.

You need more independent sources of information and insight. Clearly there were only a few financial analysts who adequately prepared their clients for the 2008 disaster.

Very few of these analysts will be included among our ranks. For insights we can better trust we'll turn to those analysts who *did* accurately foresee 2008 and are now issuing exclusive stock, commodities, and tax recommendations for our Fellowship only.

You need insights into global financial markets that are clear and straightforward—because while most investment opportunities are now found overseas, you don't want to get stuck in some offshore tar pit because you didn't know the lay of the land.

So the Fellowship connects you with senior managers in overseas companies and funds to allow you a firsthand assessment of the opportunities available to you.

Catering to the needs of entrepreneur investors is the whole purpose of the *Freeing Wealth Fellowship*. That's why we formed it, and we expect to have an exclusive core of 25,000 members by year end. Each new member adds another level of insight into the investment hurdles we face, coupled with a shared vision of the prosperous tomorrow we seek to make real for our families and our nation.

As a member of this Fellowship, you will benefit in four ways:

- You'll get inside intel on the Obamacrats' next moves and how they affect you financially.
- You'll be able to capitalize on the global business insights of fellow members.
- You'll have your own global intel service bringing you opportunities to exploit.
- You'll find your self happily among like-minded peers—people who "get you."

You'll also receive a daily email briefing that offers strategies, advice, and commentary on our confidential portfolio, tax-wise investing, entrepreneurship, and conservative character.

To learn more about the Fellowship, or to receive an invitation to join us on a complimentary basis, please visit www.FreeingWealth.com

Warm regards,
Floyd Brown and Lee Troxler
FreeingWealth.com

NOTES

1   Ronald Reagan, sourced from *Along Wit's Trail: The Humor & Wisdom of Ronald Reagan* by Lee Troxler Henry Holt, 1983.

2   Interview with the *Australian*, as reported by Mail Foreign Service, March 25, 2009.

3   John Feehery, "Biggest Single Democratic Donor Makes Billions off of Financial Crisis," *The Hill's pundit's blog*, March 26, 2009.

4   Floyd Brown and Lee Troxler, *Obama Unmasked* (Merril Press, 2008), 90.

5   John Feehery, "Biggest Single Democratic Donor Makes Billions off of Financial Crisis," *The Hill's pundit's blog*, March 26, 2009.

6   "The Decline in Manufacturing Jobs," *Economists View*, March 1, 2005, http://economistsview.typepad.com.

7   Ronald Reagan, sourced from *Along Wit's Trail: The Humor & Wisdom of Ronald Reagan* by Lee Troxler, Henry Holt, 1983.

8   Simon Johnson, "The Quiet Coup," *The Atlantic*, May 2009.

9   Manuel Roig-Franzia, "Credit Crisis Cassandra: Brooksley Born's Unheeded Warning Is a Rueful Echo 10 Years On," *Washington Post*, May 26, 2009.

10   Michael Lewis, "The End of Wall Street's Boom," *Portfolio.com*, December 2008.

11   Abraham Lincoln, "Address at Sanitary Fair, Baltimore, Maryland, April 18, 1864," *The Collected Works of Abraham Lincoln*, Roy P. Basler, ed.

12   Michael Medved, *The 10 Big Lies About America* (Crown Forum, 2008)

13   Samuel Huntington, *Who Are We? The Challenges to America's National Identity* (Simon & Schuster, 1984).

14   Michael Medved, *The 10 Big Lies About America* (Crown Forum, 2008;) Lee Troxler, *Fahrenhype 9/11* (Companion Book, 2004); Samuel Huntington, "Dead Souls: The Denationalization of the American Elite," *The National Interest*, Spring 2004.

15   Various sources, including Richard C. Cook, "War or Peace?: The World After The 2008 U.S. Presidential Election," *Countercurrents.org*, March 28, 2008, http://www.countercurrents.org/cook281008.htm.

16   Eric Dash and Julie Creswell, "Citigroup Saw No Red Flags Even as It Made Bolder Bets," *New York Times*, November 23, 2008.

17   The Who, "Won't Get Fooled Again," 1971.

18   John D. McKinnon, "Obama Team's Finances Released," *Wall Street Journal*, April 6, 2009.

19   Neil King Jr., "Rattner Net Worth Disclosed," *Wall Street Journal*, May 28, 2009.

20   Ben Bernanke, Chairman of the Federal Reserve, www.federalreserve.gov/ newsevents/speech/Bernanke20060612a.htm.

21   Bruce Wiseman, "Hitler's bank goes global," *Canada Free Press*, May 9, 2009.

22   Ibid.

23   "Year in Review 2008," *The Deal Magazine*, December 2008.

24   Federal Reserve Chairman Alan Greenspan testimony at hearing of the House Committee on Oversight and Government Reform, October 2008.

25   David Sirota, *The Uprising* (Three Rivers Press, 2008), 55.

26   Michael Flynn, "Anatomy of a Breakdown," *Reason*, January 2009.

27   Phil Gramm, "Deregulation and the Financial Panic, *Wall Street Journal*, February 20, 2009.

28   Ibid.

29   Testimony of Chairman Alan Greenspan before the Committee on Banking, Housing, and Urban Affairs, U.S. Senate, February 13, 2001.

30   "Year in Review 2008," *The Deal Magazine*, December 2008.

31   Steven Gjerstad and Vernon L. Smith, "From Bubble to Depression?" *Wall Street Journal*, April 6, 2009.

32   2006 Office of Federal Housing Enterprise Oversight report.

33   http://en.wikipedia.org/wiki/Barney_Frank.

34   Phil Gramm, "Deregulation and the Financial Panic," *Wall Street Journal*, February 20, 2009.

35   Ronald D. Utt, PhD, "The Subprime Mortgage Market Collapse: A Primer on the Causes and Possible Solutions," Heritage Foundation, April 22, 2008.

36   Phil Gramm, "Deregulation and the Financial Panic," *Wall Street Journal*, February 20, 2009.

37   Floyd Brown and Lee Troxler, *Obama Unmasked* (Merril Press, 2008), 98.

38   Sebastian Rotella, "Europeans on left and right ridicule U.S. money meltdown," *Los Angeles Times*, September 20, 2008.

39   Michael Flynn, "The Roots of the Crisis," *Reason*, October 1, 2008.

40   Floyd Brown and Lee Troxler, *Obama Unmasked* (Merril Press, 2008), 165–174.

41   "Prof: I want U.S. off the planet," *WorldNetDaily.com*, February 7, 2005.

42   Kirk Johnson and Katherine Q. Seelye, "Jury Says Professor Was Wrongly Fired," *New York Times*, April 2, 2009.

43   Mark Goldblatt, "Citrus College Letters," *NationalReview.com*, March 11, 2003.

44   Matt Barber, "Palin Bashing Professor Andrew Hallam Exposed by Fox News on *The O'Reilly Factor*," *The National Ledger*, September 19, 2008.

45   Bruce Tinsley, Mallard Fillmore, King Features Syndicate, March 21, 2009.

46   Christopher Chow, "New Study Reveals Extreme Partisan Bias Among Faculty," *Academia.org*, October 2002.

47   Don Feder, "Obama's Hatemonger Helpers," *FrontPageMagazine.com*, March 20, 2008.

48   http://www.youtube.com/watch?v=NdXEQgU8G9E&feature=related.

49   http://www.depts.drew.edu/wmst/corecourses/wmst111/timeline_bios/ Vsolanas.htm.

50   http://www.amazon.com/SCUM-Manifesto-Valerie-Solanas/dp/1859845533.

51   http://www.radicalwomen.org/intro.html#purpose.

52 Philip Howard, "How Modern Law Makes Us Powerless," *Wall Street Journal*, January 26, 2009.

53 Donna Huffaker, "Legal Profession Edges Out Other Industries in Campaign Contributions," LawCrossing, http://www.lawcrossing.com/article/403/Legal-Profession-Edges-Out-Other-Industries-in-Campaign-Contributions.

54 Stephan Fender, *50 Facts That Should Change the USA*, (New York: Disinformation Company Ltd., 2008).

55 National Center for State Courts and Siegel Law Firm, http://www.siegel-legal.com/hammer.htm.

56 Media Research Center, http://www.mrc.org/biasbasics/biasbasics1.asp; and Pew Research Center for the People & the Press, http://people-press.org/report/?pageid=1269.

57 http://www.famous-quotes.com/author.php?aid=2873.

58 http://blog.dreamthisday.com/2009/01/anais-nin-we-dont-see-things-as-they.html.

59 Floyd and Mary Beth Brown, "Duck-and-Run Obama," Cagle Cartoons Newspaper Syndicate, December 11th, 2009.

60 Shobhana Chandra, "Payrolls Fall More Than Forecast, Unemployment Rises," *Bloomberg.com*, July 2, 2009.

61 Kevin Mooney, "ACORN drops tarnished name and moves to silence critics," *Washington Examiner*, June 21, 2009.

62 The Harrington Report, "Folks, the ACORN Fraud is Unraveling," May 12, 2009, http://matthewharrington.wordpress.com.

63 John Fund, "More Acorn Voter Fraud Comes to Light," *Wall Street Journal*, May 9, 2009.

64 Ginger Adams Otis, Susan Edelman, and Melissa Klein, "7-Yr.-Old Gets an ACORN Vote," *New York Post*, March 12, 2008.

65 Bill Dolan, "County rejects large number of invalid voter registrations," *NWI.com*, March 2, 2008.

66 John Fund, "More Acorn Voter Fraud Comes to Light," *Wall Street Journal*, May 9, 2009.

67 Ibid.

68 http://www.fightthesmears.com/articles/20/acornrumor.html.

69 Brody Mullins, "House Earmark Requests Risk Clash With Obama," *Wall Street Journal*, April 6, 2009.

70 Greg Morcroft, "Fraudsters eye huge stimulus pie," *MarketWatch*, June 12, 2009.

71 "Pig-odor study passes smell test," Associated Press, May 5, 2009.

72 Rob Hotakainen, "Earmark critics are up in arms over tattoo removal funds," McClatchy Newspapers, March 10, 2009.

73 Phillip Rucker, "Earmark for Mormon cricket isn't pork to ranchers in Utah," *Washington Post*, March 18, 2009.

74 Kimberley A. Strassel, "Pelosi's Pork Problem," *Wall Street Journal*, June 5, 2009.

75 Ken Connor, "America For Sale," *Townhall.com*, December 14, 2008.

76 For more information, see http://www.usconstitution.net/creed.html.

77 Dave Kopel, Research Director, Independence Institute, http://www.davekopel.com/Terror/Fiftysix-deceits-in-Fahrenheit-911.htm.

78 Jeff Hays and Lee Troxler, Executive Producers, *FahrenHYPE 9/11* (Michael & Me LLC, 2004).

79   Susie Madrak, "Michael Moore goes after Wall Street in next film," *USA Today*, June 12, 2009.

80   Michelle Malkin, "Peggy the Moocher," *Townhall.com*, May 08.

81   Aaron Lucchetti and Stephen Grocer, "Wall Street On Track to Award Record Pay," *Wall Street Journal*, March 14, 2009.

82   Neal Gabler, "Desperately Seeking Celebrity," *Los Angeles Times*, August 11, 2002.

83   Simona Covel, "Slump Batters Small Business," *WSJ.com*, December 25, 2008.

84   Jeffrey McCracken and Vishesh Kumar, "Wave of Bad Debt Swamps Companies," *Wall Street Journal*, February 13, 2009; and Bankruptcy Home, http://www.bankruptcyhome.com/Five-Major-Corporate-Bankruptcies-2009.htm.

85   Maurice Tamman and David Enrich, "Local Banks Face Big Losses," *Wall Street Journal*, May 19, 2009; Greg Morcroft, *MARKETWATCH*, March 24, 2009.

86   Maurice Tamman and David Enrich, "Local Banks Face Big Losses," *Wall Street Journal*, May 19, 2009.

87   Damian Paletta and Joe Bel Bruno, "BankUnited Fails in Year's Biggest Bust," *Wall Street Journal*, May 22, 2009.

88   Cari Tuna, "Small Firms Wait for a Credit Thaw," *Wall Street Journal*, May 20, 2009.

89   Ibid.

90   Pui-Wing Tam, "Venture Capitalists Head for the Door," *Wall Street Journal*, June 5, 2009.

91   Remarks by President Barack Obama at Georgetown University in Washington, D.C., April 14, 2009. See http://www.whitehouse.gov/the_press_office/Remarks-by-the-President-on-the-Economy-at-Georgetown-University.

92   Remarks by President Barack Obama at George Mason University in Washington, D.C., January 8, 2009. See http://www.cnn.com/2009/POLITICS/01/08/obama.conference.transcript/index.html.

93   Simona Covel and Kelly K. Spors, "U.S. Proposal Aims to Aid Smaller Companies," *Wall Street Journal*, March 17, 2009.

94   Conn Carol, "Progressive Corporatism in Action," *BeyondBailouts.org*, January 28, 2009.

95   Laura Meckler and Jonathan Weisman, "Obama Warns of Lost Decade," *Wall Street Journal*, February 10, 2009.

96   Source verified from http://www.exposeobama.com/2009/01/30/beware-an-obama-bearing-gifts.

97   Brian M. Carney, "Elections Have Consequences," *Wall Street Journal*, April 24, 2009.

98   Gerald F. Seib, "Obama Goes for It All in Budget," *Wall Street Journal*, March 27, 2009.

99   Statistics provided by Alan Reynolds, "$646,214 Per Government Job," *Wall Street Journal*, January 28, 2009. Mr. Reynolds is a senior fellow with the Cato Institute and author of *Income and Wealth* (2006).

100   David Brooks, "The Quiet Revolution in Education," *New York Times*, March 22, 2009.

101   Mary Anastasia O'Grady, "Now Is No Time to Give Up on Markets," *Wall Street Journal*, March 21, 2009.

102   Randy Fardal, "Hit and Run," *American Thinker*, March 28, 2009.

103   Brad Heath, "Billions in aid go to areas that backed Obama in '08," *USA Today*, July 9, 2009.

104 Dick Morris and Eileen McGann, "Beware Obama's Trojan Horse," *Townhall.com*, February 2, 2009.

105 Gerald F. Seib, "Obama Goes for It All in Budget," *Wall Street Journal*, March 27, 2009.

106 Brett J. Blackledge and Matt Apuzzo, "Stimulus jobs overstated," Associated Press, March 29, 2009.

107 Robert J. Barro, "Government Spending Is No Free Lunch," *Wall Street Journal*, January 22, 2009. Professor Barro is author of *Macroeconomics: A Modern Approach* and teaches economics at Harvard University. He is a senior fellow at Stanford University's Hoover Institution.

108 David Leonhardt, "The Big Fix," *New York Times*, January 27, 2009.

109 Bill Bonner, "Wall Street Gets the Boot," *Daily Reckoning*, January 30, 2009.

110 Niall Ferguson, "Keynes can't help us now," *Los Angeles Times*, February 6, 2009.

111 John Carney, "The Warning: Brooksley Born's Battle With Alan Greenspan, Robert Rubin and Larry Summers," *Business Insider*, March 21, 2009.

112 Simon Johnson, "The Quiet Coup," *The Atlantic*, May 2009.

113 NPR.org, November 2008, http://www.npr.org/templates/story/story.php?storyId=96643808.

114 *Daily Mail*, editorial, January 26, 2009, http://www.canadafreepress.com/index.php/article/7705.

115 http://www.military-quotes.com/Churchill.htm.

116 Various sources, including IMF and Demographica.com (http://www.demographia.com/db-ppp60+.htm).

117 Peggy Noonan, "Obama's Domestic Agenda Gains Clarity," *Wall Street Journal*, April 3, 2009.

118 Interview With Peter Orszag, State of The Union With John King, *CNN.com*, March 8, 2009.

119 See Bureau of Economic Analysis and TheFreeEnterpriseNation.org.

120 Senator Tom Coburn, "Budget Debate Shows Washington Politicians in Denial," *RealClearPolitics.com*, April 2, 2009.

121 According to Moody's Economy.com.

122 Michael M. Phillips and Ruth Simon, "Mortgage Bailout to Aid 1 in 9 U.S. Homeowners," *Wall Street Journal*, March 5, 2009.

123 *Mark Calabria, "A Fake Financial Fix,"* Cato.org, June 18, 2009.

124 Dick Morris and Eileen McGann, "Obama's Mortgage Rescue Plan Is a Failure," *DickMorris.com*, June 9, 2009.

125 Deborah Solomon, Jon Hilsenrath, and Damian Paletta, "U.S. Plots New Phase in Banking Bailout," *Wall Street Journal*, January 17, 2009.

126 Ibid.

127 Tunku Varadarajan, "Nouriel Roubini: 'Nationalize' the Banks," *Wall Street Journal*, February 21, 2009.

128 *Mark Calabria, "A Fake Financial Fix,"* Cato.org, June 18, 2009.

129 Blogpost by W-31, *HuffingtonPost.com*, August 18, 2009, http://www.huffingtonpost.com/users/profile/W-31?action=comments.

130 Betsy McCaughey, "Dissecting the Kennedy Health Bill," *Wall Street Journal*, June 19, 2009.

131 Dr. Hieb has given several interviews, including with one of the authors for another nonaffiliated project, *Hillary The Movie*. We sought to capture the flavor of those interviews.

132   Thomas Sowell, "Alice in Medical Care," *Townhall.com*, June 30, 2009.

133   Opinion Page Editors, "ObamaCare Sticker Shock," June 19, 2009; "The Massachusetts Health Mess," *Wall Street Journal*, July 11, 2009.

134   Ibid.

135   Robert Knight, "Call It What It Is: Rationed Health Care," *American Thinker*, June 10, 2009.

136   Estimated by The Lewin Group, a health-care policy research and consulting firm.

137   John C. Lechleiter, "Health-Care Reform and the 'Innovation Test,'" *Wall Street Journal*, May 14, 2009.

138   Liz Rappaport and Jon Hilsenrath, "Fed Moves to Free Up Credit for Consumers," *Wall Street Journal*, March 4, 2009.

139   Michael J. Boskin, "Obama's Radicalism Is Killing the Dow," *Wall Street Journal*, March 6, 2009.

140   Michael Reagan, "Where's the Beef?" *Townhall.com*, February 25, 2009.

141   http://quotes.liberty-tree.ca/quotes_by/benjamin+franklin.

142   Thomas Jefferson, letter to Joseph Milligan, April 6, 1816, http://www.marksquotes.com/Founding-Fathers/Jefferson/index8.htm.

143   Dennis Cauchon, "Leap in U.S. debt hits taxpayers with 12% more red ink," *USA Today*, May 28, 2009.

144   Mary Anastasia O'Grady, "Don't Monetize the Debt," *Wall Street Journal*, May 23, 2009.

145   Terry Easton, "*Human Events* Quizzes Bernanke at London School of Economics," *Human Events*, January 16, 2009.

146   Mary Anastasia O'Grady, "Don't Monetize the Debt," *Wall Street Journal*, May 23, 2009.

147   Patrick Barron, "Dumping the Dollar: A Case of Government Schizophrenia," *PatrickBarron.blogspot.com*, June 18, 2009.

148   Milton Friedman, *Money Mischief* (Mariner Books, 1994).

149   http://www.hoover.org/publications/digest/2939401.html.

150   Russian President Dmitry Medvedev interview with CNBC, June 1, 2009.

151   Oliver Biggadike and Chris Fournier, "Dollar Declines as Nations Mull Reserve Currency Alternatives," *Bloomberg News*, June 2, 2009.

152   Gerald F. Seib, "Taxes Test Obama's Support Among Higher-Income Voters," *Wall Street Journal*, February 27, 2009.

153   http://en.wikipedia.org/wiki/John_Stuart_Mill.

154   Ari Fleischer, "Everyone Should Pay Income Taxes," *Wall Street Journal*, April 13, 2009.

155   Source verified at http://en.wikipedia.org/wiki/Income_tax_in_the_United_States.

156   Ari Fleischer, "Everyone Should Pay Income Taxes," *Wall Street Journal*, April 13, 2009.

157   Alan Reynolds, "How's Obama Going to Raise $4.3 Trillion?" *Wall Street Journal*, March 24, 2008.

158   Opinion Page Editors, "The Missing Obama Tax Cut," *Wall Street Journal*, February 10, 2009.

159   Arthur Laffer and Stephen Moore, "Soak the Rich, Lose the Rich," *Wall Street Journal*, May 18, 2009.

160   James Pethokoukis, "10 Reasons to Whack Obama's Stimulus Plan," *US News & World Report*, January 27, 2009.

161   Tax calculations based on similar calculations made by Lawrence B. Lindsey, "Obama Turns FDR Upside Down," *Wall Street Journal*, June 20, 2008.

162   Tom Herman, "What I Learned in My 16 Years on the Tax Beat," *Wall Street Journal*, April 15, 2009.

163   David Cay Johnston, *Perfectly Legal* (Penguin Group, 2003).

164   Kim Dixon, "Obama seeks to double tax law enforcement budget," Reuters, May 7, 2009.

165   John D. McKinnon, "White House Unveils Tax-Rate Details," *Wall Street Journal*, May 12, 2009.

166   Ibid.

167   http://www.freerepublic.com/focus/f-news/1973711/posts.

168   Kimberley Strassel, "The Union Agenda," *Wall Street Journal*, April 14, 2008.

169   Center for Union Facts sponsored poll, http://laborpains.org/index.php/2009/02/04/new-poll-82-of-americans-dont-want-to-join-a-union.

170   Matthew Continetti, "Obama, labor's lackey," *Los Angeles Times*, March 7, 2009.

171   Arthur Laffer, Stephen Moore, and Jonathan Williams, *Rich States, Poor States: ALEC-Laffer State Economic Competitiveness Index*, American Legislative Exchange Council, March 2009.

172   Remarks of President Barack Obama—As Prepared for Delivery by Video to AFL-CIO Executive Council, Miami, FL, March 3, 2009, http://www.whitehouse.gov/the_press_office/Remarks-of-President-Obama-to-AFL-CIO-Executive-Council.

173   Newt Gingrich, "None Dare Call it Scandal," *HumanEvents.com*, June 10, 2009.

174   Ibid.

175   Neil King Jr., Jeffrey McCracken, and Mike Spector, "Potential Conflicts Abound in Government Role," *Wall Street Journal*, June 1, 2009.

176   http://unionfacts.org/cardcheck/introduction.cfm.

177   Service Employees International Union: http://www.seiu.org/2009/07/statement-by-seiu-president-andy-stern-on-the-employee-free-choice-act.php.

178   Remarks of the President at AFL-CIO Convention in Pittsburgh, September 15, 2009, http://www.aflcio.org/aboutus/thisistheaflcio/convention/2009/sp091509.cfm.

179   G. Harrison Darby and Margaret R. Bryant, "When Unions Knock, How Should Employers Answer?" *HR Magazine*, July 1997.

180   Marc J. Lane, *Legal Handbook for Small Business*, AMACOM, 1989. Quoted from the *Encyclopedia of Small Business*: http://www.enotes.com/small-business-encyclopedia/labor-unions-small-business.

181   Office of Speaker of the House Pelosi, http://speaker.house.gov/issues?id=0010.

182   Drew Zahn, "Obama: Spike energy costs to make people go green," *WorldNetDaily.com*, November 1, 2008.

183   Ronald D. Utt, Ph.D., "Obama Administration's Plan to Coerce People Out of Their Cars," Heritage Foundation, July 10, 2009.

184   Keith Koffler, "Obama, in Radio Address, Looks for Momentum for Climate Bill," *RollCall.com*, July 27, 2009.

185   "Greenhouse taxes to raise cost of everything," *WorldNetDaily.com*, January 20, 2009.

186   David Kreutzer, Ph.D., "The Economic Impact of Cap and Trade," Heritage Foundation, May 7, 2009.

187   Martin Feldstein, "Tax Increases Could Kill the Recovery," *Wall Street Journal*, May 14, 2009.

188   Kate Galbraith, "Buffet: Cap-and-Trade Is a 'Regressive' Tax," *New York Times*, March 9, 2009.

189   http://goliath.ecnext.com/coms2/gi_0199-10568347/The-great-global-cooling-myth.html.

190   Marc Gunther and Adam Lashinsky, "Al Gore's next act: Planet-saving VC," *CNN Money.com*, February 12, 2008.

191   Opinion Page Editors, "Whose Ox Is Gored?" *Wall Street Journal*, March 19, 2007.

192   Sourced from contacts in Silicon Valley, and Marc Gunther and Adam Lashinsky, "Al Gore's next act: Planet-saving VC," *CNN Money.com*, February 12, 2008.

193   Justin Hibbard, "Doerr to the Environment," *Business Week*, August 14, 2006.

194   Terence Chea, "Doerr firm invests in 'green technology,'" Associated Press, April 10, 2009.

195   American Presidency Project, http://www.presidency.ucsb.edu/ws/index.php?pid=65090.

196   Russ Mitchel, "Behind the Green Doerr," *Portfolio.com*, March 2007.

197   John M. Broder, "Gore's role as a goad for a cause and an investor draws spotlight," *New York Times*, November 3, 2009.

198   Daniel Henninger, "Democrats Bid Business Adieu," *Wall Street Journal*, March 26, 2009.

199   Lee Troxler, *Out of Order*, 1999.

200   Jake Tapper, "Do You Want Your OTV?" ABC News, May 20, 2009.

201   Bernard Goldberg, *A Slobbering Love Affair: The True (And Pathetic) Story of the Torrid Romance Between Barack Obama and the Mainstream Media* (Regnery Press, 2009).

202   Michelle Oddis, "Obama Official Linked to Racially Charged Boycott of Glenn Beck," *HumanEvents.com*, August 13, 2009.

203   http://www.whitehouse.gov/blog/Facts-Are-Stubborn-Things.

204   Michael Sluss, "Obama throws political muscle to Deeds," *Roanoke Times*, August 7, 2009.

205   Carrie Budoff Brown, "White House to Democrats: 'Punch back twice as hard,'" *Politico.com*, August 6, 2009.

206   Andrew Breitbart, "Have You Heard Ken Gladney's Story?" *RealClearPolitics.com*, August 10, 2009.

207   Gerald F. Seib, "GOP Tries to Dig Out of Its Hole," *Wall Street Journal*, May 5, 2009.

208   Lanny J. Davis, "The Obama Realignment," *Wall Street Journal*, November 6, 2008.

209   Opinion Page Editors, "A 40-Year Wish List," *Wall Street Journal*, January 28, 2009.

210   See Bud Conrad, "Assessing How Serious the Financial Crisis Can Get," *WhiskeyAndGunpowder.com*, April 23, 2009.

211   Kerry Hannon, "Best advice: Stay invested even in turbulent times," *USA Today*, November 7, 2008.

212   Gregory Bresiger, "Life Will Be Good Again—But When?" *FA Magazine*, November 2008. For updates on total national debt, see www.usdebtclock.org.

213   See www.caseyresearch.com.

214   James Howard Kunstler, "Shoveling Money into the Deceased Economy," *WhiskeyAndGunpowder.com*, May 19, 2009.

215   Stephen Fidler and Neil Shah, "Bonds Hit by Ratings Fears," *Wall Street Journal*, May 22, 2009.

216   Henry Blodget, "PIMCO's Gross: Yes, We Will Lose Our AAA," *The Business Insider*, May 22, 2009.

217   Bill Bonner, "O! Bama!" *Fleet Street Daily*, January 20, 2009.

218   Peter Schiff, "The Mother of All Bubbles," *Barron's*, February 8, 2008.

219   Bill Bonner, "An Avalanche of Claptrap," *Daily Reckoning*, May 22, 2009.

220   Various sources, including http://www.abovetopsecret.com/forum/thread505319/pg1.

221   James B. Stewart, "With Taxes, Who Wants to Be a Millionaire?" *Wall Street Journal*, March 18, 2009.

222   Emily Maltby, "Need Funding? Better Get Creative," *Wall Street Journal*, March 15, 2009.

223   Warren E. Buffett, "Buy American. I Am.," *New York Times*, March 16, 2008.

224   Peggy Noonan, "Who We (Still) Are," *Wall Street Journal*, December 19, 2008.

225   Robert A. Hall, "I'm Tired," *Tartanmarine.blogspot.com*, February 19, 2009.

226   Ken Connor, "America For Sale," *Townhall.com*, December 14, 2008.

227   Kimberley A. Strassel, "Mr. Burd Goes to Washington," *Wall Street Journal*, June 19, 2009.

228   Stephen Moore, "The Conscience of a Capitalist," *Wall Street Journal*, March 3, 2009.

229   Carl Schramm, "Schumpeter's Moment," *Wall Street Journal Europe*, May 29, 2009.

230   Judy Shelton, "A Capitalist Manifesto," *Wall Street Journal*, March 13, 2008.

INDEX

A

Accuracy in Academia, 40
ACHA (Affordable Health Choices Act), 109, 113, 117
ACORN (Association of Community Organizations for Reform Now), 14, 50–53, 122, 198
Advanced Energy Initiative, 181–82
Affordable Health Choices Act (ACHA), 109, 113, 117
AFL-CIO Executive Council, 164
AIG, 218
Akon (rapper), 36
Alexandria, Virginia, xvi
alternative energy, 176, 181–83, 219–20, 241
American Bar Association, 45, 186
American Dream, ix
American empire, 11
American Labor Movement, 159
American's Creed, The, 58–59
Amtrack, 80
Ant and the Grasshopper, The (Traditionalist and *Revisionist* versions), 123–24
Ascent of Money, The (Ferguson), 90
asset bubbles
  commercial real estate, 128
  derivatives, 128
  government debt, 128–29, 132–34, 183
  green, 183–84, 211
  inflationary cycle of, 128–29
  residential housing, 128

tech, 28, 128
U.S. Treasury market as, 215
  See also housing bubble
Associated Press, 86
Association of Community Organizations for Reform Now (ACORN), 14, 50–53, 122, 198
Atlantic, The, 93
automobiles of the future, 219–20

B

baby boomers and 1960s, 11–12, 21, 59–60, 216–17. See also *Revisionists*
Bailout (Waggoner), 208
bailouts
  bonuses paid with funds, 62–63
  Fed's control and business scrambling, 133
  killionaires use of, 72–76
  overview, xii
  as payback for Democratic supporters, 204
  permanent nature of, 107–8, 118
  recipients of, 70–72, 100, 218–19
  sectors supported with, 99–100
  TARP, 67–72
  See also Obama Stimulus Package
Baker, Charlie, 113
Bangkok, Thailand, 2–3
banking holiday, 212
Bank of America, 106
Bank of England and Soros, 25

bankruptcy protection for name brand companies, 68

banks

bank failures, 69–70

banking holiday, 212

Bank of England and Soros, 25

losses on toxic loans, 105–6

nationalization of, 106–8

reforms and destabilization, 91–93

risk management, 18

and small businesses, 68–69

"too big to fail" list, 108

See also bailouts

BankUnited of Florida, 69

Barro, Robert J., 251n107

Barrow, Robert J., 88–89

BDS (Bush Derangement Syndrome), 23–24

Bear Stearns, 106

Beck, Glenn, 198

Becker, Gary, 82

Bernanke, Ben, 18, 131–34

big business

bankruptcy protection, 68–69

and Financial Stability Board, 19

health assessment by S&P, 68

mega-company regulations, xvi–xvii

nationalization of weakest businesses, 218–19

Obama's courting of, 187

small business policies versus, 71–72, 74–76, 143, 145

and Sugar part of sugar/sugar/shaft, 75–76

tax rate, 145

See also bailouts

black liberation theology, 40–41

Blackwell, Ken, 41

Blattmachr, Jonathan, 152

Blood, David, 179

BNSF railroad, 176

Bonner, Bill, 90, 218

Bonnie and Clyde (movie), 21

borders, xiii. *See also* illegal immigrants

Born, Brooksley, 9–10, 92

Boskin, Michael, 122

breakaway states, 148

Brown, Gordon, 114

Bryant, Margaret, 169–72

bubbles. *See* asset bubbles; housing bubble

Buchanan, Patrick, 6

budget deficits

and big government, 90, 130

Bush's inheritance, 15–16

foreign financing of U.S. deficits, 135–37, 212

and health care overhaul, 109–11

and inflation, 234

Obama's campaign promises versus, 78, 85–86, 97–98, 143–44

Obama's inheritance, 98

of states, 146–48

from stimulus spending, 84, 126, 133

Buffett, Warren, 135, 176, 233

Burd, Steve, 242

Bush, George W.

and bank bailouts, 106

and budget deficit, 15–16

cost to conservatives, 139, 140, 143

on energy, 181–82

and financial crisis, 23

and Republican Party, 13

and unions, 158

Bush Derangement Syndrome (BDS), 23–24

C

Calabria, Mark, 103, 108

California, 56, 146, 148

Canada, 112

Cantor, Eric, 140, 198

cap-and-trade policy, xii, 174–78

capital, hiding from the IRS, 8

capital gains taxes, 145–46, 149

Capitalism: A Love Story (film), 61

carbon-capture demonstration project funding, 82

"card check" fight, 166, 168–69

Carlson, Robert C., 153–54

Carol, Conn, 75–76

cars of the future, 219–20

Carter, Jimmy, 23

Casey, Doug, 210

"cash for clunkers" program, 83–84

Casteel, Roberta, 51

Catastrophe (Morris and McGann), 104

Cerberus Capital Management, 16

Cerberus Capital Partners, 17

Cheney, Dick, 23

Chesterton, G.K., 238

childcare subsidies, 81

China

growing economy of, 230–32

ownership of U.S. dollars, 134

China (*cont.*)
  and Soros, 3
  U.S. tariff on tire imports from, 167
Chomsky, Noam, 14
Christie, Chris, 203
Chrysler, 17, 68
Churchill, Ward, 38–39
Circuit City, 68
Cisco, 155–56
CIT Group, 70
Citibank, 218
Citigroup, 14, 17
Civil Rights Act (1964), Title VII, 185–86
clawback. *See* Personal Clawback Strategy
clean-energy research, 181–82
Clinton, Bill, 7, 15, 121–22, 158
Closing the Gap: A Guide to Equal
  Opportunity Lending (Federal Reserve
  Bank of Boston), 24–25
Coburn, Tom, 99
Cold War years, 135
collateralized debt obligations, 22
college professors, 38–43
commercial property values, 68–69
commercial real estate bubble, 128
Community Reinvestment Act (CRA), 23,
  24–25
company policy on unionization, 170
Congressional Budget Office, 109
con jobs, 2–4, 9
Connolly, John, 135–36
Connor, Ken, 58, 239–40
construction sector and stimulus money,
  80
Consumer Price Index, 232
consumers
  borrowing, 209–10
  personal financial goals, 225–26, 228
Continetti, Matthew, 159
Conyers, John, 53
Cooling, The (Ponte), 178–79
corporations. *See* big business
Cortez Masto, Catherine, 51
Corzine, John, 203
Cougar Town (TV program), 36
Council of Economic Advisers, 86
Countrywide, 106
CRA (Community Reinvestment Act), 23,
  24–25
creative destruction, authors' plan for, 131
credit, contraction of, 5, 70–72, 106,
  214–15, 219

credit companies' financial scams, 209–10
credit default swaps, 8

D
Darby, Harrison, 169–72
Daschle, Tom, 155
Davis, Lanny, 203
demand-side economics, 88–92
Democratic Party
  and black president, 195–96
  and deficits, 90–91
  energy, environment, and, 219–20, 241
  and lawyers, 44–45
  meaninglessness of, x
  script for recruiting immigrants, 49
  and Soros, 2
  See also ACORN; *Revisionists*
deregulation, 8, 26–27
derivatives bubble, 128
derivatives market, 9–10, 92
destabilization of banks, 91–93
Dobbs, Lou, 61
doctors and the health care overhaul,
  114–15, 241
Doerr, John, 180–81, 182
dollar, freeing our, 239
dollar defense strategy, 137
dollars, value of U.S., 134–38
Donilon, Tom, 17
Dorfman, Margot, 67
Dr. Zhivago (movie), xiii

E
earned income credit, 81
Earnhardt, John, 155–56
Easton, Terry, 133, 212
economics
  the building of bubbles, 128–29
  demand-side view, 88–92
  financial services-based economy of
    U.S., 5–7, 9, 22, 29–30, 128–29, 223
  history of economic meltdowns, 207–8
  hyperinflation, 134–38
  inflationary bubble cycle, 128
  Keynesian Multiplier, xiv–xv, 88–92,
    234
  Obama's balancing act, 129–31
  seignorage, 135–36
  supply-side view, 87–88
  ultimate balance sheet, 215–16
  See also asset bubbles; budget deficits;
    rolling stall period

Eddie Bauer, 68
Education, Department of, 81
education sector and stimulus money, 80
Edwards, John, 189–90
EFCA (Employee Free Choice Act), 166,
    168–69
Elmendorf, Douglas, 176
Emanuel, Rahm, 78, 195
employee benefits, nonunion, 171–72
Employee Free Choice Act (EFCA), 166,
    168–69
energy and the environment, 219–20
energy producers, freeing, 240–41
England, 112, 134
entrepreneur investors
    carryback tax break, 76
    and credit contraction, 5, 70–72, 106,
        214–15, 219
    as driving force and tax target, xv–xvi
    freeing, 243–45
    jobs created by, xi, 74
    and labor unions, 160–61
    lawyer-initiated destruction, 187–89
    and Obama-unleashed lawyers, 185–
        87, 189
    opportunities, 118–19
    regulations versus, xvi–xvii
    and SBA loans, 74–75
    and shaft part of sugar/sugar/shaft,
        66–67, 70–72, 74, 117–18, 129, 243
    taxation of, 140–41, 144, 218–19
    as wire in Obama's balancing act,
        129–31
    See also small businesses
Environmental Defense Fund, 181
environmentalists, 174, 181, 219–20, 241
equality of opportunity, xvii
Europe and Europeans
    dependence on United States, 95
    and European style of social democracy,
        96, 140–41, 145, 204–5, 242–43
    medical care rebellion, 114
    quality of life measures, 95–96
    social democracy versus opportunity,
        95
evil, 237. See also Revisionists

F
Faber, Marc, 128–29, 141–43
Fahrenheit 9/11 (film), 31, 60–61
Fannie Mae, 30
Fardel, Randy, 83–84

Federal Deposit Insurance Corp. (FDIC),
    69
Federal Election Commission, 44
federal funds rate, 28–29
Federal Housing Administration, 103
Federal Reserve
    Bernanke and, 18, 131–34
    co-opting of, 131–34, 218
    creating money, 5
    increasing power of, 108
    survey of bank loan officers, 71
    and Treasury bills, 29, 134, 215, 232–33
Feehery, John, 1
Feldstein, Martin, 105
Ferguson, Niall, 90–91
Fillmore, Millard, 39–40
financial crisis
    beneficiaries of, 18
    causes of, 17–18, 20–24
    federal funds rate leading to mortgage-
        backed securities, 28–29
    global nature of, 18–19, 90–91, 131,
        206–7
    killionaires' plan for, 25, 32–34, 128
    presidents' policy advisors leading to,
        14–17
    script for, 4–6
    Soros's argument against regulations,
        25–26
    wealth changing hands, 1–2, 25, 67–68
    See also service sector
financial sector
    manufacturing sector versus, 6–9, 128
    U.S. as paper-based economy, 5, 9,
        29–30, 128–29, 223
    See also banks
Financial Stability Board, 18–19
Financial Times, 3
Fisher, Richard W., 134
Flake, Jeff, 57
Fleischer, Ari, 142
Florida's BankUnited, 69
Flynn, Michael, 33
food stamp programs, 81
forecasting the future, 206–11. See also
    rolling stall period
Fortunoff, 68
fossil fuel dependence of U.S., 175,
    176–77
France, 95–96, 114
Frank, Barney, 31
Franklin, Benjamin, 125

Freddie Mac, 30
Freeing Wealth Fellowship
    freeing our country, 238–39
    freeing our dollar, 239
    freeing our energy producers, 240–41
    freeing our entrepreneurs, 243–45
    freeing our health care system, 241–42
    freeing our laws, 239–40
    freeing our taxes, 242–43
    freeing our teachers, 240
    overview, 226, 236, 245–46
    rules for, 226–27
freeloaders
    and black liberation theology, 40
    dependence from welfare, 79
    as Obama's base of support, xiv–xv,
        65–66, 128–29, 204–5
    permanent subclass of, 121–25, 129,
        243
    refusing to succumb to, 140
    the rich as, 152
    and union organizers, 170–71
Friedman, Milton, 135
Frontline (PBS program), 92

G
G-20 meeting in London (April 2, 2009),
    18–19
Gabler, Neal, 63
GDP (gross domestic product) per capita,
    France and U.S., 95–96
Geithner, Timothy, 16, 75–76, 102–4, 155
General Growth Properties, 68
Generation Investment Management, 179
Gettelfinger, Ron, 165
Gingrich, Newt, 164–65
Gladney, Ken, 200
Gladstone, William, 47
Glass-Steagall Act (1999), 8, 26
global markets
    and financial crisis, 18–19, 90–91, 131,
        206–7
    and tax rates, 155–57
    trade conflicts, 166
global-warming research funding, 82
glut of dollars on the market, 134–38
Goldberg, Bernard, 197
Goldman Sachs, 15, 16, 17, 29, 30, 105
Goodyear Tire & Rubber Co., Ledbetter v.,
    185–86
Gore, Al, 178–81
Gorelick, Jamie, 31

government debt bubble, 128–29, 132–
    34, 183
government of the United States parody,
    100
government regulations
    on banks, 107–8
    free enterprise promoting, 7–9
    for mega-companies versus
        entrepreneurs, xvi–xvii
    with taxation and spending, 129–31
government workers, 80, 98
Graham, Lindsey, 107
Gramm, Phil, 26, 32
Gramm-Leach-Bliley Act (1999), 26–27
greater good concept, 43
Great Financial Panic of 2008. *See*
    financial crisis
green bubble, 183–84, 211
green movement, 180–84
Greenspan, Alan
    and derivatives, 10
    and era of cheap credit, 132
    fall from grace, 33
    and housing bubble, 18
    and interest rates, 27–29
    and nationalization of banks, 107
    on subprime market, 23
Gregg, Judd, 78
Gross, Bill, 212
gross domestic product (GDP) per capita,
    France and U.S., 95–96
Guo Shuqing, 136
Gutmann, Amy, 14

H
Hall, Robert, 237–38
Hallam, Andrew, 39
Hartford Courant, 168
Harvard-Pilgrim (Massachusetts health
    insurance company), 113
health care system
    abusers of, 112
    doctors' concerns, 114–15
    end-of-life concerns, 111
    freeing, 241–42
    incentives-based approach to medicine,
        111–12
    Massachusetts plan, 113–14
    overview, xii–xiii, 108–10
    rationing care, 110–11
    Safeway Stores plan, 242
    Whole Foods plan, 242

health sector
    cost of, 109
    politics surrounding reform efforts,
        199–200
    research and development concerns,
        115–17
    and stimulus money, 80
Henninger, Daniel, 186–87
herd mentality in financial advice-giving
    business, 208–9
Hess, Steven, 212
Hieb, Lee, 111–12, 251n131
Hollywood, 36–38, 237
Holmes, Oliver Wendell, Jr., 239
Homeland Security Department, 163
homeowners, help for, 103–4
Horowitz, David, 39
housing bubble
    CRA, subprime market, and, 23, 24–25
    financial beneficiaries of, 18
    green bubble compared to, 183, 184
    in killionaire's plan, 128
    market collapses, 31–32, 102–5, 208,
        213–14
    subprime mortgages, 32, 33–34
housing market, 22, 30
Howard, Philip, 43–44
How to Disappear from the IRS (Carlson),
    153–54
Huffington Post website, 109–10
Human Events, 84
Huntington, Samuel, 13
hyperinflation, 134–38, 213–14

I
illegal immigrants, xiii, 122
Illinois, 146
immigrants, 13–14, 49–50
income distribution, 81, 139–41
Inconvenient Truth, An, 180–81
India, 231–32
inflation, 135, 213–14
inflationary bubble cycle, 128
investment banks, 8
investment profit taxes, 145–46, 149
investors in Chrysler and GM, 164–65
Ireland, 134
IRS audits, 154
IRS enforcement procedures, 153–55

J
Japan, 101, 134, 151

Jefferson, Thomas, 125
Jensen, Robert, 14
Johnson, Chalmers, 14
Johnson, Simon, 93
Johnston, David Cay, 152
Jones, Van, 198
Joseph, Peggy, 61–62
J.P. Morgan Chase, 71, 106

K
Kahn, Rosalyn, 39
Kansas, 45
Kashkari, Neel, 93
Keating, Raymond, 74–75
Kelly, Tom, 71
Keynes, John Maynard, xiv, 90
Keynesian Multiplier, xiv–xv, 88–92, 234
killionaires
    and bailouts, 72–76
    choosing capital purchases, 92–93
    complexity of plan, 119–20
    execution of heist, 65–66
    and national leaders, 119
    and Obama, 129
    and partisanship, 22–23, 54–55
    plan for financial crisis, 25, 32–34, 128
    and politics, 24, 25–26
    profits from bank failures, 69–70
    success of, 225
    and tax system, 151–52
    See also Soros, George
King, Martin Luther, Jr., 41
Kish, Dan, 176
Kopel, David, 60–61
Kornafel, Peter, 83
Kreutzer, David, 176
Krugman, Paul, 92
Kunstler, James Howard, 210–11
Kvamme, Floyd, 181

L
Labor, Department of, 167–68
labor unions
    at Amtrack, 80
    current tactics, 159–60
    and Employee Free Choice Act,
        168–69
    and Obama, 161–68
    paying teachers well without, 240
    role in U.S. history, 159, 161
    for teachers, 81–82
    and U.S. presidents, 158

Laffer, Arthur, 147, 160
LaHood, Ray, 175
Lane, Marc J., 171–72
Las Vegas, Nevada, 56
laws, freeing our, 239–40
lawsuits, increase in, 45
lawyers
    Clinton, 190
    and Democratic Party, 44–45
    Edwards, John, 189–90
    nationalizing, xii
    and Obama, 185–87, 189
    and tax codes, 152
Leftstream media, 46
Legal Handbook for Small Business (Lane),
    171–72
legal profession, 43–46
Leonhardt, David, 89–90
Letterman, David, 37
Levenson, Scott, 51
Lewis, Michael, 10
Liar's Poker (Lewis), 10
Lifestyles of the Rich and Famous (television
    program), 63
Life Without Lawyers (Howard), 43–44
Lilly Ledbetter Fair Pay Act, 185–86
Lincoln, Abraham, 10
Lowell, Francis, 222–23
Luxembourg, 134

M
Mackey, John, 242
Madoff, Bernard, 141–42
"Make Work Pay" tax cut, 142
Malkin, Michelle, 62
manufacturing sector
    financial sector instead of, 6–9, 128
    freedom to invent from, 223
    job losses and unemployment rate, 80,
        176
    real versus artificial production, 22
Marshall, John, 139, 243
martial law in the United States, 221–22
Marxism, 40, 41
Massachusetts, 113
Matthews, Chris, 48
McCain, John, 48
McDonald's, 128
McDonnell, Bob, 203
McGann, Eileen, 84, 104
McKinnon, John, 156–57
media

on Employee Free Choice Act, 168
    and green movement, 183
    Hollywood, 36–38, 237
    Leftstream and Rightstream views,
        46–49
    and Obama, 91, 122–23, 195–200
    and Reagan, 87–88
    television programs, 36–37, 63, 220
Medicaid, 81
Medved, Michael, 12
Medvedev, Dmitry, 136
Meet the Press (television program), 46
mega-company regulations, xvi–xvii. *See
    also* big business
Mellon, Jim, 213
Merrill Lynch, 106
Messina, Jim, 199
Mill, John Stuart, 141
Miller, Dennis, 85
Mills, C. Wright, 11
minimum wage increase, 56
minority in America, Europeans as, 13,
    220–21
monetizing the debt, 132–34
Money Meltdown (Shelton), 244–45
Moody's rating of United States, 212
Moore, Michael, 60–61
Moore, Stephen, 147, 160
Morris, Dick, 36, 84, 104
mortgage-backed securities, 22, 29
Mourdock, Richard, 165
MoveOn.org, 24
movie industry, 36
movie star paychecks, 63
Murtha, John, 57
Muzak, 68

N
nation. *See* United States
National Campaign to Prevent Teen and
    Unplanned Pregnancy, 37
National Center for State Courts, 45
National Endowment for the Arts, 82–83
nationalization
    of banking industry, 106–8
    of lawyers and bankers, xii
    of weakest businesses, 218–19
National Labor Relations Act, 171
National Labor Relations Board, 171–72
natural gas reserves in the United States,
    219
natural resources, investing in, 231–32, 233

neo-Marxist redistribution, 40
New Hampshire, 148
New Jersey, 203
Newman, Paul, 141
news media, 46–49, 122–23
New York City, New York, 146
New York Times, 48
Nin, Anaïs, 47
9/11 terrorist attacks, 28
Noonan, Peggy, 85, 96–97, 236–37
Nortel, 68
notehall.com, 229
Nussbaum, Martha, 14

O
Obama, Barack
    and ACORN, 53–54
    and Cap-and-Trade bill, 175–76
    and CEO bonuses, 62–63
    distancing from longtime friends, 53
    and economic-stimulus bill, 55
    and European style of social democracy,
        96, 140–41, 145, 204–5, 242–43
    "house upon a rock" speeches, 72–76
    intentions of, xiv–xv
    and labor unions, 161–68, 169
    livewire act, 129–31
    Ponzi scheme, 141–43
    senior policy appointees, 16–17, 101–2
    on stimulus-created jobs, 48–49
    takeovers of businesses, 99–100
    and terrorism, 238–39
Obama Stimulus Package
    bank destabilization, 91–92
    credit crunch from, 214–15
    fuzzy math, 87–91
    goal and actions, 79–84
    and housing collapse, 102–5
    job creation, 86–87
    killionaires' benefits from, 92–93
    paying for, 85–86
    and size of government, 98–99
    stimulus plan speech, 77–78, 79
Obama Unmasked (Brown and Troxler),
    32, 36, 40–41, 206
O'Brien, Conan, 46, 48
off-budget obligations, 209
offshore tax cheating, 155–57
Off With Their Heads (Morris), 36
oil industry in Ukraine, 2
Olson, Mancur, 89–90

Opel imports, 165
Open Society Institute, 25
Opinion Research Corporation, 159
opportunity from danger, 28–29
optimism versus pessimism, 35–36
Orszag, Peter, 98
Out of Order (Patterson), 190–94

P
Palin, Sarah, 47–48
paper-based economy, 5, 9, 29–30,
    128–29, 223
partisanship in Congress, 203–5. See also
    Revisionists
patriotism, *Revisionists on,* 14
Patterson, Thomas E., 190–94
Patton, Doug, 176
Paul, St., 237
Paulson, Henry, 16, 30
Paycheck Fairness Act (2009), 186–87
payroll tax surcharge, 145
peanut storage, 55
Pelosi, Nancy, 56–57, 203–4
Perfectly Legal (Johnston), 152
Personal Clawback Strategy
    invest in real assets, 227, 230–34
    overview, 225–27
    putting your house in order, 227–28
    starting your own business, 228–30
    stocks as real assets, 233–34
pessimism versus optimism, 35–36
Pew Research Center, 47
pig odor research, 55
Pilgrim's Pride, 68
PMA Group, 57
political contributions and payback, 84
political realignments, 205
Pontek, Lowell, 178–79
poor people, xi, xiv–xv. *See also*
    freeloaders
Power Elite, The (Mills), 11
predictions. *See* forecasting the future
private sector versus public sector, 98–99
productivity loss from tax incentives, 149–51
progressive taxation, 141
prosperity versus absence of war, 216–17
public sector versus private sector, 98–99,
    167

Q
Quinn, Patrick, 146

R

Race to the Top program in schools, 81
radical feminist liberation, 40, 41–43
radio "actualities," 197
Raines, Franklin, 30–31
Rangel, Charles, 155
Rathke, Wade, 50
Rattner, Steven, 17
Reagan, Michael, 123
Reagan, Ronald, 7, 48, 158
real assets, 227, 230–34
real estate, income producing, 230, 232
Real Estate Roundtable, 68
Reason (Flynn), 33
recovery. *See* rolling stall period
redistribution of wealth, 18, 40, 177,
    242–43
regulations. *See* government regulations
Reich, Robert, 14
Reinhart, Carmen, 207
renewable energy project funding, 82
Republican Party
    Bush II's legacy, 139, 140, 143
    decline in power, 200–201
    energy, environment, and, 219–20, 241
    and killionaires, 121
    meaninglessness of, x
    See also *Traditionalists*
residential housing bubble, 128
Revisionists
    absence of war as preference over
        prosperity, 216–17
    The Ant and the Grasshopper, 123–24
    beliefs of, 11–15, 216–17
    college professors, 38–43
    lawyers, 43–46
    news media, 46–49
    political operatives, 49–55
    protesting in the streets, 201–3
    self-centered demands, 59–60
    and taxpayer privacy, 152–57
    turning against America, 21–22,
        35–36, 59–60
    on Wall St. and in Washington, 14
    See also Democratic Party
Reynolds, Alan, 86, 144
rich, 152. *See also* killionaires
Rich States, Poor States (Laffer, Moore, and
    Williams), 147, 160
Rightstream media, 46
right-to-work states, 160

riots in the United States, 221–22
Roanoke Times, 199
Rogoff, Kenneth, 207
rolling stall period
    asset deflation and price inflation,
        213–14
    bank holiday, 212
    credit-crunched consumers, 211
    fall from energy leader to laggard,
        219–20
    government's inability to function as
        provider, 222–24
    loss of hegemonic interests, 220–22
    nationalization of industries, 218–19
    no government rescue, 214–16
    overview, 210, 223–24
    war against America, 216–17
Romer, Christina, 149
Romney, Mitt, 113
Roosevelt, Franklin D., 79
Rossotti, Charles O., 151
Roubini, Nouriel, 106
Rubin, Robert, 10, 14
Rush, Bobby, 162
Russia, 134
Ryan, Paul, 200

S

Safeway Stores health care plan, 242
Safire, William, 235
Santelli, Rick, 202
Sarkozy, Nicolas, 96, 114, 244
SBA (Small Business Administration)
    loans, 74–75
Schiff, Peter, 215
Schumpeterian creative destruction,
    authors' plan for, 131
Science News, 178
script for financial crisis, 4–6
SCUM (Society for Cutting Up Men),
    41–43
SCUM Manifesto (Solanas), 41–43
Securities and Exchange Commission, 8
Seib, Gerald, 86
SEIC (Service Employees International
    Union), 50–51, 163–64, 169, 200
seignorage, 135–36
Seoul, Korea, 2–3
September 11, 2001, terrorist attacks, 28
Service Employees International Union
    (SEIC), 50–51, 163–64, 169, 200

service sector, 223. *See also* banks; financial sector
Shelton, Judy, 244–45
Siegelo, Marc, 114–15
Silvia, John, 48
Sirius-XM Radio, 68
Sirota, David, 23
Six Flags, 68
16 and Pregnant, 37
Small Business Administration (SBA) loans, 74–75
"Small Business Emergency Rescue Plan" (Obama website), 145–46
small businesses
    company policy on unionization, 170
    jobs created by, xi, 74
    lawsuits, liability insurance, and, 45
    starting your own, 228–30
    and union organizers, 167
    value of, xi
    See also entrepreneur investors
Smith, O'jahnae, 51
Smithsonian Institute, 83
Snow, John, 16
social democracy, 96, 140–41, 145, 204–5, 242–43
Social Security Administration, 131
society, ix, 2–3, 43
Society for Cutting Up Men (SCUM), 41–43
Solanas, Valerie, 41–43
Solis, Hilda, 168
Soros, George
    argument against regulations, 25–26
    and Bank of England, 25
    on capitalism, 27
    and China, 3
    and Democratic Party, 25–26
    and MoveOn.org, 24
    as original killionaire, 1–2
    See also ACORN
spending
    monetizing the debt, 132–34
    with taxation and regulations, 129–31
    See also Obama Stimulus Package
sports star paychecks, 63
Standard & Poors, 68
StarKist Tuna, 56
startup funders, 229. *See also* venture capital firms
states' right-to-work laws, 160
state taxes, 146–48

state-wide competition, xiii–xiv
Stern, Andy, 163–64, 169
stimulus plan. *See* Obama Stimulus Package
strategy. *See* Freeing Wealth Fellowship; Personal Clawback Strategy
subprime market, 23, 24–25, 32, 33–34
Summers, Larry, 10, 17, 92
supply-side economics, 87–88
surtax, 145
Sussman, Brian, 176–77
sweetheart deals, xii

T
Taft-Hartley Act (1947), 166
tariffs on imports to U.S., 167
TARP (Troubled Asset Relief Program), 67–72. *See also* Obama Stimulus Package
taxation
    "ability to pay" concept, 140–41
    carryback tax break for small businesses, 76
    Democratic plan, 139–42
    effect of tax increases, 149–51
    of entrepreneur investors, 140–41, 144, 218–19
    freeing our taxes, 242–43
    IRS enforcement procedures, 153–55
    Obama's campaign not to tax 50 percent of Americans, 122–23
    offshore tax cheating, 155–57
    overview, xv–xvi
    with regulations and spending, 129–31
    state taxes, 146–48
    surtax, 145
tax incentives, 149–51
tax shelters, overseas, 155–56
tax system, replacing, 151
tax-wise money policies, 157
teachers, freeing, 240
tea parties, 200, 201–3, 242
tech bubble, 28, 128
television programs, 36–37, 63, 220
television watching funding, 82
Tennessean, The, 180
Ten Biggest Lies About American, The (Medved), 12
terrorists and terrorism, 238–39
Thoma, Mark, 6–7
Thomas, Evan, 48
Tinsley, Bruce, 39–40

trade agreements, 166
Traditionalists
  The Ant and the Grasshopper, 123–24
  beliefs of, 10–11
  living by a code, 35
  losing power, 220–22
  on Wall St. and in Washington, 14–15
  See also Republican Party
Treasury market, 29, 134, 215, 232–33
tribalism, 12. *See also* Revisionists
Tribune Company, 68
Troubled Asset Relief Program (TARP),
  67–72. *See also* Obama Stimulus
  Package

U
UBS Investment Bank, 27
Ukraine, 2
Un-American Activities Committee, 216
unemployment compensation, 81, 167
unemployment rate, 48, 81, 87, 145,
  207–8, 221
UniFoil Corp., 70–71
United Auto Workers (UAW), 164
United States
  European descendants as minority, 13,
    220–21
  as experiment for 230 years, 222–24
  freeing the country, 238–39
  illusion of hope, 126–28, 143–44
  the "it could never happen here" myth,
    3–4, 217
  Moody's rating of, 212
  natural gas reserves, 219
  overview, ix
  as paper-based economy, 5, 9, 29–30,
    128–29, 223
  quality of life measures, 95–96
  state of the union, 208–11
University of Colorado, 38–39
USA Today, 84
U.S. Census Bureau, 220
U.S. Congress
  earmarks, 55–56, 57, 98
  partisanship, 22–23, 54–55, 73–74,
    203–5
  Un-American Activities Committee,
    216

U.S. dollars, value of, 134–38
U.S. Treasury market, 29, 134, 215,
  232–33
Utah, 56

V
values, personal
  effect of changing culture, 220–21
  finding our way back to, 211
  loss of, 13–14
  of *Traditionalists,* 11
Vazza, Diana, 68
Vedder, Richard, 147
venture capital firms, 71–72, 180–81, 229
Virginia, 203
voter registration fraud, 51–53

W
Wachovia, 106
Waggoner, John, 208
Walker, David, 209
war, prosperity versus absence of, 216–17
"Warning, The" *(PBS Frontline),* 92
Washington Mutual, 106
welfare, dependence from, 79. *See also*
  freeloaders
Wells Fargo, 106
"When Unions Knock, How Should
  Employers Answer?" (Darby and
  Bryant), 169–72
White, Alan M., 103–4
white minority in the United States, 13,
  220–21
*Who Are We? The Challenges to America's
  National Identity* (Huntington), 13
Williams, Brian, 48
Williams, Jonathan, 147, 160
Winfrey, Oprah, 60
world currency, 136
World War II multiplier, 89
Wyoming, 56

Y
Yuma, Arizona, 111–12

Z
Zandi, Mark, 86
zinc mine on Gore's property, 180

Dangerous winds are blowing across America's culture today,
creating an atmosphere of extreme anxiety.

So why is the government making things worse?

Former TV meteorologist turned talk show host Brian Sussman wondered that for years,
and a decade's worth of investigation has yielded one of the most shocking stories of our time.

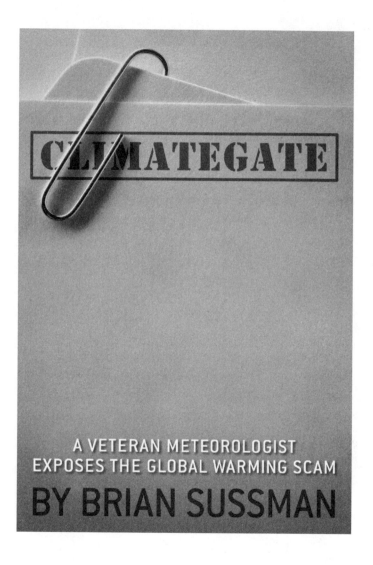

CLIMATEGATE

A VETERAN METEOROLOGIST
EXPOSES THE GLOBAL WARMING SCAM

BY BRIAN SUSSMAN

WND BOOKS

WND Books   •   A WorldNetDaily Company   •   Washington, DC   •   www.wndbooks.com